THE TRUTH ABOUT WATERGATE

A TALE OF EXTRAORDINARY LIES AND LIARS

NICK BRYANT

THE TRUTH ABOUT WATERGATE: A TALE OF EXTRAORDINARY LIES AND LIARS
COPYRIGHT © 2023 NICK BRYANT

Published by:
Trine Day LLC
PO Box 577
Walterville, OR 97489
1-800-556-2012
www.TrineDay.com
TrineDay@icloud.com

Library of Congress Control Number: 2023940331

Bryant, Nick.
–1st ed.
p. cm.

Epub (ISBN-13) 978-1-63424-429-9
Trade Paperback (ISBN-13) 978-1-63424-428-2
1. Watergate Affair, 1972-1974. 2. United States Politics and government 1969-
1974. 3. Nixon, Richard M. 1913-1994 Friends and associates. 4. POLITICAL
SCIENCE/American Government/Executive Branch. I. Bryant, Nick. II. Title

FIRST EDITION
10 9 8 7 6 5 4 3 2 1

Printed in the USA
Distribution to the Trade by:
Independent Publishers Group (IPG)
814 North Franklin Street
Chicago, Illinois 60610
312.337.0747
www.ipgbook.com

For Chaton…

Acknowledgements

I would especially like to thank Len Colodny and Jim Hougan whose pioneering work and subsequent conversations with me have been indispensable in the writing of *The Truth About Watergate*. The books and research of Robert Gettlin, Ray Locker, James Rosen, Phil Stanford, and Adrian Havill have also been indispensable. Collectively, Hougan, Colodny, Gettlin, Locker, Rosen, Stanford, and Havill have dedicated decades to researching the subject matter of *The Truth About Watergate*. I would also like to thank Mark Gorton and Mike Graves for their support.

"I mean, it doesn't take a genius to figure out that Watergate was a C.I.A. setup. We were just pawns."

– Frank Sturgis, Watergate burglar.

CONTENTS

DRAMATIS PERSONAE

IN ORDER OF THEIR APPEARANCE

Richard Nixon was 37th president of the United States who resigned because he faced imminent impeachment for his role in the Watergate cover-up. Prior to becoming president, he represented California as a U.S. representative, senator and served as vice president to President Dwight D. Eisenhower.

John Mitchell, a close friend of Richard Nixon, served as Richard Nixon's campaign manager in 1968 and 1972. After Nixon was elected president in 1968, Mitchell became Nixon's attorney general before resigning in 1972 to become Nixon's campaign manager. Mitchell served 19 months in prison for his actual and fabricated Watergate crimes.

H.R. Haldeman was Nixon's chief-of-staff from 1969 to 1973. Haldeman served 19 months in prison for his actual and fabricated Watergate crimes.

John Ehrlichman initially served as Nixon's counsel to the president, and Nixon elevated him to be the president's chief assistant on domestic affairs. Ehrlichman served 18 months in prison for his actual and fabricated Watergate crimes.

Richard Helms was the director of the C.I.A., and he had intense antipathy for Richard Nixon.

Admiral *Thomas Moorer*, chairman of the Joint Chiefs of Staff, who initiated the "Moorer-Radford affair," which was an espionage ring designed to spy on the Nixon administration as it made overtures of amity to the Soviet Union and Communist China.

Charles Radford was a Navy Yeoman who Moorer deployed to pilfer top-secret documents from the National Security Council.

Rear Admiral *Robert Welander* was a co-conspirator in the "Moorer-Radford affair."

Alexander Haig would eventually become Nixon's chief of staff, even though he was complicit in the "Moorer-Radford affair." He would usher Nixon's presidency to ruin.

E. Howard Hunt had allegedly retired from the C.I.A., and he was one of the architects of the Watergate break-ins.

G. Gordon Liddy, a former F.B.I. agent, was general counsel of the Committee to Re-elect the President and one of the architects of the Watergate break-ins.

James McCord had allegedly retired from the C.I.A. and then served as the security director for the Committee to Re-elect the President. He was also one of the architects of the Watergate break-ins.

John Dean was council to the president under Nixon, and his factual and fabricated testimony were integral to the toppling of the Nixon administration.

John Caulfield was a retired N.Y.P.D. detective who specialized in dirty deeds for the Nixon administration.

Heidi Rikan was a close friend of John Dean and his wife, and she was also the madam of a brothel that served as a honey trap.

Maureen "Mo" Dean is the wife of John Dean and close friend of madam Heidi Rikan, and, according to G. Gordon Liddy, Maureen Dean was a prostitute who had worked with Rikan.

Phillip Bailley was a Washington, D.C. attorney, who became enmeshed in Heidi Rikan's brothel/honey trap at the Columbia Plaza apartments.

Lou Russell, a former F.B.I. agent and overseer of the brothel/honey trap at the Columbia Plaza apartments.

Jeb Magruder was the acting chairman of the Committee to Re-elect the President, and unbeknownst to his superiors in the Nixon administration he funded the Watergate break-ins.

Alfred Baldwin, a former F.B.I. agent, was retained by James McCord to serve as a security operative for the Committee to Re-elect the President. He was also the lookout for the second Watergate break-in, and, according to Jim Hougan's *Secret Agenda*, tipped off the police about the Watergate burglary.

The Watergate burglars: *Eugenio Martinez, Bernard Barker, Felipe De Diego, Ronaldo Pico, Virgilio, Gonzalez*, and *Frank Sturgis*. With the exception of Sturgis, all of the burglars were born in Cuba and all of the burglars had been or were C.I.A. assets.

Carl Shoffler, a former Army intelligence agent, and undercover D.C. police officer, who was improbably near the Watergate on the night of the second burglary and arrested the burglars.

Richard Kleindienst became U.S. attorney general after John Mitchell relinquished the position.

L. Patrick Gray was the acting director of the F.B.I.

General Vernon Walters was the deputy director of the C.I.A.

Bob Woodward, a reporter for the *Washington Post* and serial liar.

Carl Bernstein, a reporter for the *Washington Post* and serial liar.

John Sirica was the U.S. district court judge who presided over the Watergate adjudication and trials.

Sam Dash, a distinguished professor at the Georgetown University Law Center, was appointed to be the chief counsel of the Senate Watergate Committee.

Fred Buzhardt simultaneously served as counsel for the Department of Defense and Nixon's special counsel for Watergate. Buzhardt and Haig were old friends, and Buzhardt would help Haig usher Nixon's presidency to its ruin.

Ben Bradlee was the former propagator of C.I.A. propaganda and was also the executive editor of the *Washington Post* who abetted Woodward and Bernstein's lies throughout their Watergate reporting. Bradlee also repeatedly lied about his affiliation to the C.I.A.

Alexander Butterfield disclosed Nixon's secret taping system to the Watergate Committee, which ultimately toppled the Nixon administration. He was a former Air Force colonel who acted as liaison to the C.I.A., and he lied to Haldeman to infiltrate the Nixon administration. Butterfield also committed perjury when testifying before the House Judiciary Committee but was not prosecuted.

Elliot Richardson replaced Richard Kleindienst as the U.S. attorney general.

Archibald Cox was the first special prosecutor of the Watergate Special Prosecution Force.

Leon Jaworski was the second special prosecutor of the Watergate Special Prosecution Force. He, too, lied about his affiliation to the C.I.A.

Maxie Wells was the D.N.C. secretary who allegedly provided Democratic V.I.P.s with a directory of call girls from Heidi Rikan's brothel/honey trap at the Columbia Plaza apartments.

PROLOGUE

A *delusion* is a strong belief or conviction despite superior evidence to the contrary. The Watergate delusion, embraced by millions, is that swashbuckling Bob Woodward and the left confronted the malevolent Nixon administration as it cast a sinister pall over America and slew it with the lance of truth, thereby saving democracy. But the actual evidence demonstrates that Watergate was not a shining example of democracy, and Bob Woodward's place among the pantheon of journalistic immortals is a grift.

One of the grand deceptions of Watergate is that Nixon's enemies on the left razed his presidency when it was actually his enemies on the right – the far right – who initially had the means, motive, and opportunity. And although Bob Woodward and Carl Bernstein told numerous lies throughout their Watergate reporting, Woodward's Big Lie was that he didn't meet Alexander Haig until 1973. As I take the reader on a guided tour of the extraordinary lies and liars of Watergate, I will prove that Woodward's fabrication about Haig has seismic implications. If Woodward's Big Lie about Haig had been exposed, then the synergistic mythologies of Bob Woodward and "Deep Throat" would have been shattered and swept away by gusts of veracity.

Jim Hougan's 1984 *Secret Agenda: Watergate, Deep Throat, and the C.I.A.* was the Big Bang in revisiting Watergate fictions, and seven years later Len Colodny and Robert Gettlin published *Silent Coup: The Removal of a President,* which further augmented our understanding of Watergate. In the wake of *Secret Agenda* and *Silent Coup,* several books have been published demonstrating that the version of Watergate prepped and served for public consumption is a fiction.

When writing *The Truth About Watergate,* I've conducted zero original research on Watergate to demonstrate that additional research is not required to declare the Watergate cover story a grand fabrication. But the book is fortified by 2,328 citations that have been gleaned from books about Watergate, revisionist and non-revisionist, primarily mainstream media articles, and government documentation.

As I've written *The Truth About Watergate*, I've trolled the internet looking for various viewpoints on both the revisionist and non-revisionist accounts of Watergate, and I've come across the phrase "conspiracy theory" with regard to *Silent Coup*. The *Washington Post* has scorned *Silent Coup* as a conspiracy theory, but I'll demonstrate that the *Washington Post* has fervent, utilitarian motives for banishing *Silent Coup* to the conspiracy theory ghetto. *Silent Coup* is a remarkable example of scholarship. A mainstream publisher, St. Martin's, published *Silent Coup*, and the book has sold more than 100,000 copies. Texas A&M also features the Colodny Collection, which is a medley of the research materials utilized by *Silent Coup's* authors. These facts by themselves should dissuade people from summarily banishing *Silent Coup* to the conspiracy theory ghetto.

The "call girl theory" plays an integral role in *The Truth About Watergate*. I've written one book and co-authored a second book about sexual, political blackmail in American politics. I've found that Americans have a collective naiveté about their politicians' sexcapades, believing that they are the dalliances and moral failings of a select few. My fellow Americans have great difficulty accepting that many of our politicians are endowed with a potent psychological alchemy of power, arrogance, and lust that fluently translates into extramarital affairs, aberrant behavior, and even illicit deeds.

Sexual, political blackmail is a time-honored tradition in America. The husband of Alexander Hamilton's 23-year-old mistress financially extorted Hamilton to ensure that his affair remained surreptitious, but a muckraking journalist exposed Hamilton's affair.[1,2] Hamilton and Jefferson were antagonists, and the muckraker who outed Hamilton's extramarital affair felt that Jefferson owed him a political appointment when Jefferson became president.[3] But Jefferson declined, so the muckraker disseminated news about Jefferson's affair with one of his slaves.[4] Although a procession of hagiographies have elevated America's Founding Fathers to saint-like status, they, nonetheless, had their sexual foibles that made them susceptible to blackmail.

In the previous 20 years, the following U.S. senators and representatives have been entangled in sexual scandals: Gary Condit, (D-CA),[5] Ed Schrock (R-VA),[6] Steven C. LaTourette (R-OH),[7] David Dreier (R-CA),[8] Don Sherwood (R-PA),[9] Mark Foley (R-FL),[10] David Vitter (R-LA),[11] Larry Craig (R-ID),[12] Tim Mahoney (D-FL),[13] Vito Fossella (R-NY),[14] John Edwards (D-NC),[15] John Ensign (R-NV),[16] Chip Pickering (R-MS),[17] Eric Massa (D-NY),[18] Mark Souder, (R-IN),[19] Christopher Lee (R-NY),[20] Anthony

Weiner (D-NY),[21] Scott DesJarlais (R-TN),[22] David Wu (D-OR),[23] Vance McAllister (R-LA),[24] Blake Farenthold (R-TX),[25] Dennis Hastert (R-IL),[26] Tim Murphy (R-PA),[27] Al Franken (D-MN),[28] Joe Barton (R-TX),[29] Trent Franks (R-AZ),[30] Matt Gaetz (R-FL),[31] Katie Hill (D-CA),[32] Cal Cunningham (D-NC),[33] John Conyers (D-MI)[34] and, last but probably not least, Pat Meehan (R-PA).[35]

The aforementioned names are merely the U.S. representatives and senators whose sexcapades have pierced the mainstream media. The majority of Americans are probably cognizant of Hollywood Babylon, but Sodom and Gomorrah on the Potomac seems to be largely overlooked. I'll comment on two of the formerly esteemed men that I've cited, and they should give the reader an idea of the relative ease a third party would have compromising a politician and also of the mindboggling risks politicians will take to satiate their lusts.

Former U.S. Senator Larry Craig was in Washington, D.C. as a congressman for more than 25 years.[36] During his tenures as a U.S. representative and a senator, his voting record for gay-rights legislation was deplorable, even though he used the services of a gay escort service.[37] Craig was an unrepentant conservative, so, if his homosexual endeavors were exposed, his political career would ignominiously crash and burn. But, nonetheless, Craig was arrested for lewd conduct in a restroom at the Minneapolis-St. Paul International Airport: He propositioned an undercover male police officer in a bathroom stall.[38]

Republican Dennis Hastert was the former Speaker of the House from 1999 to 2007.[39] During those years, he was constitutionally the third most powerful man in the country, and he established a reputation in the House as being a strong-arm specialist.[40] Hastert, however, had concealed pedophilic predations for decades throughout his meteoric political ascent.[41] As the revelations about Hastert became increasingly sordid, and the story incited a media feeding frenzy, a federal judge, siding with federal prosecutors, ruled that discovery in the case would not be made public.[42] Then, suddenly, the news about Hastert's predatory behavior quickly evaporated.

Hastert's illicit sex with minors stunned a nation. But in a 2006 investigation, the House Ethics Committee ruled that Hastert and other Republicans were "willfully ignorant" for months in their response to recurring warnings that U.S. Representative Mark Foley was preying on teenage, congressional male pages.[43] In 2009, an F.B.I. whistleblower testified during a deposition that the F.B.I. was cognizant of Hastert visiting a Chicago townhouse for "not very morally accepted activities" during his speakership.[44] If the whistleblower's revelations are true, then F.B.I. personnel were aware of Hastert's shadow life, yet, he was publicly unscathed by it during his years as Speaker of the House.

Political blackmail is rarely made public, and if it becomes public, then it generally occurs years after the fact. J. Edgar Hoover is a prime example: He was a blackmail artist for decades, and his blackmailing only emerged years after his death.[45] Blackmail marks, especially politicians, have zero incentive to turn to the authorities if the blackmailer has pictures of their extramarital flings and/or aberrant behavior. Those pictures, released to the public, would doom their careers, probably destroy their families, and reduce their lives to public ignominy.

Watergate, as promulgated by the government, has been devoid of all sexual blackmail nuances and packaged as a straightforward tale of good versus evil. But the accurate account of Watergate is profoundly complex – a conspiracy within a conspiracy. A collective delusion about Watergate is inextricably woven into America's ontological lore, so I've meticulously sourced *The Truth About Watergate*. I've also streamlined and simplified some of its complexities, which includes omitting a myriad of names from the book's narrative. But those respective names are referenced in the book's Endnotes section.

When Nietzsche initially declared that "God is dead" in *Die fröhliche Wissenschaft*, he was extremely forlorn about the prospect of living without God. When I declare that Watergate is a delusion, I, too, feel extremely forlorn: For years, I embraced the jubilant fabrication that an incorruptible Fourth Estate and an unassailable democracy saved America from Richard Nixon and his unholy minions. Unfortunately, the incorruptible Fourth Estate was quite corrupt and the unassailable democracy was the fountainhead of numerous fabrications.

CHAPTER 1

WELCOME TO THE JUNGLE

R ichard Milhous Nixon is ostensibly the alpha and omega of Watergate. He was born on January 9, 1913, in rural Orange County, California into a Quaker family.[1] A flush of misfortune resulted in the family's citrus ranch failing.[2] Nixon's mother, Hannah, came from a family that was comfortably entrenched in the middle class, but she and her husband, Frank, toiled at menial labor to provide for their family after the failure of their citrus ranch.[3] Young Richard helped to prevent the family from capsizing by working as a child laborer in the bean fields and citrus groves of Southern California.[4] Hannah's relatives ultimately came to the family's rescue and backed Hannah and Frank on a loan that enabled Frank to open a gas station and grocery store in Whittier, California, a Quaker enclave, about 30 miles southeast of Los Angeles.[5]

Nixon's labor was indispensable for the family business to remain afloat. Before attending high school, he awoke at 4:00 A.M. and drove the family truck to Los Angeles where he purchased fresh vegetables.[6] After driving back to Whittier, he would wash the vegetables and carefully put them on display.[7] Nixon had four brothers, and his volatile father eschewed the Quaker ethos of nonviolence with his sons: He routinely shouted at them and punished them via "the strap."[8] Tragically, two of his brothers died of the tubercular scourge.[9,10]

Despite Nixon's daily grind during high school, he excelled in academics, acting, debating, orchestra, and as a benchwarmer on the football team.[11] He graduated third in a high school class of 207 students.[12] Harvard and Yale offered him tuition "grants."[13] But he declined the offers proffered by the Ivy League, because his hard work was too indispensable for his family to remain in the black during the unforgiving Depression.[14]

After high school, he enrolled in Whittier College.[15] Nixon was a scrawny 5'11" and utterly devoid of athleticism, but he was on the football, basketball, and track teams.[16] He was also in a series of collegiate plays that he reveled in.[17] He shined at debate and public speaking, too.[18] Nixon was even elected student body president during his senior year, and he graduated second in his class.[19,20] Though he was showered with accolades and

honors, his classmates viewed him as shy, solitary, very tense, and painful-
ly uncertain of himself.[21] He was an indelible loner.[22]

The family gas station and market ultimately became relatively lucra-
tive, which enabled Nixon to attend Duke University School of Law on
a scholarship.[23] Nixon was hard-wired for politics: He was elected president of Duke's Student Bar Association.[24] Nixon also graduated third in
his class, and he qualified for the Order of the Coif, the national law honor
society.[25] With an auspicious tailwind of achievements, he pursued employment with monolithic New York City law firms and the F.B.I.[26] But
he found no takers.

A small firm in Whittier that specialized in probate and estate litigation
and also represented small petroleum companies assimilated Nixon.[27] He
felt that the Whittier law firm was anticlimactic when juxtaposed to his
grand Duke odyssey, but his zeal and work ethic enabled him to become
a full partner in the firm after two years.[28] Nixon, however, burning with
ambition, coveted a career in politics, so he cultivated relationships with
various civic organizations that could serve as a political springboard.[29]
During this period, he met Patricia Ryan, his future wife.[30] Ms. Ryan was a
schoolteacher, and she had endured a hardscrabble childhood that made
Nixon's childhood look like a vacation to Xanadu.[31]

Nixon's courtship of the beautiful, taciturn, and mysterious Patricia
Ryan was extremely unorthodox: She repeatedly rebuffed Nixon's awk-
ward attempts at romantic overtures, but she granted him the privilege of
chauffeuring her to Los Angeles on Friday nights and retrieving her on
Sunday nights.[32] In Los Angeles, she lodged with her stepsister and routinely dated a variety of suitors.[33] After Nixon's relentless pursuit of Pat,
which today might garner a restraining order, the couple married in 1940.[34]

Nixon opted for the navy in 1942 to enhance his chances at a political
career.[35] Although he served in the Pacific, he managed to avoid the hellish
realities of the frontlines by specializing in transport and logistics.[36] When
Nixon exited the navy, a group of Orange County shakers and movers
tapped him to make a run for the U.S. House of Representatives in 1946.[37]
The wealthy men who conscripted Nixon desperately sought to vanquish
the ten-term incumbent Democrat whose New Deal egalitarianism was
anathema to their tacit embrace of social Darwinism.[38,39]

It would've been difficult for Nixon not to embrace the Hobbesian
outlook that life is solitary, nasty, brutish, and short. His formative years
had forged a zealous resolve that placed a premium on survival, which
translated into personal achievement, and then, ultimately, into political

achievement: He would eagerly engineer the downfall of his political foes to ensure his survival in the jungle of American politics.

Nixon deployed his boyhood ethos of blood, sweat, and grit to become an indefatigable campaigner and a no-holds-barred in-fighter: He pounded his Democratic opponent as an unrepentant Pinko.[40] Nixon's scorched earth tactics enabled him to be swept into congress – he was 33 years old.[41] After the election, Nixon confessed that his opponent wasn't a Pinko. "I had to win," he said. "The important thing is to win."[42]

The freshman representative had a foothold in the august arena of Washington, D.C. politics, but his rapacious ambition yearned to be more than a one-term trick pony. America's grand witch-hunt for Communists, the House Un-American Activities Committee, offered Nixon a carpe diem opportunity. After Nixon had embedded himself in the House Un-American Activities Committee, he would evolve into a red-baiter par excellence. He eventually lined up former State Department official and diplomat Alger Hiss in his crosshairs and accused him of being a Soviet agent.[43] A dissolute editor of *Time* magazine had fingered Hiss as a Soviet agent.[44,45]

Hiss had emerged from the elite, East Coast leisure class, a stratum of society that Nixon tacitly detested, and he graduated from Harvard Law School.[46] The evidence against Hiss was initially flimsy, but Nixon had become an outspoken proponent of Hiss' guilt, even though President Harry Truman and the majority of the media had pronounced Hiss innocent of the charges.[47] Nixon's binary political cogitation concluded that his political survival was contingent on Hiss' guilt – and annihilation.

Initially, Hiss testified that he had never met his accuser.[48] However, after evidence to the contrary surfaced, Hiss acknowledged meeting his accuser.[49] Hiss' accuser eventually coughed up State Department documents that he said Hiss had purloined and passed to him.[50] One of the documents was in Hiss' handwriting, and Hiss' typewriter had been shown to reproduce some of the documents.[51] Hiss was indicted on two counts of perjury: His first trial ended in a hung jury, but a second trial found him guilty on both counts.[52] He was sentenced to five years in prison.[53] The Hiss case had been a wild rollercoaster ride for Nixon, especially when the star witness turned out to be a perjurer, but it catapulted him to the status of a national personage.

Nixon next coveted the exalted status of U.S. senator, and California's 1950 race for the U.S. Senate pitted Nixon against Democrat Helen Gahagan Douglas. The former actress was a three-term U.S. Representative, unabashed champion of the New Deal, and the wife of a famous actor.[54] Her devotion to the New Deal and other progressive platforms meant that the Nixon campaign had little difficulty forging a sobriquet for her – "Pink Lady."[55] Nixon welcomed Douglas to the jungle with his characteristic zeal and ruthlessness, and he proceeded to rout her by nearly 20 percentage points.[56] Nixon, however, did not emerge from the mêlée utterly unscathed, because he had been christened "Tricky Dick," a moniker that would stalk him to the bitter end.[57]

The Republicans anointed World War II hero General Dwight (Ike) Eisenhower as their 1952 presidential candidate.[58] The 61-year-old Eisenhower emanated a benign, grandfatherly aura.[59] His campaign handlers felt that he should avoid the political mosh pit and assume the mantle of an elder statesman throughout the campaign.[60] So, as Eisenhower incarnated into the modern-day embodiment of Pericles, his campaign concluded that a vice presidential attack dog would benefit him significantly.[61] The 39-year-old freshman senator from California was a political pit bull who fit the bill, and Nixon surfaced from the Republican convention as Ike's running mate.[62]

As Nixon was poised to make an ascent to the rarified air of Mount Olympus, he was served a cold dish of his comeuppance: the New York Post reported that a cadre of affluent Californians had created a slush fund "exclusively for the financial comfort of Sen. Nixon."[63] Stories and editorials on the fund quickly ignited throughout the country, creating a mushroom cloud that cast a dark pall over Nixon.[64] Eisenhower's aides and friends sowed the seeds of doubt in Ike's mind about the merit of running with the freshman senator.[65] Nixon felt the jungle looming, and he initially plummeted into fear and trembling.[66] But his next move was one of the great political Houdini acts in history.

The Republican National Committee and the Senate Republican Campaign Committee ponied up $75,000 and purchased a half hour of primetime on N.B.C., where Nixon casually delivered the "Checkers Speech."[67] Before an audience of 60 million Americans, Nixon delivered the first-ever nationally televised political address.[68] He explained that his boosters had established a fund following his 1950 election to assist with his various expenses.[69] After stressing that the fund was both legal and transparent, he gave America a shameless financial strip tease of his various assets.[70]

In the speech's tear-jerking crescendo, Nixon cynically pilfered a Roosevelt trope and focused on the family dog. "We did get something, a gift, after the election," said Nixon.[71] "It was a little cocker spaniel dog.... And our little girl Tricia – the six-year-old – named it Checkers.[72] And you know the kids love a dog, and I just want to say this right now that regardless of what they say about it, we're gonna to keep it."[73] On the homestretch of the Checkers' Speech, Nixon, naturally, assailed the Democrats as being negligent about the Red Menace.[74] A tsunami of telegrams, phone calls, letters, and cards – estimated to be around four million – deluged the Republican National Committee, Eisenhower's campaign, newspapers, etc., and the vast majority urged Ike not to dump Dick.[75]

A poll of eminent communication scholars has ranked the Checkers Speech as the sixth most important American speech of the 20th century, and Nixon parleyed the Checkers Speech into eight years as Ike's vice president.[76] He was Ike's heir apparent for the presidency in 1960, but he had a formidable opponent – John Fitzgerald Kennedy. Nixon lost a tightly contested presidential race to Kennedy.

Despite the defeat, politics continued to course through Nixon's veins: He quickly jumped back into the jungle and made a California gubernatorial bid in 1962, but he lost to the incumbent Democrat.[77] Nixon's concession speech was laced with vitriol.[78] He told the audience that he was bowing out of politics for the duration: "You won't have Dick Nixon to kick around anymore, because, gentlemen, this is my last press conference."[79]

Nixon ostensibly resigned from politics and eventually resurfaced as a senior partner in a powerhouse, Wall Street law firm during the turbulent 1960s.[80] For Americans, the race riots that ignited American cities and the massive demonstrations raging against the Vietnam War were signs of apocalyptic cataclysm, but the upheaval was a Siren song for Nixon, summoning his return to the jungle.[81] He began coast-to-coast stumping for Republicans of all stripes.[82]

When Nixon decided to make a dash for the presidency, he tapped one of his law partners, John Mitchell, to be his campaign manager, even though Mitchell had never run a political campaign.[83] Mitchell was a burly and bald 55-year-old who emanated self-confidence. A pipe was an omnipresent, inorganic extension of his face. Mitchell, like Nixon, came from a working-class family: Mitchell's father had been a meat salesman during the Great Depression.[84] He came of age in the blue-collar hamlet of Blue Point, New York on Long Island's southern shore.[85] He had two brothers and a sister.[86] Also like Nixon, death had purloined two of Mitchell's siblings.[87]

When Mitchell's family relocated to Queens, New York, he attended Jamaica High School.[88] In high school, Mitchell was a superlative athlete; hockey was his sport of choice.[89] Jamaica High School was a hockey juggernaut in the 1920s and 1930s, winning the city championship 13 years in a row.[90] Mitchell even played semi-pro hockey.[91] After he graduated from Fordham University Law School, he started practicing law in 1938.[92]

Mitchell quickly became an expert on a New Deal policy enabling the hawking of municipal and state bonds, which were often tax exempt and quasi guaranteed by the federal government if the private or public entity issuing the bonds ensured their repayment.[93] Wall Street eventually welcomed the bonds, and, according to Mitchell, "They sold like hotcakes."[94]

The future looked friendly for the wunderkind: He had married his high school sweetheart, a prestigious law firm had made him a partner, and he was afloat in cash.[95] Mitchell took a sabbatical from the American Dream and answered the call of duty for World War II.[96] Ensign Mitchell served in the South Pacific on a P.T. boat.[97] He quickly distinguished himself as a leader and was promoted to lieutenant and given command of a P.T. boat.[98] After the war, Mitchell returned to his wife and two children in New York, and he resumed his deft touch in the bond market, morphing into a Wall Street virtuoso.[99, 100]

As Mitchell's wealth escalated, his expertise in bonds attracted clients nationwide, and he became peripatetic.[101] His perpetual motion took a toll on his marriage, and he started to stray.[102] The ink was barely dry on his divorce papers when he married Martha Beal – a curvaceous, blonde Arkansan – five years his junior.[103] Love can be highly irrational, and Mitchell's friends were perplexed by his choice of Martha, because she was a drunk who had the potential to be seismically obnoxious.[104] The couple would have a daughter, and also raise Martha's son from her previous marriage.[105]

Mitchell had a larger-than-life persona that captivated Nixon. He hadn't descended from the East Coast leisure class, but he nonetheless adroitly navigated it.[106] Though Nixon and Mitchell were approximately the same age, the former looked upon the latter as a mentor.[107] Mitchell took Nixon under the wing of his Brooks Brothers' suit.

In the spring of 1968, in Washington, D.C., a cadre of pro-Nixon congressmen questioned Mitchell's qualifications to run a presidential campaign. "I'm his campaign manager, and I'm running the show," Mitchell responded. "When I tell Dick Nixon what to do, he listens. I'm in charge. So, if you have any questions about the campaign, call me. But you won't be able to reach me because I'll be busy electing a president of the United States."[108] After Nixon won the presidency, Mitchell became the attorney general. In Greek tragedies, the protagonist has a hitherto unforeseen flaw that ultimately sows his ruinous fate. Mitchell's flaw was his friendship with Richard Nixon.

CHAPTER 2

THE TRICKY DICK DOUBLE CROSS

Nixon's perpetual barnstorming around the country on behalf of his fellow Republicans enabled him and Mitchell to call in markers during the 1968 primaries, and he crushed his various challengers for the Republican nomination.[1] During the Republican primaries and convention, the media and political bystanders perceived a kinder, gentler Nixon, especially when discussing the Red Menace.[2] The formerly unabashed Cold Warrior now talked about extending olive branches to both the Soviet Union and China.[3] Onlookers wondered if Nixon's new rhetoric was a cynical campaign ploy or if America was witnessing a leopard changing his spots.[4]

Nixon's Democratic foe was Hubert Humphrey, President Lyndon Johnson's vice president. Humphrey's campaign was fettered by Johnson's unrepentant escalation of the Vietnam War and a disastrous 1968 Democratic Convention in Chicago, which erupted into a nationally televised blood bath that showed Chicago police mercilessly bludgeoning anti-war demonstrators.[5] The pundits declared that Nixon's ascent to Mount Olympus would be an unencumbered fait accompli, but then Humphrey started to vociferously advocate against raining bombs on North Vietnam.[6] Suddenly, Humphrey's campaign started to surge.[7]

In early September of 1968, Nixon had watched the Humphrey campaign from the summit of a commanding frontrunner.[8] But as Nixon and Humphrey were darting towards the campaign's homestretch, they were running neck and neck.[9] The ghosts of 1960 haunted Nixon, and Tricky Dick, his alter ego, emerged. Nixon had an intermediary clandestinely convey to the President of South Vietnam that his administration would force greater concessions from the North Vietnamese towards the South Vietnamese than the Johnson administration was willing to concede at the Paris Peace Accords.[10] Nixon's treasonous intervention convinced the South Vietnamese to embargo the Paris Peace Accords until after the 1968 election.[11] Nixon ultimately thumped Humphrey by a lopsided margin in the Electoral College – 301 to 191 – but the race was too close to call the night of the election.[12] He was finally named President-elect the following morning. Nixon would ultimately discover that heaven and hell had the same address – 1600 Pennsylvania Avenue.

Nixon conscripted a pair of aides who would form the "Berlin Wall" to ensure that he wasn't troubled by mundane trivialities. The Berlin Wall's building blocks included H.R. Haldeman – Nixon's chief-of-staff. Haldeman was married and had four children – two boys and two girls.[13] The 42-year-old Haldeman had been a high-powered advertising executive prior to becoming Nixon's chief-of-staff.[14]

He was tall, thin, and a brown, bristly flattop crowned his long, stern face. His scowl was so omnipresent that it appeared as if his face might crack, or possibly shatter, if he ever smiled. Haldeman could be a cyclone of hostility and an unyielding taskmaster: His movement was brisk and mechanical – like Robocop, sans the exoskeleton hardware. "Every president needs a son-of-a-bitch, and I'm Nixon's," Haldeman would proudly say.[15]

Haldeman grew up in Southern California, which is noted for mass-producing archetypal slackers, surfers, and stoners. But Southern California also mass-produces rabid right-wingers, and Haldeman definitely fell into the latter category. His paternal grandfather founded the Better American Foundation, which was a precursor to the John Birch Society.[16] Haldeman, like a young Nixon, harbored unbridled contempt towards Communism.[17] As a student at the University of Southern California, before transferring to the University of California, Los Angeles, he attempted to expunge students that he perceived were Communist from influencing the school's newspaper.[18]

Haldeman quickly became a Nixon devotee as Nixon used the pulpit of the House Un-American Activities to seemingly cleanse the country of the insidious Red Menace.[19] Haldeman initially worked for Nixon as an advance man in 1956, when Nixon was stumping for Ike and seeking re-election as Ike's vice president.[20] Haldeman's dedication and grey matter impressed the vice president, so Haldeman was appointed Nixon's chief advance man when Nixon made his ill-fated presidential bid in 1960.[21] Two years later, Haldeman managed Nixon's miscarried run for California governor.[22] Haldeman's loyalty to Nixon was unequivocal. After Nixon lost his California gubernatorial bid, Haldeman was subjected to hours of Nixon's scathing retorts about his foes – real and imagined.[23]

As Nixon's chief-of-staff, Haldeman became a daunting barricade to those who sought an audience with the president.[24] Even cabinet officers had to persuade Haldeman to grant them an audience.[25] He was Spartan-like and puritanical, and he created Nixon's staff in his own image – obsequious and dour.[26] His unyielding loyalty to Nixon had a significant fault: He relinquished freethinking that may have offset Nixon's more egregious or self-destructive traits.[27]

The 43-year-old John Ehrlichman consummated the Berlin Wall. He was married with three sons and two daughters.[28] Ehrlichman had a round face with dark, intense eyes and receding black hair. He was tall and slightly corpulent. Like Haldeman, Ehrlichman came of age in Southern California – Santa Monica – and his teenage years were dedicated to becoming an Eagle Scout.[29] After graduating from high school, Ehrlichman majored in political science at U.C.L.A.[30] Ehrlichman met Haldeman at U.C.L.A., and they became fast friends.[31] Both were Christian Scientists.[32]

As a freshman at U.C.L.A., Ehrlichman enlisted in the Air Force in 1943.[33] He was a B-24 navigator during World War II and flew 26 missions over Germany – he was even awarded a Distinguished Flying Cross.[34] Upon his return to California, he graduated from U.C.L.A. and enrolled in Stanford Law School.[35] After graduating from law school, he and his wife ultimately opted for Seattle.[36] As Ehrlichman was en route to becoming Seattle's premier zoning lawyer, Haldeman recruited him to work on Nixon's 1960 presidential bid.[37]

Prior to the Republican Convention, Ehrlichman was directed to clandestinely infiltrate a rival Republican candidate's campaign.[38] When Nixon's Republican foes had been vanquished, Ehrlichman infiltrated the Democratic Convention and wrote a dossier on the Kennedy campaign machine.[39] Ehrlichman proved to have a panache for surreptitious exploits, which wasn't lost on Haldeman or Nixon.

After Ehrlichman worked on Nixon's doomed 1962 California gubernatorial bid, he returned to his Seattle law practice.[40] He thought his days in politics were in the rearview mirror.[41] But like the Phoenix, Nixon's political career arose from its ashes, and both Haldeman and Ehrlichman plunged into his presidential campaign.[42]

In the aftermath of Nixon's victory, Nixon appointed Ehrlichman to be counsel to the president.[43] Nixon then elevated him to be the president's chief assistant on domestic affairs.[44] Domestic issues didn't enthrall Nixon like reshaping the geo-political landscape, and he intended to devote an inordinate breadth of his energies to foreign policy.[45] Accordingly, Ehrlichman harnessed tremendous domestic power, because all domestic initiatives and legislation were funneled through his office.[46] Though Nixon was a ferocious pit-bull from the pulpit, his violent, abusive father had imbued him with a near phobic skittishness about one-on-one face-to-face confrontations. [47] Haldeman and Ehrlichman enabled Nixon to avoid such confrontations, because they acted as his button men.

During Nixon's inaugural speech, he repeatedly alluded to peace. "The greatest honor history can bestow is the title of peacemaker," he said. "The honor now beckons America – the chance to help lead the world at last out of the valley of turmoil and onto that high ground of peace that man has dreamed of since the dawn of civilization."[48]

Nixon was determined to become the peacemaker with his mortal foe – the Red Menace. But Nixon wasn't naïve about the powerful forces that he would confront to become the architect of harmony with the Soviet Union and China, because he had once been firmly entrenched in the dominion of the hawks. He realized that he would have the onus of literally re-inventing the government to actualize his foreign policy objectives.

Shortly after Nixon became president, he signed National Security Decision Memorandum 2, which sounds like an innocuous bureaucratic directive, but it transformed the National Security Council from an advisory organization into an organization that would determine and control foreign policy.[49] By re-inventing the National Security Council, Nixon decisively excluded the State Department, C.I.A., and Defense Department from his major geo-political moves.[50]

Nixon issued decrees via his National Security Advisor, and those decrees were relayed to the State Department, C.I.A., and Defense Department.[51] Nixon distrusted the C.I.A.: He would allow C.I.A. Director Richard Helms to brief the National Security Council at the commencement of meetings, but, after his briefing, Helms was then persona non grata.[52]

Helms was the tall, lean, and arrogant scion of East Coast patricians. In the world according to Richard Nixon, Helms belonged to a subgenus of humanity who were guilty until proven innocent. Moreover, Nixon felt he had been burned by the C.I.A. in his 1960 presidential campaign against Kennedy.[53] He was cognizant that Cubans were being trained in the U.S. to invade Cuba, but that knowledge was top secret, and he couldn't utter a word of it during the presidential campaign.[54] And Kennedy hammered Nixon throughout the 1960 campaign for the Eisenhower administration's lax policy towards Cuba.[55] Nixon felt that C.I.A. operatives had edified Kennedy about the impending invasion, and Kennedy used that information against Nixon, because Nixon was handcuffed and couldn't discuss the administration's actual policy towards Cuba.[56]

Indeed, when Helms briefed the National Security Council, Nixon gratuitously interrupted him or corrected him on insignificant facts.[57] Nixon's low opinion of the C.I.A. also surfaced at the Council's meetings. "What are those idiots out in MacLean doing?" Nixon wondered aloud. "There are forty thousand people out there, reading newspapers."[58]

Nixon's reinvention of the National Security Council essentially created a secret apparatus for him to reshape the world's geo-political landscape by launching diplomatic overtures to the U.S.S.R. and the People's Republic of China.[59] Nixon had concluded that the strategy of containment regarding the Red Menace had been, in general, a failure, and he felt that the time had come for an earnest dialogue with the U.S.S.R. and People's Republic of China.[60] Conservatives who promoted a strong military had been Nixon's base.[61] Moreover, the Defense Department and C.I.A. jingoes almost certainly thought that Nixon would revert to Tricky Dick when he was elected president and the war machine would feast.[62] But Nixon double-crossed his base and the militaristic hawks in the government, because he actually sought to become a peacemaker.

Nixon's collaborator in his crusade for peace would be Henry Kissinger, who he elevated to National Security Advisor.[63] The 45-year-old, former Harvard professor came to Nixon's attention through Kissinger's Machiavellian machinations: Kissinger was an advisor to a Republican candidate who Nixon had vanquished in the primaries, and Kissinger leaked information to Nixon about the American and Vietnamese peace negotiations that he had gleaned from Nixon's defeated adversary.[64] So, Kissinger scored an assist in Nixon's treasonous act of undermining the U.S.-mediated peace negotiations between North Vietnam and South Vietnam.

CHAPTER 3

THE TABERNACLE CHOIR

The Pentagon and Langley jingoes did not trust Russia or China, and Nixon's sudden metamorphosis from cold warrior to peace-maker draped the Defense Department and C.I.A. hawks with a patina of disdain.[1] In fact, Nixon relayed to the Soviets that he was willing to relinquish America's involvement in Vietnam to advance the two countries diplomatic rapport.[2] To monitor Nixon's secretive peace mongering, the Joint Chiefs of Staff and C.I.A. tenaciously infiltrated the Nixon administration.

The Joint Chiefs of Staff conducted the first documented infiltration of the Nixon administration by military or intelligence entities.[3] In 1970, Nixon appointed Admiral Thomas Moorer to be chairman of the Joint Chiefs of Staff.[4] The 58-year-old Moorer was a tall, stout Alabaman.[5] A 1933 graduate of Annapolis, Moorer was a Navy fighter pilot who was stationed at Pearl Harbor when the Japanese executed their aerial banzai against the U.S. Pacific fleet.[6]

A few months later, the Japanese shot down Moorer's plane near Australia.[7] After the Japanese sent the recue vessel that was to retrieve Moorer and his crew to Davy Jones' Locker, he guided his crew and the rescue vessel's crew to an uninhabited island, where they erected an immense S.O.S. in the sand.[8] Moorer ultimately became a highly decorated war hero, and he rose through the ranks of the Navy.[9] He was appointed Chief of Naval Operations, which is the highest-ranking officer in the Navy, before Nixon tapped him to be chairman of the Joint Chiefs of Staff.[10]

Although Moorer had a seemingly relaxed demeanor and a slow drawl that were the byproducts of his rural Alabama roots, he was a frothing at the mouth anti-Communist. Moorer was stunned by Nixon's affable comportment towards the Russians and Chinese.[11,12] Nixon also utilized the Navy's top-secret communications system – SR-1 – as a backchannel for his secret negotiations with the Red Menace.[13]

The latter added insult to injury, so Moorer ultimately initiated a treasonous espionage campaign that focused on infiltrating Nixon and Kissinger's clandestine negotiations.[14] The espionage campaign has been coined the

"Moorer-Radford affair," because Admiral Moorer and a subordinate rear admiral conscripted Navy Yeoman Charles Radford to pilfer top-secret documents from the National Security Council.[15] Radford was a stenographer in the Joint Chiefs liaison office to the National Security Council.[16]

Yeoman Radford's father was Native American, and his mother was of Eastern European descent.[17] Radford's fragmented family was nomadic, and he had been intermittently tossed into foster homes, so, as a child and a teenager, he felt perpetually estranged.[18] He was a convert to Mormonism, which assuaged the estrangement he had endured throughout his youth.[19] Radford was elated to be working for the Joint Chiefs: He told the authors of Silent Coup that his assignment was "a long way from the Indian reservation…"[20] The Joint Chiefs had zero difficulty transforming Radford's yearning for praise and belonging into their treasonous hijinks.

Though Yeoman Radford would have a panache for purloining top-secret documents, he received a helping hand from the Joint Chiefs' inside man at the National Security Council – U. S. Army Colonel Alexander Haig, who served as a military aide to Kissinger.[21] Haig was Moorer's ace up his sleeve, because he enabled Radford to intersect with top-secret documents from the National Security Council.[22] Haig had Radford join him on two sojourns to Southeast Asia, and Haig's briefcase was "always" accessible to Radford.[23] When the authors of Silent Coup asked Radford about the primary objective of the Joint Chiefs' espionage, Radford replied "bringing Nixon down" and "getting rid of Kissinger."[24]

As Radford was engaged in stealing top-secret documents, Rear Admiral Robert Welander ultimately became Radford's principal handler at the Joint Chiefs liaison office to the National Security Council.[25] After Admiral Welander wedged himself into the espionage ring, Radford accompanied Kissinger on a jaunt to Southeast Asia, India, Pakistan, and Paris.[26] Kissinger's jaunt was purportedly to advance the peace process in Vietnam and buttress relations between India and Pakistan, who were locked in a clash over Bangladesh breaking away from Pakistan.[27] The United States and India were allies, but Nixon had covertly backed Pakistan in its 1971 war against India, because Pakistan's bloodthirsty president was an ally of China, and he provided Nixon and Kissinger with a conduit to the Chinese.[28]

In addition to Tricky Dick's duplicity against India, Nixon had Kissinger secretly skirt from Southeast Asia to China and firm up the administration's negotiations for the rapprochement of China.[29] As Kissinger was engaged in Nixon's clandestine ventures, Radford managed to leaf through Kissinger's briefcase, where he uncovered an "EYES ONLY" document earmarked for Nixon that was an overview of Kissinger's negotiations with the Chinese Premiere.[30]

The Joint Chiefs' espionage against Nixon and Kissinger was producing a windfall of unsavory secrets for the military, and Nixon's double-dealing with Pakistan and India was leaked to syndicated columnist Jack Anderson.[31] The Pakistan duplicity was a colossal scoop for Anderson, and he was awarded a Pulitzer Prize for the story.[32] Nixon had a pathological hatred of leaks, so he immediately scoured his administration for the leak: Radford promptly appeared on the radar due to his casual association with Jack Anderson – both were Mormons – and Radford was ordered to take a lie detector test.[33] Nixon was erroneously convinced that Anderson and Radford were homosexual lovers.[34] The fact that Radford and his wife had eight children was apparently lost on Nixon.[35]

As Radford was being polygraphed, he was asked if he furnished classified information to uncleared individuals.[36] Radford recoiled from answering the query, and the polygraph registered major fluctuations in his blood pressure, pulse, and respiration.[37] In a state of acute duress, Radford told his interrogators that he had to have a chat with Admiral Welander before he made additional disclosures.[38]

When Radford phoned Welander, he informed him that the investigators were inquiring about "our" activities.[39] Welander mistakenly thought that Radford had been Anderson's source, and he presumed that Radford was only being grilled about the information provided to Anderson.[40] He ordered Radford to be truthful.[41] Welander was utterly oblivious to the fact that he had just authorized Radford to cough up the full monty on the Joint Chiefs' espionage: Radford then sang an aria that rivaled the Mormon Tabernacle Choir.[42]

After Nixon was briefed on Radford's revelations, he met with Attorney General John Mitchell to deliberate on Radford's confession.[43] Nixon was seething over the Joint Chief's treachery, but Mitchell insisted that Nixon bury the matter and offered a number of rationales.[44] Nixon ultimately concluded that it was prudent to bury the Moorer-Radford affair, because he didn't trust his Secretary of Defense and frequently circumvented him by issuing orders directly to Admiral Moorer.[45] Publicizing the Moorer-Radford affair would also undercut public opinion of the military and military morale, which was scraping rock bottom due to the Vietnam debacle.[46] Nixon, moreover, was concerned that his top-secret negotiations with the Russians and Chinese would seep out of the subsequent investigation.[47]

So Nixon, ever the practitioner of realpolitik, used Moorer-Radford as a Damoclean sword over Moorer's treasonous head.[48] Nixon ultimately crushed Moorer's authority, but he retained a neutered Moorer as the Chairman of the Joint Chiefs.[49] Nixon then had Welander and Radford banished from D.C.[50] And last but not least, he decided to punish the Mormons en masse: He ordered that Mormon clergy be banned from performing services at the White House.[51]

The day after Nixon and Mitchell decided to bury the Moorer-Radford affair, Ehrlichman and a subordinate were slated to question Admiral Welander about his role in the affair, and their interview unfolded as scheduled in Ehrlichman's West Wing office.[52] At first, Welander attempted to evade his role in the spy ring, but then he largely fessed up to his complicity – and he implicated Haig.[53]

Although Welander's confession implicated Haig, Ehrlichman rightfully surmised that his subordinate and Haig had "bad blood."[54] Ehrlichman's subordinate was a Kissinger protégé, and he divulged to Ehrlichman that Haig had repeatedly betrayed Kissinger to the military.[55] Ehrlichman played the tape for Kissinger and Haig, but the investigator's animus towards Haig may have obfuscated Haig's role in the spy ring.[56] Nixon had decided to quash the affair, so he opted not to listen to the Welander confession or read the transcripts.[57]

When the authors of *Silent Coup* interviewed Admiral Welander, he wasn't very accommodating, but he disclosed that he thought Haig was privy to Radford reporting the various machinations of the National Security Council to the Joint Chiefs via Welander.[58] Welander also disclosed that Haig would reveal information to him that was specifically earmarked for Moorer.[59] The authors of *Silent Coup* also questioned Moorer about Haig's participation in the espionage scheme, and Moorer wasn't very accommodating either, even though he divulged that he returned the top-secret documents Radford had pinched to Haig via Welander.[60] Moorer's disclosure indicates that Moorer felt Haig would be mute on Radford's extracurricular activities, and Haig didn't relay Radford's pilfering to either Nixon or Kissinger.

Astonishingly, Haig was not tainted by the Moorer-Radford affair, because of Nixon's expeditious resolution of the matter. Nixon even shielded Haig from Kissinger's wrath about the Joint Chiefs' hijinks.[61] By safeguarding Haig, Nixon had armed a thermonuclear bomb whose epicenter was his presidency.

Chapter 4

The Plumbers

The hawks at the C.I.A. shared the same sentiments about Nixon's covert negotiations with the Red Menace as Moorer et al., and a fortuitous chain of events for the C.I.A. enabled its agents to infiltrate the inner sanctums of the Nixon White House. The first of those events was the *New York Times* publishing a May 1969 article about the Nixon administration's clandestine bombing of North Vietnamese sanctuaries in neutral Cambodia.[1] The leak to the *New York Times* made Nixon and Kissinger absolutely livid.[2] At Nixon's behest, Kissinger contacted F.B.I. chieftain J. Edgar Hoover, and the F.B.I. tapped the phone of a National Security Council employee who had a dovish repute.[3] Over the next two years, Kissinger and Haig directed the F.B.I. to tap the phones of government officials, Democratic powerbrokers, and even journalists.[4]

Two years after the Cambodian bombing leak, in June of 1971, the *New York Times* published excerpts from the "Pentagon Papers," a secret Defense Department study about the Vietnam War that belied the government's Vietnam propaganda.[5] Daniel Ellsberg, a former military analyst, leaked the Pentagon Papers.[6] Nixon thought that the F.B.I. and Defense Department were dragging their collective heels on investigating the leak, so he directed Ehrlichman to assemble a crew of White House personnel to investigate the genesis and motives behind the Pentagon Papers' leak.[7]

The crew, christened the Special Investigations Unit, was formed in July of 1971, and its raison d'être was to plug leaks.[8] The Unit quickly acquired the epithet of the Plumbers.[9] The Plumbers' mandate was buttressed that July, because the *New York Times* published highly classified information about the Nixon administration's ongoing Strategic Arms Limitations Talks with the Soviets, which made Nixon apoplectic.[10]

C.I.A. agent E. Howard Hunt was hired to be a Plumber in July of 1971.[11] The 52-year-old Hunt had receding blond hair, and his thin, sharp face was ferret-like. He had a svelte, medium-height frame, and he was fond of sporting opaque, black sunglasses and fedoras. He was married with four children. Hunt's connection to the Nixon administration was via Charles Colson, the special counsel to the president.[12] Both Hunt and Colson were Brown University alumni, and Hunt initially approached Colson about White House employment in the autumn of 1969, when the C.I.A. overtly employed him.[13] Hunt then pestered Colson for more than a year about employment at the White House.[14] Colson eventually introduced Hunt to Ehrlichman.[15] Hunt and C.I.A. Director Richard Helms were old friends, and Helms put in a good word for Hunt to Ehrlichman.[16] Hunt told Ehrlichman that he had retired from the C.I.A. the previous year, and Ehrlichman hired him to be a Plumber.[17]

But Hunt lied to Ehrlichman about his severed association with the C.I.A., because the record is replete with illustrations of his continued affiliation with the Company. For example, he reported his contacts with Colson and ultimate conscription by the White House to the C.I.A.[18] The F.B.I. also reported that Hunt worked for the C.I.A. on an "ad hoc basis" even while the White House employed him.[19]

Though E. Howard Hunt is primarily remembered as a Watergate burglar, he had a legendary career as a globetrotting spy. He was born in upstate New York.[20] His father was an attorney, and his mother a classically trained pianist.[21] Before being conscripted by the C.I.A., Hunt had been an intelligence officer in China during World War II, a novelist, and a screenwriter.[22] A former U.S. ambassador extolled Hunt's virtues when he declared that Hunt was "totally self-absorbed, totally amoral, and a danger to himself and anybody around him."[23] Hunt was a "black operative," which implies that his life was a tapestry of fabrications and fictitious covers.[24]

Prior to Hunt's "retirement" from the C.I.A. in 1970, he had fraudulently retired in 1960 and 1965.[25] In 1960, Hunt was issued bogus C.I.A. retirement papers that afforded the Company plausible deniability for Hunt's clandestine liaisons with anti-Castro Cubans prior to the Bay of Pigs.[26] After the ill-fated Bay of Pigs invasion, Hunt ostensibly skipped back to the C.I.A., even though he had never truly left its payroll.[27]

Hunt's second bogus retirement from the C.I.A. was in 1965, when a "flap" was deceptively created between the C.I.A. and Hunt.[28] After Hunt "retired" from the C.I.A. in 1965, he authored a series of spy novels under a nom de plume.[29] The books included thinly veiled depictions of various domestic and international political figures, and the C.I.A.'s objective was to manipulate the K.G.B into believing that the books contained various security breaches that were shrouded in the cloak of fiction.[30]

After Hunt's "retirement" in 1970, he worked for the Robert R. Mullen Company, a public relations firm that served as a C.I.A. front.[31] The C.E.O. of the Robert R. Mullen Company was either a C.I.A. agent or asset.[32] The

Robert R. Mullen Company also provided covers for C.I.A. agents, like Hunt, and launched various C.I.A. initiatives like Radio Free Cuba, which broadcast anti-Communist propaganda on Cuban radio waves.[33] In fact, the Robert R. Mullen Company hired Hunt at the behest of C.I.A. Director Richard Helms.[34] Hunt's track record of bogus retirements from the C.I.A., his unencumbered contact with the agency, and his employment by the Robert R. Mullen Company imbues his 1970 retirement from the C.I.A. with unequivocal reservation.

Approximately four months before Hunt was hired as a Plumber, he ventured to Miami in April of 1971, allegedly to service an account for the Robert R. Mullen Company, but, in actuality, he attended the 10th commemoration of the Bay of Pigs.[35] Hunt's attendance at the commemoration would ultimately turn out to be a recruitment drive: He inquired about the status of various Cubans who had been participants in the Bay of Pigs and formerly worked with the C.I.A.[36] Hunt's recruitment drive in Miami for Cubans, who would eventually become Watergate burglars, occurred before the Watergate break-in had even been conceived .[37]

The Bay of Pigs commemoration marked Hunt's first meeting with Eugenio Martinez.[38] Martinez was a Bay of Pigs veteran who had become a legend in the Cuban underground, because he had helmed more than 200 covert, maritime missions to Cuba.[39] He also continued to be employed by the C.I.A. after the Bay of Pigs.[40] At one point, a troubled Martinez met with his C.I.A. case officer to discuss Hunt.[41] His C.I.A. case officer then bumped up Martinez's concerns to the C.I.A.'s Miami station chief, who was well aware of Hunt's role as a "black operative."[42] The station chief expressed his reservations about Hunt's interactions with Martinez to a superior at Langley, but his C.I.A. overlord quashed his concerns.[43]

The Plumbers also conscripted former F.B.I. agent G. Gordon Liddy.[44] The 41-year-old Liddy was 5'9" and lean with receding brown hair and piercing brown eyes. Describing Liddy to denizens of the 21st century is a difficult task. In fact, describing an extraterrestrial to 21st century denizens may be easier than describing Liddy. With extraterrestrials, at least, there's a point of reference due to the myriad of movies and television shows about them, whereas it's difficult to find a 21st century point of reference for Liddy.

Liddy possessed numerous extremely unorthodox beliefs that superseded standard issue insanity, which I believe is the misinformation each successive generation imparts to the next generation. As a child, growing up in Hoboken, New Jersey, Liddy feared rats.[45] But he overcame his fear of the rodents by finding a dead rat that his sister's cat had mauled to death.[46] Liddy then proceeded to broil the rat and turn it into a fine dining experience.[47] Libby wrote in his autobiography that masticating on the rat neutralized his fear of the rodents.[48]

Liddy also had an affinity for all things Germanic. Given Liddy's early culinary predilections and his Teutonic enchantments, it's not surprising that movie night at the Liddy household would be bizarre, too: He was fond of taking his five kids to see Leni Reifenstahl's homage to the Nazis – *Triumph of the Will*.[49]

Liddy graduated from Fordham Law School, and he joined the F.B.I. in 1957.[50] Liddy viewed the Bureau as America's "elite corps … its Schutzstafel."[51] The Schutzstafel was the Nazi's dreaded S.S. After resigning from the F.B.I. in 1962, Liddy worked at his father's law firm for about four years before becoming an assistant district attorney for Dutchess County, New York.[52] As an assistant D.A., Liddy was often seen driving his Jeep around Poughkeepsie, New York and packing a revolver.[53] In one case he prosecuted, the defense claimed that a handgun was inoperable, but, in his closing arguments, Liddy shot a bullet from the gun into the courthouse ceiling.[54]

In 1966, Liddy spearheaded a raid on a sprawling Dutchess County estate that had been inherited by a trio of trust fund siblings, who had permitted Timothy Leary to use the estate as the fountainhead for his "Turn on, tune in, and drop out" revolution.[55] The bust ultimately proved fruitless: Liddy's case was tossed out of court due to a technicality.[56] However, I should note that Liddy and Leary became debate partners and highly improbable pals in the 1980s.[57]

Ever the man of action, Liddy tried his hand at politics in the tempestuous 1960s.[58] He made an ill-fated attempt to wrangle the Republican nomination for U.S. Representative of New York's 28th congressional district from the incumbent.[59] In 1969, Liddy incarnated as an U.S. Treasury Department agent in Washington, D.C.[60] He was then conscripted to organize a Treasury Department initiative to put the kibosh on drug smuggling across the Mexican border.[61]

But Liddy's storm trooper tactics sowed pandemonium, because traffic at border communities was subjected to extensive searches and delayed for hours, hampering tourism.[62] Liddy attempted to appeal to the distressed border communities with patriotic speeches that included advocacy for absolutely no gun control – as the best form of gun control.[63] His very public stance on gun control – or lack thereof – precipitated his estrangement from the Treasury Department, but he quickly found employment as a Plumber.[64]

So, now, the Plumbers had managed to collect the dynamic and frightening duo of E. Howard Hunt and G. Gordon Liddy. Hunt and Liddy shared the same jingoistic convictions, and they quickly became fast friends, even though Hunt would be less than candid with Liddy that his overriding affiliation was to the C.I.A. – not the Nixon administration.

Hunt and Liddy had an industrious symbiosis. In a July 1971 memorandum, after the Pentagon Papers' publication, Hunt recommended that the C.I.A. prepare a psychological profile of the Pentagon Papers' leaker Daniel Ellsberg, and C.I.A. Director Richard Helms authorized the profile.[65] After completion of the C.I.A. profile, Hunt and Liddy met with the C.I.A. shrinks who created the profile.[66] The page-and-a-half profile proved to be a rather insipid document, distilling Ellsberg's motives for spilling national secrets into a problem with authority, a mid-life crisis, and as a patriotic act.[67]

To excavate the darkest recesses of Ellsberg's psyche, Liddy wrote, Ehrlichman ultimately approved a break-in into the office of Ellsberg's Los Angeles-based psychiatrist – Dr. Lewis Fielding.[68] (Ehrlichman, however, adamantly denied sanctioning the break-in.[69]) Hunt and Liddy decided to reconnoiter Dr. Fielding's office before the actual break-in.[70] Prior to Hunt and Liddy's sojourn to Los Angeles, they visited a C.I.A. safe house in D.C., where they were supplied with sundry espionage accessories.[71]

Liddy was provided with the credentials of one "George Leonard" from Kansas and a miniature spy camera that was hidden in a tobacco pouch.[72] For his secret agent man *pièce de résistance*, he was outfitted with a wig, dentures sans an incisor, a pair of coke bottle glasses, and an implement that gave him a pronounced limp.[73] Misters "Leonard" and "Warren" packed their various C.I.A. accouterments and flew to Los Angeles.[74]

Once on the West Coast, Hunt and Liddy conducted daytime and nocturnal reconnaissance of the psychiatrist's office.[75] Neither Hunt nor Liddy had lock-picking expertise. But Hunt spoke to the cleaning woman in Spanish and conveyed to her that he and Liddy were physicians who wished to leave a message for Dr. Fielding.[76] The cleaning woman, apparently accustom to incisor deficient physicians, granted Liddy access to Dr. Fielding's second-story office, where he snapped a myriad of pictures with his miniature C.I.A.-issued camera.[77] With his personal Minolta camera, Hunt snapped pictures of Liddy standing outside of Dr. Fielding's office.[78] The pictures showed Liddy standing in front of a Volvo, and, printed on the background wall, above the Volvo, was "Dr. Lewis J. Fielding."[79] When Hunt and Liddy returned from the West Coast, they were greeted by a C.I.A. employee at the airport who took custody of both cameras to develop their film.[80] The C.I.A. claimed that the miniature spook camera used by Liddy had malfunctioned and yielded no photographs.[81] The C.I.A., moreover, would disseminate the pictures taken by Hunt's Minolta camera at a very inopportune interlude for the Nixon administration, sowing irrevocable damage to Nixon.

After Hunt and Liddy's L.A. adventure, the C.I.A.'s deputy director phoned Ehrlichman and said that the C.I.A. would discontinue backing Hunt's White House activities.[82] The phone call befuddled Ehrlichman, because he had not been hitherto aware of the C.I.A.'s assistance for Hunt.[83] The C.I.A.'s deputy director also wrote a note to C.I.A. Director Helms stating that Hunt had been cut-off by the C.I.A.[84]

As I've previously mentioned, Hunt had kept the C.I.A. apprised of his various White House activities, so the C.I.A. was almost certainly cognizant that the next move for the Plumbers was a break-in into Dr. Fielding's office. Consequently, the note from the C.I.A.'s deputy director to its director provided the C.I.A. with plausible deniability regarding the upcoming break-in. But, according to Liddy, the C.I.A.'s disconnection from Hunt and his White House shenanigans was pure malarkey: The C.I.A. continued to assist Hunt and Liddy.[85]

CHAPTER 5

IN THE COMPANY OF MEN

John Ehrlichman was the Plumbers' capo, but a subordinate who oversaw the Plumbers was flabbergasted that Hunt and Liddy had ventured to Los Angeles without his blessing: The thought of White House personnel being busted breaking into Dr. Fielding's office was extremely disconcerting.[1] He demanded that Hunt and Liddy use surrogates for the break-in.[2] Hunt subsequently contacted the Cuban soldiers of fortune he had cultivated for dirty deeds: Hunt, Liddy, and three Cuban operatives – Eugenio Martinez, Bernard Barker, and Felipe De Diego – then converged on Los Angeles, September 1, 1971.[3] They hit Dr. Fielding's office on September 3.[4]

The burglars were well-equipped: In addition to a plethora of photographic equipment, they had surgical gloves, a glass cutter, a crowbar, black plastic to cover the office windows, four walkie-talkies, and a nylon cord, so they could rappel from the second-story should they be detected.[5] The burglars also had a Polaroid camera.[6] The rationale for the Polaroid camera was ostensibly to take photographs at the onset of the burglary and then to use the photographs to return Dr. Fielding's office to its former pristine state before the burglars departed.[7]

The Polaroid pictures quickly became a moot issue: The Cubans shattered the window on the ground floor, and crowbarred Dr. Fielding's office door ajar.[8] The Cubans then ransacked the psychiatrist's office as they searched for Ellsberg's file.[9] The disarray sown by the Cubans made it impossible to reassemble Dr. Fielding's office to its former state, so the Cubans ultimately flung files and pills on the floor to make the burglary appear as if drug addicts had committed the crime.[10] The burglars then used the Polaroid to take pictures of the carnage.[11]

Cuban burglar Barker said that they never located Ellsberg's file.[12] However, burglar De Diego maintained that they had, in fact, located it.[13] He said that he paged through the file as Martinez photographed each of its pages with a miniature camera, even though Martinez also said the burglars never found the Ellsberg file.[14] Dr. Fielding corroborated De Diego's account, because the following morning he found Ellsberg's file on the office floor and said that it had been undoubtedly "fingered."[15] Martinez gave the camera to Hunt in front of Liddy, but the camera was destined for a black hole: Liddy was never apprised of the film's fate.[16]

The viewpoint that Hunt and at least two of the Cubans intentionally botched the break-in into Dr. Fielding's office shouldn't elicit too many reservations. Veterans of spycraft like Hunt and the Cubans had extensive experience with black bag jobs, but the Dr. Fielding break-in was an utterly ramshackle exploit. Hunt also had access to a skilled locksmith in the cadre of Cubans from whom he recruited Martinez, Barker, and De Diego.[17] The fact that the burglars had a Polaroid camera in tow so they could return Dr. Fielding's office to its formerly pristine condition after it had been burgled demonstrates that ransacking his office wasn't in their covert game plan.

Ehrlichman was "appalled" by the carnage when he leafed through the Polaroid pictures of Dr. Fielding's office after the break-in.[18] The burglary was potentially a gushing catastrophe for the White House, because participants of that bizarre escapade could firmly place the prime mover of the burglary at the doorsteps of the White House. Moreover, the C.I.A.'s deputy director's note to C.I.A. Director Helms, stating that Hunt had been cut-off by the C.I.A., wholly exonerated the C.I.A. of malfeasance related to the break-in.

Odds are that the C.I.A. hawks who had antipathy for Nixon looked upon the Dr. Fielding break-in as a windfall. The botched burglary potentially incriminated the Nixon administration and, chances are, those very hawks were the recipients of Dr. Fielding's notes on Ellsberg – and the White House underwrote the expenses for their windfall. The C.I.A., however, had not finished penetrating the Plumbers.

The next documented Company man to infiltrate the Plumbers was 47-year-old James McCord.[19] He had a non-descript pasty, white face, and comb over of black hair that futilely attempted to cover his white dome. His dark eyes were like obsidian. McCord was about six feet tall, and he had a protruding paunch. His gait was not entirely dissimilar to the waddle of a penguin. He was married, and he had three children – one son and two daughters. One of his daughters was developmentally challenged.[20]

McCord, like Hunt, was jingoistic and absolutely dogmatic about the C.I.A.'s anti-Communist credo, even though he and Hunt had antithetical personality types. Hunt was bombastic and an eccentric skirt chaser, and McCord was a taciturn, monogamous Pentecostal Christian. Hunt looked upon the Red Menace as an ideological foe that had to be vanquished, but McCord looked upon it as the spawn of Satan. For McCord, the fight against the Red Menace was a crusade of cosmic proportions.

Personality types like McCord have the potential to be extremely dangerous, because they rationalize their nefarious activities as necessary evils to abet the Almighty in the cosmic crusade against Beelzebub.

McCord's entrée into the Nixon administration was via the Committee to Re-Elect the President (C.R.P.). In the fall of 1971, shortly after Hunt's botched, black bag job in Los Angeles, the C.R.P. was in the market for a security chief.[21] The White House operative who was tasked with finding the C.R.P.'s security chief was at a loss, so he sought guidance from a Secret Service supervisor at the White House.[22] The White House operative told the Secret Service agent that the C.R.P.'s security chief should be a resident of Washington, D.C., a former Secret Service agent, an accomplished security expert, and also a Nixon loyalist.[23]

The Secret Service agent relayed to the White House operative that he had made an "exhaustive" quest for Secret Service agents meeting his four requirements, and his considerable labors had yielded only McCord.[24] McCord was an electronics expert *par excellence*, but he was not a resident of the capital or a former Secret Service agent. Moreover, McCord's loyalty to Nixon was far from effusive. In fact, a former C.R.P. employee who befriended McCord said that McCord felt that "Richard Nixon wasn't a team player, wasn't an American…"[25] If the former C.R.P. employee's recollections of McCord are accurate, McCord had contempt for Nixon, and his antipathy did indeed play an integral role in delivering Nixon to the valley of the shadow of death – without a rod or staff.

In reality, numerous Secret Service agents living in or near Washington, D.C. met the requisites for the C.R.P. role, but McCord was ultimately recommended for the job.[26] In *Secret Agenda*, Jim Hougan interviewed a former C.I.A. employee who had worked for a Secret Service detachment at the White House: He said that the Secret Service agent who recommended McCord for the C.R.P. assisted additional C.I.A. agents in their infiltration of the Nixon administration.[27] The C.R.P. initially hired McCord on a part-time basis in October of 1971.[28] By January of 1972, McCord had become the C.R.P.'s security chief.[29]

Prior to joining the C.I.A. in 1951, McCord had been an F.B.I. agent – his focus was counterespionage.[30] McCord's initial charge at the C.I.A. was identifying C.I.A. personnel whose leftist leanings had the potential to be ensnared by the dragnet of Joe McCarthy and the House on Un-American Activities Committee.[31]

Throughout the balance of the 1950s and early 1960s, McCord worked for the C.I.A.'s Office of Security, a sprawling bureaucracy tasked with safeguarding C.I.A. operations, personnel, and assets.[32] The Office of Security reported directly to the C.I.A. director, so it had zero oversight beyond the C.I.A.[33] One mandate of the Office of Security was to root out agents of the Red Menace who were attempting to infiltrate or had infiltrated the C.I.A.[34] The director of the Office of Security maintained a file on 300,000 Americans, primarily homosexuals, who had been busted for various sexual offenses to ostensibly ensure that they did not become C.I.A. employees who were susceptible to blackmail.[35]

A section within the Office of Security worked closely with a D.C. police captain who helmed the department's "sex squad," which collected prurient dirt on everyone in the capital.[36] In Secret Agenda, Jim Hougan wrote that the esteemed captain "…maintained exhaustive files on the subject of sexual deviance, files said to have included the names of every prostitute, madam, pimp, homosexual, pederast, sadomasochist, and most types in between, of whatever nationality, who came to the attention of the police in the country's capital."[37] The captain, via confiscated "trick books," also had the names and sexual preferences of the prostitutes' clients, who included congressmen, diplomats, judges, and spooks.[38]

McCord had various assignments in the Office of Security throughout the 1960s. He was a cog in a branch of the C.I.A. that perpetrated domestic spying.[39] If a C.I.A. agent was suspected of being a quisling, agents of the Office of Security would conduct physical surveillance and, if necessary, break into the agent's residence and plant eavesdropping devices.[40] McCord was a "master" wireman.[41]

McCord ostensibly retired from the C.I.A. on August 31, 1970, but, like Hunt, his retirement is mired in implausibility.[42] Despite McCord's "retirement" from the C.I.A., he regularly reported to a C.I.A. contract agent about his tasks for the Plumbers.[43] The contract agent then relayed McCord's information to his C.I.A. case officer.[44] The rationale McCord offered for retiring from the C.I.A. was that his federal salary was not sufficient to meet the financial onuses posed by his developmentally delayed daughter.[45] He proffered a dubious story of augmenting his federal pension teaching industrial security part-time at a Maryland junior college.[46]

Shortly after McCord "retired" from the C.I.A., he rented a basement apartment from a septuagenarian landlady in Chevy Chase, Maryland.[47] McCord told the landlady that he was a retired C.I.A. officer who needed a second dwelling near Washington, D.C., because of his "consulting work" for the Pentagon.[48] Jim Hougan pointed out in Secret Agenda that McCord's cover story was rather flimsy, because he, most likely, was not consulting for the Pentagon.[49] And his home in Rockville, Maryland was approximately ten miles further from the Pentagon than Chevy Chase, Maryland.[50]

Prior to renting the apartment to McCord, the landlady decreed that he could not smoke in his bedroom or entertain women in the apartment.[51] McCord consented to both conditions.[52] After McCord's Watergate infamy, the F.B.I. interviewed his landlady, and she provided the F.B.I. with a number of interesting tidbits about McCord.[53] First, she said that Hunt had visited him at the apartment.[54] Second, a telephone company technician relayed to her that McCord had extensive bugging equipment in the apartment.[55] Third, the landlady said that "young girls" recurrently visited the apartment, and she had an eviction showdown with McCord as a young woman was crying uncontrollably on the bed.[56] McCord's flimsy C.I.A. retirement story and his C.I.A. background conceivably translate into the Chevy Chase basement apartment being the scene of a covert operation that entailed young women, bugging equipment, blackmail, and, perhaps, Hunt.

The working relationship between Hunt and McCord probably dated back to the early 1960s, when both men reportedly participated in a clandestine venture that involved deploying Cubans to perpetrate surreptitious actions against Cuba.[57] Hunt was a rather unsavory bloke, and he probably exposed his wife to various unsavory blokes, but McCord gave Hunt's wife a serious case of the willies.[58] She told him there was something "wrong" with McCord.[59]

In his role as the C.R.P.'s security chief, McCord came into contact with Liddy.[60] Liddy was in search of a skilled wireman, and he plied McCord with various questions about electronic gadgets and gizmos.[61] Liddy ultimately floated an offer to McCord that would augment his salary by $2,000 every month, and it also offered McCord piecework incentives – $2,000 per clandestine break-in.[62] McCord acquiesced to Liddy's offer.[63] Liddy was impervious to the fact that recruiting McCord meant sowing the seeds of his ruin and the ruin of the Nixon administration.

In April of 1972, Liddy "introduced" McCord to Hunt.[64] The two "retired" C.I.A. agents greeted each other as absolute strangers and feigned meeting for the first time.[65] Hunt had played Liddy in Los Angeles, and now both Hunt and McCord will play Liddy throughout Watergate. Unbeknownst to Liddy, Hunt and McCord will use his man of action persona against him. Liddy wasn't being played by run-of-the-mill C.I.A. agents – Hunt and McCord were legends and super spooks. In fact, a former C.I.A. director said of McCord: "This is the best man we have."[66]

CHAPTER 6

THE BOY WONDER

John Dean has been portrayed as the Nixon minion whose *blind ambition* compelled him to become awash in the moral turpitude of the Nixon administration. But, then, he beheld a burning bush and heroically unlocked the secrets that played an integral role in the demise of the Nixon presidency. Since Watergate, Dean has forged an ideal life for himself, living in Beverly Hills as an investment banker, author, and pundit. Dean has even become a darling of the left as he's excoriated the neocons for their brazen deceit and called for the impeachment of George W. Bush and Dick Cheney.[1]

John Wesley Dean, III, was born in Akron, Ohio in 1938.[2] His upwardly mobile family moved to Evanston, Illinois, which is 30 miles south of Chicago, where he attended elementary and middle school.[3] In high school, Dean enrolled in Staunton Military Academy in Virginia.[4] At Staunton, he befriended Barry Goldwater, Jr., son of the uber conservative U.S. senator and 1964 Republican presidential candidate.[5] Dean majored in political science at Wooster College in Ohio as he was becoming preoccupied by his premature balding. He washed his hair with Grampa's Wonder Soap, a proverbial snake oil to prevent baldness.[6]

After graduating from Georgetown Law School in 1965, Dean had a pair of existential misfires. [7] The first was an acrimonious marriage to the daughter of a Democratic senator that yielded a divorce and a son who sustained the Dean lineage – John Wesley Dean, IV.[8] The *New York Times* queried Dean's former mother-in-law about her former son-in-law, and she responded: "I wouldn't want to discuss John's character, because there's a chance it's changed since I knew him."[9] His second misfire was being terminated by a Washington, D.C.-based law firm that specialized in communications law.[10] Dean's employer discovered that he had been clandestinely laboring on a television broadcast license for the competitor of one of the law firm's clients. He was fired after a mere six months.[11]

In one fell swoop, however, Dean's Republican pedigree gave him the connections to reinvent himself from fallen attorney to chief minority counsel for the House Judiciary Committee.[12] Dean continued to utilize a little help from his friends after Nixon became president, and he ultimately became a deputy assistant attorney general in the Nixon Department of Justice.[13] At Justice, Dean displayed a talent for dancing with wolves, which was in vogue during the Nixon administration.[14] When Nixon decided to reconfigure his administration, Dean was tapped to be the counsel to the president in June of 1970.[15] Haldeman and Ehrlichman thought that Dean wouldn't be a threat to their supremacy, which ultimately proved to be an egregious miscalculation.[16]

Ehrlichman had preceded Dean as counsel to the president before his ascension to domestic affairs czar.[17] In the reconfigured White House, Dean's new status as counsel to the president would never harness the juice of Ehrlichman.[18] He was expected to be a loyal, competent apparatchik who would report to Haldeman and Ehrlichman.[19]

The 32-year-old Dean was a slender 5'10", and he cut a swath of pizzazz in the dour Nixon administration, wearing flashy, tailored clothes and Gucci loafers, leaving his less style conscious colleagues in the dust of the late 1950s.[20] Dean also wore contacts to accentuate his boyish good looks.[21] He owned a pricey townhouse in Alexandria, Virginia, and he careened around town in a maroon Porsche.[22] Grampa's Wonder Soap proved to be ineffective, so Dean's thinning dishwater blond hair was neatly arrayed into a comb-over. His hair almost draped his ears, which offended Haldeman's aesthetic sensibilities, and, upon hiring Dean, he quipped that Dean would be the White House's token "hippie."[23] Dean even cultivated the reputation of a playboy amongst his White House co-workers.[24] He was clearly en route to upward mobility.

As Dean champed at the bit to prove himself, Haldeman granted him the opportunity.[25] Haldeman presented Dean with a disconcerting proposal for the collection of domestic intelligence – "The Huston Plan."[26] The Huston Plan called for an interagency cabal to wage a no quarter crusade against the "New Left," which was fomenting campus riots and demonstrations.[27] The Huston Plan included various dirty deeds designed to trample on the Constitution: The illicit opening of Americans' mail, unlawful electronic surveillance of targeted Americans, illegal break-ins, etc.[28] However, F.B.I. Director J. Edgar Hoover rejected The Huston Plan.[29]

Though Hoover had a protracted track record of trampling on the Constitution, he felt that The Huston Plan impinged on his personal fiefdom of reaping domestic intelligence.[30] Hoover was also concerned about the inevitable blowback if the plan were made public.[31] Attorney General

John Mitchell was not aware of The Huston Plan as it wended through the alphabet agencies, but Hoover edified him about it.[32] Mitchell was dismayed by The Huston Plan's unconstitutional caveats, and he ultimately told Nixon to quash it.[33] Nixon had the prudence to listen to Mitchell, and The Huston Plan was relegated to the circular file – at least for the time being.[34]

After the demise of The Huston Plan, Haldeman pressed Dean for strategies to bypass J. Edgar Hoover in the quest for domestic intelligence, because the F.B.I.'s ruthless closet queen sowed fear in the hearts of D.C. bureaucrats.[35] Dean composed his vision of an interagency cabal, and he forwarded it to Mitchell the following day.[36] Dean's memo articulated that a "blanket removal of restrictions" like The Huston Plan would be "inappropriate," but it would be appropriate "to remove restraints as necessary."[37] Dean's unconstitutional proposal was never deployed.[38]

But he was undeterred: In August of 1971, he wrote a memorandum, "Dealing with our Political Enemies," that endorsed deploying the "available federal machinery to screw our enemies."[39] Before the Senate's Watergate Committee, Dean testified that he was "asked to prepare a strategy for dealing with political enemies."[40] Dean, however, neglected to reveal who sanctioned the rather alarming memorandum. He testified that he routed the memorandum to Haldeman and Ehrlichman for approval.[41] But Ehrlichman subsequently testified that he had never seen Dean's memorandum.[42]

As counsel to the president, Dean inherited a couple of Ehrlichman operatives, who were former, hard-boiled New York Police Department detectives, and they specialized in clandestine ventures.[43] The first was John Caulfield.[44] The 40-year-old Caulfield was born in the Bronx to Irish immigrants.[45] He attended Wake Forest University in North Carolina for two years on a basketball scholarship.[46] Caulfield then served in the Army during the Korean War before becoming a N.Y.P.D. cop.[47] Within two years, Caulfield was promoted from a beat cop to a detective.[48] He ultimately joined an elite unit of the N.Y.P.D. that was tasked with protecting visiting dignitaries.[49] The unit also investigated dissident organizations and deftly penetrated left-wing and black groups.[50]

Caulfield essentially acted as a cutout for Ehrlichman and then Dean, and he conscripted a second former N.Y.P.D. detective who specialized in dirty deeds.[51] At Ehrlichman's behest, Caulfield's underling was tasked with finding the dirt on Nixon's enemies, which included Democrats, especially Ted Kennedy, anti-war groups, entertainers, etc.[52] Dean essential-

ly disavowed having knowledge of Caulfield's subordinate and his shenanigans, but Caulfield told the authors of *Silent Coup* that Dean was "full of
shit."[53]

He said that Dean renegotiated his subordinate's contract.[54] In fact, at
Dean's bidding, the former N.Y.P.D. detective specializing in dirty deeds
said he investigated a New York City madam whose stable of exquisite
prostitutes catered to a high-powered clientele that were potentially
blackmail fodder.[55] But the information proved to be fruitless, because
her clientele was bipartisan – Democrats and Republicans were equally
represented in her "little black book."[56]

Caulfield maintained that Dean's hunger for political intelligence became increasingly ravenous, and he started taking "greater chances" in the
hopes of greater intelligence windfalls.[57] In November of 1971, Caulfield
said that Dean instructed him to evaluate the viability of harvesting intelligence at the D.N.C. headquarters in the Watergate, and his subordinate
cased the D.N.C. – seven months before the Watergate break-in.[58] Dean,
initially, denied sanctioning the assignment to the authors of *Silent Coup*,
but then he backpedaled when confronted with the accounts of the two
former N.Y.P.D. detectives: Dean said that Caulfield may have recommended casing the Watergate when he was in the midst of multitasking
and distracted, and he may have replied: "Whatever you think…"[59]

Caulfield thought that plundering the D.N.C. was quite hazardous:
He recalled thinking that botching such an assignment could conceivably
"bring down the president."[60] But Caulfield, nonetheless, directed his subordinate to case the D.N.C. headquarters, and he reported to Caulfield
that it would yield a scant dividend of intelligence.[61]

In the spring of 1971, Caulfield, at Ehrlichman's behest, proposed
leaving the White House and launching a security firm that specialized
in campaign intrigue.[62] Caulfield's intrigue would be named "Operation
Sandwedge," and it included collecting derogatory scuttlebutt on the
Democrats, black bag jobs, and surveillance of the Democratic primaries
and the D.N.C. convention.[63] Caulfield told the authors of *Silent Coup* that
the operation's particulars were forged from various discussions that he
had with Dean.[64] Caulfield sent a memo to Dean delineating Sandwedge's
various ploys, and stating its estimated price tag – $500,000.[65] Dean lob-
bied Mitchell and Haldeman for the implementation of Sandwedge, but
both put the kibosh on it.[66]

CHAPTER 7

HONEY TRAP

In the 1970s, the procurers of prostitutes had to take risks and/or subject themselves to unanticipated pitfalls: They had to phone escort services, visit brothels, troll for prostitutes on the streets, etc. In these various milieus, the potential for encountering unsavory individuals or vice cops was invariably a threat. So, some industrious D.N.C. employees made it easy for visiting dignitaries and V.I.P.s to circumvent the pre-internet pitfalls of procuring prostitutes by providing them with call girls who were in the stable of D.C. madam Heidi Rikan.

Rikan had a black book that was a who's who of "famous athletes, mobsters, movie stars, bookies, playboy millionaires, and, of course, politicians and government officials of every stripe…"[1] Her black book also had listings for Watergate whistleblower John Dean and his future wife Maureen.[2] But before examining John Dean's purported role in the Watergate break-in, I want to focus on Rikan's fascinating yet tragic background, and her relationship with Maureen Dean, John Dean's wife.

Rikan was a flawless, blonde voluptuary who had the eroticism to elicit a double-take from a near-sighted eunuch at fifty yards. But like legions of prostitutes, her childhood was most likely disfigured by incest and other cataclysms that decimated her self-esteem, compelling her to deploy her exquisite beauty in the skin trade.[3] Rikan was born in Kiel, Germany in 1937, which wasn't a superlative time to be born in Germany.[4] Her father was in the Nazi navy and her mother labored in a torpedo factory.[5]

According to Rikan's mother, allied bombings had reduced the Rikan family to a near nomadic state.[6] The Nazis were never enthusiasts of family values, and Rikan was placed in a state run camp as a child, so her mother could unabatedly toil long hours at the torpedo factory.[7] After the war, Rikan was eight years old when the Red Cross repatriated her with her parents.[8] She had undergone a dark metamorphosis at the camp: She spent protracted hours sitting in a corner, sucking on her thumb.[9]

The Rikan family emigrated to Reading, Pennsylvania in 1951, where Rikan graduated from high school in 1956.[10] In December of 1956, Rikan signed on for a hitch in the army, and her hometown newspaper featured a

1958 article on her: The article noted that even an army uniform couldn't obscure her "beautiful streamlined curves."[11] The article also reported that she had been crowned Miss Fort Myers and Miss Military District of Columbia, but the article neglected to mention that she had commenced on a nude modeling career.[12]

Rikan fell in love with a fellow soldier – a helicopter pilot – and they were married in September of 1958.[13] Rikan's marital status enabled her to opt out of the army.[14] Shortly thereafter, her husband was able to vacate his commission, because the Eisenhower administration was significantly reducing military expenditures and streamlining army personnel.[15] After a few months of matrimony, Rikan's husband found employment flying helicopters in South America for an oil company, and Rikan moved back to Pennsylvania to live with her mother who had divorced her father and remarried.[16]

Rikan's husband then found himself flying helicopters in California where he received a call from a D.C. attorney who said Rikan sought a divorce, and her husband ultimately signed the divorce papers.[17] Rikan's lawyer had apparently taken an amorous interest in the buxom beauty, because he told Rikan that her husband had died in a helicopter accident.[18] Throughout her lawyer's skullduggery, Rikan was in the midst of reinventing herself as a D.C. stripper.[19]

As a stripper, Rikan found a sugar daddy whose largesse included all of the accouterments of a kept woman – apartment, cars, furs, lingerie, etc.[20] She eventually rendezvoused with D.C.'s criminal overlord, Joe Nesline, and became a mobster moll.[21] She had an affair with Nesline and also befriended Nesline's mistress who was a stripper, too.[22] Although Rikan and Nesline's mistress became fast friends, the mistress noticed that Rikan was unequivocally taciturn about the various machinations of her life.[23] The latter quality wasn't lost on Nesline, and he put her to work, because, after all, in the bygone days of the underworld omertà reigned supreme.

One of Nesline's primary rackets was gambling on professional football, and Rikan garnered a royal flush of Hall of Fame gridiron greats in her little black book.[24] A pair of Nesline's underworld cohorts told police investigators that Nesline used Rikan to glean the lowdown on various football players, which gave him an edge over his gaming competition.[25] Rikan also became a globetrotting bagwoman for Nesline. On a junket to Antigua with Nesline, Rikan met a dapper, dashing scout for the Dallas Cowboys who was the consummate playboy, and they quickly became a libidinal whirlwind.[26] He, too, was mob connected.[27]

After the affair between Rikan and the scout fizzled out, he met a blonde voluptuary by the name of Maureen "Mo" Kane – or the future Mrs. John Dean.[28] Mo Kane grew up in a middle class Los Angeles neighborhood, and she was voted "Best Looking" by her high school classmates.[29] Shortly after Mo graduated from high school, she met an affluent suitor who became enamored with her.[30] She was 18 years old, and he was in his "early forties."[31] The age gap put a damper on her amour, but her suitor, nonetheless, gave her a 9½ carat diamond ring.[32] Mo refused to relinquish the ring in the aftermath of their break up. Her suitor sued, but Mo triumphed in court.[33]

In *White House Call Girl,* Phil Stanford interviewed an L.A. dentist to the stars who had been a brief paramour of Mo, and he reminisced about her: "She was looking for bigger potatoes. Millionaires. I had a house in Bel Air, a Porsche. But she was looking for something more."[34] In fact, she dated two superstar actors, but neither endeavor yielded matrimony.[35] Despite her blonde ambition, Mo became a flight attendant, based in Dallas, Texas.[36]

At the time Mo met the Cowboys' scout, who had so captivated Rikan, he was married to a popular singer. [37] The scout's former wife told Phil Stanford that Mo claimed to be pregnant, even though Mo rebuffs the insinuation.[38] The scout ultimately opted for a rather idiosyncratic form of chivalry: He married Mo but didn't divorce his wife.[39] Mo must have been utterly baffled by this ripple effect, because she returned to Los Angeles and married a high school beau in a Tijuana Blue Light Special.[40] Both Mo and the scout had become bigamists without the slightest indications of converting to Mormonism. Apparently, her second marriage proved to be problematic too, and she rebooted her marriage to her first husband, who had become a scout for the New Orleans Saints.[41]

The scout was the catalyst for Mo meeting Rikan.[42] After Mo's marriage to the scout went south for a second time, Mo and Rikan whiled away a few months in Lake Tahoe before Mo rejoined husband number two in L.A. and Rikan ventured back to D.C.[43] Though Mo received an annulment from the scout, her second marriage remained rocky.[44] So Mo eventually made a sojourn to D.C., and Rikan accommodated her.[45] Mo and Rikan then made a cross country trek to L.A. in Rikan's new Corvette.[46] When Mo and Rikan were en route to the West Coast, Mo's husband had a fatal car accident.[47] By the age of 23, Mo had been twice married and also become a widow. She then purportedly rented a Beverly Hills apartment with a woman who was separated from a gridiron great.[48]

Mo had seemingly become disillusioned with the City of Lights regarding matrimonial prospects, because she reportedly said: "I'm sick of Hollywood. Everybody here is so phony. I'm going to Washington. See if I can get a congressman or a senator or something. I've been trying for the longest time."[49] And as fate would have it, according to Mo's account, she received a phone call from John Dean, who was in L.A. on business.[50] Dean had ostensibly gleaned Mo's number from a mutual friend.[51] Dean was not quite a "congressman or a senator," but he was the counsel to the president of the United States, which wasn't too bad vis-à-vis the D.C. food chain. Dean apparently invited her to dinner.[52]

In *Mo: A Woman's View of Watergate*, Mo wrote that their dinner was a tempest of pheromones, and she was smitten.[53] Mo maintains that Dean invited her to the Virgin Islands for Thanksgiving.[54] And then he ostensibly flew to L.A. where they spent New Year's together.[55] Mo wrote that she accompanied him back to D.C., and she moved in with him, using Rikan's condo as a mailing address.[56] Mo's life quickly became a bouquet of dazzling D.C. parties.[57] Mo and Dean were a resplendent couple when they arrived at a White House function, featuring a famous opera singer, in Dean's Porsche.[58] Mo was draped in Rikan's full-length sable coat.[59] When Mo's mother was informed about her daughter's upward mobility, she roared: "I always knew my daughter would make it to the White House!"[60]

Mo's account of her courtship with Dean is very heartwarming. However, a *Washington Post* article reported that Mo met Dean when she was working for the "National Committee [sic] on Marijuana and Drug Abuse" in Washington, D.C. If the *Washington Post* is correct about Mo meeting Dean when she was in D.C., then her chronology collapses.

CHAPTER 8

THE TALENTED MR. BAILLEY

The Watergate saga is brimming with winners and losers, and one of its foremost losers was an attorney named Phillip Bailley, a Rikan associate and former seminarian.[1] Bailley had an imperious id and insurmountable libidinal appetites: His calling to be a priest inevitably resulted in a disconnected number. After graduating from Catholic University, Bailley attended Catholic University Law School, where he was voted "Most Likely to be Disbarred."[2]

As the reader will quickly discern, Bailley is a deeply flawed man. The accounts of Bailley that Phil Stanford has included in *White House Call Girl* have been liberally plumbed for this chapter. Though Bailley seems to be a highly suspect source, his story has been a constant over the years, and vast swaths of it have been corroborated. Indeed, a former assistant U.S. attorney for D.C. confessed that the Justice Department viciously napalmed Bailley's credibility to compromise his integrity as a witness.[3] As the Watergate saga unfolds, you, the reader, will be the ultimate arbitrator of whether or not Bailley is being truthful.

Bailley, in his late twenties, was a svelte 5'6", and he had sparkling blue eyes and a cherubic face that was framed by curly locks of black hair. He was an accomplished reprobate who possessed a talent for seducing women and coaxing them to be photographed in the nude.[4] His fledging law practice included petty criminals, prostitutes, and indigents who the court assigned to him.[5] The closest Bailley came to family values was employing his 17-year-old sister as his dutiful secretary.[6]

Bailley was a dedicated Democrat, but his political idols weren't J.F.K., L.B.J., or even R.F.K. Bailley had a special affinity for L.B.J. bagman Bobby Baker who oversaw the Quorum Club, where he pandered a harem of young women to D.C.'s high flyers.[7] Emulating Bobby Baker, Bailley orchestrated soirees for his buddies that included excessive drinking and sex with young women whom Bailley conscripted by placing ads in various college newspapers.[8] A University of Maryland graduate student was a very eager participant at the soirees, and, according to Bailley, she aspired to be a glamorous call girl.[9]

As Bailley loitered around the courthouse hustling up penny-ante cases, he met a seasoned criminal defense attorney whose clientele of criminals and prostitutes were in a much higher socioeconomic stratum than his.[10] And he was benevolent enough to start showing Bailley the ropes.[11] Bailley's mentor, or perhaps I should say dementor, introduced Bailley to the vice squad cops who would forgo their testimony in exchange for $50.[12]

Bailley's new mentor also spoke highly of an upscale brothel in D.C. that was stocked with a bevy of German and French knockouts.[13] Almost as a rite of initiation, Bailley made a pilgrimage to the brothel, where he was dazzled by its plush interior and superlative service.[14] A few days later, Bailley returned to the brothel, where he was greeted by a blonde, Teutonic goddess with a German accent, who introduced herself as "Erika."[15] Bailley also encountered two other women and two men. "Erika" then displayed her consummate managerial skills as she became the director of a "daisy chain gangbang."[16] Bailley maintains that the fräulein in question, who adroitly directed the orgy, just happened to be Heidi Rikan.[17]

Rikan's presence and stunning beauty enthralled Bailley. Though Bailley realized that upscale setups like Rikan's are generally protected, he, nonetheless, handed her one of his cards as he departed the brothel.[18] As he walked to his red Camaro convertible, he noticed a telephone company van and a repairman on a telephone pole behind the brothel.[19] But on closer inspection, Bailley realized that the telephone repairman was, in actuality, a vice squad cop tapping the brothel's phone.[20] The undercover vice cop recognized Bailley from his ubiquitous presence at the courthouse and chided him about the brothel.[21]

When Bailley reacted indignantly, the cop disclosed that the brothel had hidden cameras and Bailley's amorous acts had been captured for posterity.[22] Bailley made a beeline for his office and phoned the brothel.[23] He relayed to Rikan that her brothel was on the precipice of being raided by law enforcement.[24] Rikan phoned Bailley the following week, and she told him that the brothel had, indeed, been raided by the police and thanked him for his seemingly inside scoop.[25] Bailley then impressed upon her his snug relationship with the vice squad, and its potential value for her operation.[26]

Heretofore, Bailley had primarily represented streetwalkers, so he would be on the escalator of upward mobility if he had an opportunity to represent an upscale brothel like Rikan's.[27] During the course of their conversation, Bailley informed Rikan that he had an upcoming jaunt to the West Coast, and she told him to phone her upon his return to D.C.[28] The thought of being Rikan's representative in the courtroom and in the bedroom was a two-for-one special. Bailley could see nirvana on the horizon – courtesy of the D.C. police.

When Bailley returned from the West Coast, he gave Rikan a prompt call.[29] Rikan suggested that they rendezvous at his place: Her only requisites were dinner and champagne.[30] Bailley had recently moved into a new apartment complex in southwest D.C., and his third floor apartment balcony overlooked the complex's spacious swimming pool.[31] After Rikan arrived, Bailley escorted her to the balcony, where he popped the cork on a bottle of champagne and grilled a couple of steaks.[32] Bailley ultimately divulged to Rikan that he regularly made payoffs to vice cops in lieu of their appearance at the courthouse.[33] Rikan eventually disclosed to Bailley that she felt she could trust him, so she unveiled her "real name" to him – Kathie Dieter.[34] After Rikan came clean with Bailley about her name, the two retired to the bedroom for a romp.[35]

Approximately a week after Rikan's visit to Bailley's apartment, Rikan phoned Bailley, and they met at Nathan's, a happening Georgetown singles bar.[36] During their tête-à-tête at Nathan's, Rikan unfurled information about her new operation at the Columbia Plaza, a posh apartment complex about a block from the Watergate.[37] She then offered to slip Bailley $200 every couple of weeks to pass on the activities of the D.C. vice squad.[38] Bailley joyfully accepted the terms of his new employment.[39]

Bailley had boasted to Rikan that he volunteered for Robert Kennedy's 1968 presidential campaign, and he had connections at the Democratic National Committee offices, headquartered at the Watergate.[40] Rikan subsequently inquired if Bailley could use his D.N.C. connections to enlarge her clientele.[41] Though Rikan was very enthusiastic about the prospect of pandering prostitutes to Democratic luminaries, she pointed out that they needed an inside man to syphon Democrats from the D.N.C. to the Columbia Plaza.[42] Ever the man of action, with a gift for blarney, Bailley offered to take the initiative in the winter of 1970, 1971 – approximately five or six months before the Watergate burglary bust.[43]

Bailley said that he started trolling the Watergate bar, because he was aware that D.N.C. secretaries frequented it after work.[44] He started to approach various D.N.C. secretaries about the prospect of syphoning Democratic luminaries to Rikan's prostitution ring.[45] After a week of snubs, Bailley finally found a D.N.C. secretary up to the task.[46] Bailley conveyed to her that the escort service was on the up and up, and she simply had to show prospective clients a plastic folder of the prostitutes' pictures.[47] He added that she would be compensated $50 for every client she recruited.[48]

Bailley was fond of using code names in his address book.[49] When he conscripted the secretary, she was sipping champagne, so Bailley christened her "Champagne" in his address book.[50] When Bailley subsequently met Rikan at Nathan's, he informed her of conscripting Champagne.[51] He and Rikan then worked out the particulars for a Rikan underling to meet Champagne at the Watergate bar and provide her with pictures of the prostitutes and a contact number.[52] Afterwards, Bailley accompanied Rikan to the Columbia Plaza, where Rikan showed him a one-bedroom apartment. The apartment's interior decorating – Tiffany lamps, red and blue furnishings – corresponded to the décor of the brownstone housing her former enterprise.[53]

Once in the apartment, Bailley attempted to grope Rikan, but he was summarily rebuffed.[54] Rikan informed Bailley that their amorous liaisons were now verboten.[55] She was exclusively dedicated to commerce: She had additional questions about the D.N.C., and she also received a briefing on the vice squad.[56] Rikan also informed Bailley that the Columbia Plaza operation would be expanding in the near future.[57]

After Bailley's visit to the Columbia Plaza, Rikan phoned him and left a message with his sister, requesting that they meet again at Nathan's.[58] At Nathan's, Rikan was accompanied by a blonde voluptuary who wore a taut white blouse and jeans that looked "painted on."[59] Bailley recalled seeing her and Rikan in a photograph that was taken at Lake Tahoe.[60] According to Bailley, Rikan introduced the future Mrs. John Dean as "Mo Biner."[61] Rikan told Bailley that Mo's boyfriend was employed at the White House, and he had vast clout.[62] Bailey gave Mo the codename "Clout" in his address book and also wrote her initials – "M.B."[63] In a 1996 deposition, Mo testified that she had never met Bailley.[64] Bailley's sister, however, remembered "Clout" leaving numerous messages for her brother.[65] She also recalled that the same woman left messages as "Ms. Biner" and "Mo."[66]

Bailley began reporting to Rikan on a bi-weekly basis about vice squad activity.[67] Recruiting additional prostitutes for Rikan's operation was a topic of discussion, too.[68] In addition to her stable of seasoned pros, Rikan wanted to enlist "first-timers," because she felt they had an enthusiasm that was lacking in "experienced bitches."[69] Bailley attempted to recruit the University of Maryland graduate student who aspired to be a glamorous, high-priced call girl and had eagerly serviced Bailley and his friends at Bailley's soirees.[70] But Rikan didn't think she had the requisite class to be in her brothel – she didn't make the cut.[71] Bailley would rue the day that he became involved with the graduate student.

In September of 1971, according to Bailley, Rikan left a message for him, requesting a 2:00 P.M. rendezvous at her new, three-bedroom digs in the Columbia Plaza.[72] After Bailley knocked on the door, "Lou" greeted him and introduced himself.[73] Lou was, in fact, Lou Russell, a swarthy hulk of a man in his late fifties.[74] Years of alcoholism and dirty deeds had engraved deep burrows on his face, which looked like twenty miles of bad road. Russell was fortunate to be broaching the ripe age of a sexagenarian, because alcoholic thugs like him generally sport toe-tags at a relatively young age. In *Secret Agenda*, Jim Hougan noted that Russell's life was "devoted to booze, whores, and anti-Communism (roughly in that order)."[75] Russell lends credence to the adage that patriotism is the last refuge of scoundrels.

Russell had a pedigree that supplanted the typical mercenary thug who call-girl rings recruit for protection: He was a former minor league baseball player and F.B.I. agent.[76] The F.B.I. sacked Russell for alcoholism, but he made a comeback as an investigator for the House Un-American Activities Committee.[77] However, his tenure at H.U.A.C was curtailed when he attempted to blackmail H.U.A.C. witness Edward G. Robinson.[78]

As the Columbia Plaza operation was up and running, Russell ultimately worked for McCord and Associates.[79] In McCord's capacity as a Red Menace stalker and huntsman in the 1950s, he had daily interactions with Russell, when the latter worked for H.U.A.C.[80] Though Russell was an alcoholic and all-purpose reprobate, McCord apparently forgave his wages of sin, because the pair remained close for at least two decades.

Russell told Bailley that "Kathie" was running late, and he encouraged Bailley to help himself to various liquors that were stocked on the breakfast bar and to the deli sandwiches in the refrigerator.[81] Bailley made himself a J&B and water and sat at the breakfast bar, which overlooked the living room, where Russell was on the phone, talking to a bookie.[82] Bailley also encountered a fit man in his fifties, donning a turtleneck, who was eating a sandwich on the sofa.[83] When the man in the turtleneck dispensed with the sandwich, he walked into a bedroom at the end of the hall.[84]

Bailley's gaze followed the man into the bedroom, where he partially caught sight of a brass bed with a canopy.[85] Although the bedroom door remained ajar, and Bailley repeatedly glanced into the bedroom, he lost sight of the man.[86] After Bailley fortified himself with a second J&B and water and a few tokes from a joint, he felt primed to investigate the whereabouts of the disappearing man.[87] He checked out the bathroom but didn't see him.[88] On a lark, Bailley opened the closet door of a bedroom, and he encountered the disappearing man, who was ensconced with a reel-to-reel camera clandestinely aimed at the bedroom's bed.[89]

The disappearing man was furious when Bailley discovered his secret lair.[90] He pushed Bailley away from the closet and warned him that voicing a word about his recent discovery would have deleterious consequences.[91] Bailley then wandered back to the breakfast bar in a bewildered state.[92] Russell's haggard face yielded a smirk, and he commented on Bailley discovering "part of the set-up."[93] Russell said that it was now mandatory for Bailley to wait for "Kathie."[94]

Rikan arrived about 30 minutes after Bailley's discovery, and Russell gave her the low-down at the door.[95] After imbibing a few more J&B and waters, Bailley was stewing with questions when he confronted Rikan.[96] She explained to Bailley that the Columbia Plaza was like her previous operation in the brownstone.[97] Rikan referred to the men behind the blackmail operation as "cowboys."[98] She said that the cowboys compromise politicians and other V.I.P.s, because they're working so assiduously to "save the country."[99] Rikan also attempted to assuage Bailley's fears by telling him that their operation was "protected by the big guys."[100]

CHAPTER 9

TRIUMPH OF THE NIL

The next Nixon apparatchik to propel the Watergate saga forward was 36-year-old Jeb Stuart Magruder, who had been acting chairman of the C.R.P. until Mitchell resigned as attorney general and took the helm of the C.R.P. Magruder then became deputy director of the C.R.P.[1] Magruder had model looks and a svelte, 6'2" athletic physique, and his name among Nixon minions was "Steve Stunning."[2] He also had a beautiful wife and four beautiful children.[3]

Magruder was born on Staten Island, and his father owned a print shop.[4] At Williams College in Massachusetts, the dashing Magruder shined as a tennis player and swimmer.[5] Magruder's collegiate career was interrupted by a two-year stint in the Army, which he served in Korea.[6] After the war, he returned to Williams College and studied ethics, which he, apparently, disregarded upon entering the Nixon administration.[7] Upon graduation from college, Magruder eventually moved to Chicago and worked for the national security adjunct Booz Allen Hamilton.[8] He also earned an M.B.A. from the University of Chicago.[9]

Magruder became involved in Republican politics when he was in college.[10] After moving to Illinois, he worked on Donald Rumsfeld's successful bid for the U.S. House of Representatives in 1962.[11] He also toiled on the presidential campaign of Senator Barry Goldwater in 1964.[12] Magruder eventually relocated to Southern California, and he became the Southern California coordinator for Nixon's 1968 presidential campaign.[13] After Nixon's victory, Magruder moved east, with his wife and four children in tow, to work in the Nixon administration.[14] However, Magruder was a faint-hearted, fear-based individual who never quite acclimated to the Nixon administration's dances with wolves.

Magruder's status as deputy director of the C.R.P. forced his collision with two men who were proficient at dancing with wolves – John Dean and G. Gordon Liddy. Magruder had been tasked with finding a general counsel for the C.R.P.: He pressed Dean to ante up an attorney who worked for Dean to be the C.R.P.'s general counsel but Dean balked at the idea.[15] An Ehrlichman aide suggested to Dean that Magruder conscript

Liddy to be the C.R.P.'s general counsel, because Liddy could serve the function of a general counsel and also direct the collection of political intelligence.[16]

According to *Will*, Liddy became acquainted with Dean when he worked for the Treasury Department and Dean worked for the Justice Department.[17] Liddy wrote that a colleague who worked at the Justice Department informed him about Dean's reputation for deception.[18] In *Will*, Liddy discussed his inherent distrust of Dean, but he nonetheless met with him.[19] Liddy wrote that Dean quickly dispensed with formalities and broached the idea of Liddy being the architect of an "absolutely first-class intelligence operation."[20]

Liddy was cognizant of Sandwedge, and he inquired if Dean were referring to it.[21] Liddy wrote that Dean urged him to have a grander vision than Sandwedge, because Sandwedge had been considered inadequate.[22] Liddy recounted that he, in effect, said extravagant thinking required extravagant expenditures, and Dean replied "half a million for openers."[23] Liddy recalled that Dean assured him that a new and improved, highly sophisticated intelligence operation would receive funding to the tune of $1 million.[24] Conversely, when Dean testified before the Senate's Watergate Committee, a special committee established by the United States Senate to investigate Watergate, he couldn't remember whether or not that meeting with Liddy entailed the discussion of an intelligence operation.[25]

E. Howard Hunt's autobiography, *Undercover*, corroborated Liddy: He wrote that when Liddy returned from the meeting with Dean, he enthusiastically relayed to Hunt that the attorney general requested that Liddy "set up an intelligence operation for the campaign" that involved a "half million for openers."[26] Though Hunt may have been telling the truth, he is a dubious source, because his life was predicated on misdirection and deceit. But the subsequent actions of Dean are ultimately a superlative arbitrator of the truth.

So, now, Liddy had become the C.R.P.'s general counsel, and Magruder found the onus of supervising him to be a nightmare. Liddy's disdain for Magruder became palpable and boiled over into verbal assaults and threats of bodily harm.[27] Shortly after Dean and Liddy's initial meeting, the pair met with Mitchell to confer about the myriad responsibilities that Liddy would assume as the C.R.P.'s general counsel.[28] The meeting's agenda, prepared by Liddy, also included a discussion on "intelligence."[29] Liddy, however, asserted that they became mired in the preceding issues and never discussed intelligence.[30] But Dean testified to the Senate's Watergate Committee that they had a brief discussion about intelligence, and they concurred "Liddy would draw up some sort of plans."[31] According to Liddy, Dean unilaterally told him to embark on an intelligence proposal forthwith, and he assured Liddy that Mitchell would vet the proposal.[32]

Liddy unfettering his imagination to the tune of $1 million in 1972 was a rather frightening prospect, and he conscripted E. Howard Hunt to unfetter his imagination, too.[33] Liddy christened his leviathan intelligence operation "Gemstone."[34] Though the C.I.A. had *officially* cut off Hunt months earlier, Liddy maintained that the C.I.A. prepared the Gemstone charts that would be shown to Mitchell.[35] If Liddy's account is correct, the latter tactic enabled the C.I.A. to be privy to the C.R.P.'s prospective intelligence operation even before Mitchell was apprised of it.

In January of 1972, Liddy presented Gemstone to Mitchell, Dean, and Magruder.[36] Gemstone was … well … certainly creative – but downright demented. As Liddy displayed the slick charts made by the C.I.A., Gemstone's various operations were identified by an accompanying precious stone:

- Emerald: The use of a "chase plane" to eavesdrop on the Democratic candidate's aircraft when his entourage used radio telephones.[37]

- Quartz: The microwave intersection of telephone traffic.[38]

- Sapphire: The use of prostitutes to compromise Democrats aboard a yacht that would be moored near the Democrats' National Convention.[39]

- Garnet: The recruitment of sloven hippies to endorse Democrats.[40]

- Turquoise: A cadre of Cubans would sabotage the air-conditioning at the Democrats' National Convention, which would make Democratic delegates appear as sweat hogs on national television.[41]

- Opal: Burglaries of various Democratic targets, where bugs would be planted.[42]

- Diamond: The kidnapping, drugging, and forced deportation of anti-war protestors.[43]

On the Diamond chart, Liddy defaulted to Third Reich terminology. The kidnapping, drugging, and forced deportation of anti-war protestors received the German epithet of *Nacht und Nebel* – English for "Night and Fog."[44] In 1941, Hitler issued the Night and Fog Decree, which secretly ordered that resistance fighters in the German-occupied territories of Western Europe were to be arrested and either shot or abducted under the cover of "night and fog."

Liddy told Mitchell that Night and Fog would be staffed by profession-al hit men, and they would constitute a "Special Action Group."[45] When Mitchell requested that Liddy delineate "Special Action Group," he re-plied, "Einsatzgruppe, General," enunciating "General" with a hard, Ger-man "G."[46] The Einsatzgruppe were the SS death squads. Liddy managed to reply to Mitchell without clicking his heels or hoisting his arm upward with a "Heil Hitler," which, in the very least, demonstrated that he did not have the neurological travails of the wheelchair bound Dr. Strangelove.

When Liddy entered Mitchell's office, he was confident that Mitchell would sanction Gemstone, because he and Hunt had traveled to Miami beforehand to interview thugs and hookers who were to be deployed in the furtherance of Gemstone.[47] At the culmination of Liddy's Gemstone presentation, Mitchell was stunned.[48] His deadpan facial expressions be-lied his bewilderment when he conveyed to Liddy that the Gemstone price tag was prohibitive.[49] He also instructed Liddy to burn the Gem-stone charts.[50] Liddy wrote that Dean and Magruder silently stared at Mitchell "like two rabbits in front of a cobra" as he explained the Gem-stone charts.[51] Liddy departed Mitchell's office in silent scorn.[52]

Before the Watergate Committee, Mitchell described Gemstone as a "horror story."[53] The Watergate Committee's chief counsel confronted Mitchell about Liddy's psychotic intrigues, and he inquired why Mitchell did not simply toss Liddy out of his office.[54] Mitchell responded that "… in hindsight I not only should've thrown him out of the office, I should have thrown him out the window."[55]

The following week, Liddy presented a scaled down version of Gem-stone to Mitchell, Dean, and Magruder.[56] Gemstone 2.0 would be a mere $500,000, and Liddy lost the chase plane, microwave interceptions, ruf-fians to pummel anti-war demonstrators, and, my personal favorite with regard to sheer insanity, Night and Fog.[57] But Mitchell, once again, did not resonate with Liddy's derring-do; and to Liddy's chagrin, Dean cut off Liddy midstream and interjected that the attorney general should not be exposed to such illegalities.[58] Liddy again departed the meeting in silent scorn.[59]

Liddy recounted that Magruder was quite enthusiastic about one facet of Gemstone 2.0: The deployment of prostitutes at the D.N.C. conven-tion in Miami Beach for the purposes of blackmail.[60] Magruder suggested to Liddy that some of the prostitutes who were to be deployed in Miami be flown to D.C.[61] According to Liddy, he told Magruder "... bringing whores to Washington was like shipping cars to Detroit."[62] Magruder then inquired about the availability of the prostitutes slated for Gemstone 2.0 if he flew to Miami.[63] In *Will*, Liddy wrote: "Jesus, I thought, the wimp can't even get laid with a hooker by himself."[64] Liddy's account of Magruder's affinity for prostitutes is supported elsewhere: Magruder's name and number just happen to be in Heidi Rikan's little black book.[65]

A second account of Magruder's affinity for ladies of the night comes from none other than the libidinous barrister – Phillip Bailley. Bailley said he had dalliances with one of the "first-timers," who Rikan recruited in lieu of the "experienced bitches."[66] The first-timer in question was a friend of Mo's, and she was employed at the Executive Office Building, which housed several offices and agencies that worked directly for the executive branch.[67]

Bailley told Phil Stanford that he was en route to an appointment with the first-timer when he spotted her on the sidewalk, talking to a dark haired man in a trench coat.[68] The man then stepped into a chauffeur driven black sedan and sped off.[69] Bailley congratulated her on the upward mobility that a chauffeured clientele entails, and she replied that Bailley should forget about seeing the man in the trench coat.[70] Bailley informed Stanford that he later noticed a picture of the man in the *Washington Post*, and, lo and behold, it was, indeed, Jeb Magruder.[71]

Stanford eventually found the first-timer, who had reinvented herself as a successful lawyer.[72] Though she said that she had lunched with Rikan and Mo "once or twice," she denied ever meeting Bailley or being a call girl.[73] But despite her disavowals, she is in Rikan's black book.[74] Moreover, the address Rikan lists for her is exactly where Bailley said she lived.[75]

Given Magruder's presence in Rikan's black book and Rikan's reported connection to blackmail, Stanford reflected on Magruder's potential conundrum in *White House Call Girl*: "Dean may already have Magruder by the balls, anyway. It's entirely speculative, of course, but considering Dean's close friendship with Heidi, it's hardly possible that he doesn't know that one of Heidi's girls is having an affair with Magruder. Dean may have even set him up in the first place. And if that's so, he also knows that the last thing the straight-laced Magruder would ever want is for his shameful secret to be exposed."[76]

CHAPTER 10

GEMSTONE 3.0 MORPHS INTO WATERGATE

After Liddy encountered the sounds of silence following his presentation of Gemstone 2.0, he became increasingly inimical towards Magruder: Magruder had the C.R.P.'s power of the purse, and Liddy looked upon him as the primary obstacle to actualizing his beloved Gemstone 2.0.[1] Magruder, however, doled out piecemeal intelligence assignments to Liddy, even though Mitchell was almost certainly never apprised of Liddy's various derring-do exploits.[2]

Liddy's frustration at Magruder's piecemeal intelligence assignments intensified as his glorious Gemstone was collecting dust in a distant corner of the Nixon administration: Liddy ultimately threatened to kill Magruder.[3] Though Liddy said the death threat was in jest, Magruder, apparently, took it rather seriously, because he told all and sundry about Liddy's brandishing of a death threat.[4] Liddy then transferred to the C.R.P. finance committee and became its general counsel.[5] Magruder was greatly relieved at the thought of banishing Liddy from his life, but he wrote that Dean and a Haldeman aide urged him to retain Liddy as the C.R.P.'s intelligence chieftain.[6] He succumbed to their entreaties.[7] Magruder was between a hammer and an anvil: He had pressure to deploy Liddy, but he was also cognizant of the fact that Mitchell thought Liddy was crazed.[8] It is also within the realm of reason that Magruder was susceptible to being leveraged, because of his penchant for prostitutes.

At the end of March 1972, Magruder flew to Key Biscayne, Florida to have a meeting with Mitchell who had resigned as attorney general to helm the C.R.P.[9] Mitchell, two of Mitchell's aides, and Magruder attended the Key Biscayne C.R.P. conclave.[10] The conferees had a myriad of issues to discuss, and Gemstone 3.0 was the last item on their agenda.[11] When they arrived at Gemstone 3.0, one of Mitchell's aides, by prior arrangement, excused himself.[12] Magruder testified to the Watergate Committee that Mitchell then sanctioned Gemstone 3.0 and also targeted the D.N.C. at the Watergate as a locus for a break-in.[13]

Conversely, Mitchell categorically rejected the idea that he ever sanctioned Gemstone and/or a break-in into the Watergate: Before the Watergate Committee, Mitchell testified that he directed Magruder to completely discard Gemstone 3.0.[14] Indeed, Mitchell testified that he told Magruder that he wanted to hear nary a word of Gemstone again.[15] The Mitchell aide who remained for the meeting between Mitchell and Magruder also testified to the Watergate Committee that Mitchell did not sanction the Watergate break-in at the Key Biscayne meeting.[16]

Magruder's account of the Key Biscayne conclave has undergone a variety of revisions: After Mitchell's aide who attended the meeting testified to the Watergate Committee that Mitchell didn't sanction the D.N.C. break-in, Magruder subsequently tweaked his account, testifying that the Mitchell aide who corroborated Mitchell was talking on the telephone when Mitchell sanctioned the Watergate break-in.[17] Magruder then confessed to the authors of Silent Coup that Mitchell never targeted the Watergate for a break-in and the caper "had been initiated by Dean."[18] The authors of Silent Coup contend that the pressure on Magruder became so inexorable that he bypassed Mitchell's approval and unilaterally funded Gemstone 3.0 with C.R.P. funds.[19]

Liddy wasn't aware of the Key Biscayne meeting, but Magruder gave him a green light on Gemstone 3.0 through a subordinate in early April.[20] Liddy thought the green light applied to the Democrats' national convention in Miami Beach, which was in July, three months in the offing.[21] Liddy conveyed the go-ahead to Hunt, and then he approached the deputy for C.R.P. finance committee about his authorized $250,000 intelligence budget, requesting a prompt $83,000.[22] Liddy quickly dispersed $65,000 to C.R.P. security chief James McCord to purchase bugging equipment.[23]

McCord made a jaunt to Chicago in early May, where he visited his wireman of choice who was a C.I.A. asset.[24] McCord ordered a room bug and various telephone bugs.[25] The wireman informed the F.B.I. that when McCord ordered the surveillance equipment, he flashed his C.I.A. credentials.[26] In addition, McCord's wireman presented a letter from the C.I.A. when he sought assistance from a business that specialized in high-tech bugs.[27]

As the triumvirate of Liddy, Hunt, and McCord were in the initial phases of planning to breach the Democratic convention in April, the talented Mr. Bailley reentered the Watergate narrative. Bailley was in the midst of an opening statement for a misdemeanor case when the court clerk's phone started to ring.[28] The clerk then handed the phone to the judge.[29] The judge listened to the person on the other end of the phone for thirty seconds or so before handing the phone to Bailley: Bailley's sister told him that the F.B.I. was in the midst of raiding his office and apartment.[30] Bailley requested that the judge grant him a sudden adjournment.[31] After the judge acquiesced, Bailley holed up in the back room of a bail bondsman's office, struggling to fathom the motive for the raid.[32]

The F.B.I. was investigating Bailley for violating the Mann Act, which prohibits the transportation of individuals across state lines for immoral purposes.[33] In Chapter 8, I mentioned the graduate student who attended Bailley's amorous soirees and Bailley's attempt to conscript her for Rikan's operation. Though Rikan rejected the young woman, because she lacked the requisite class, Bailley did not tell her about Rikan's verdict and continued to invite her to his soirees.[34]

The graduate student rightfully started to feel exploited, and she made a visit to the authorities.[35] She told D.C. vice squad detectives that one of the participants at Bailley's soirees slipped Bailley $20 for her amorous amenities.[36] The vice squad detectives took a sharp interest in the graduate student's story when she discussed Bailley's association with a high-class prostitution ring.[37] Hell hath no fury like a female graduate student scorned.

After the F.B.I. descended on Bailley, former F.B.I. man, thug, and alcoholic, Lou Russell made his Watergate reappearance. Bailley's bust prompted Russell to emerge from the shadows: He revealed to the assistant U.S. attorney for D.C. prosecuting Bailley's case that a D.C. brothel near Dupont Circle was equipped with hidden video cameras, and the blackmail targets included an elite clientele of judges and lawyers.[38] Though the assistant U.S. attorney found Russell's tip to be accurate, he thought that Russell's information was an attempt to divert his interest from Bailley and the Columbia Plaza.[39] The Justice Department ultimately dissuaded the assistant U.S. attorney from pursuing a case against the brothel near Dupont Circle.[40]

As Russell was attempting to distract the assistant U.S. attorney, Magruder directed Liddy to infiltrate the D.N.C. at the Watergate and plant a bug in the D.N.C. chairman's office and also photograph relevant documentation.[41] Liddy was both miffed and perplexed by Magruder's directive, because Liddy had been planning to infiltrate the Democratic convention in Miami Beach.[42] Liddy thought that bugging the office of the D.N.C. chairman would be a colossal squandering of resources: As of April, the D.N.C. chairman had, for all intents and purposes, encamped in Florida, organizing the Democratic National Convention, and he wouldn't return from Florida on a fulltime basis until after the convention in July.[43]

It was evident to Liddy that Magruder was not the prime mover sanctioning the Watergate break-in.[44] Magruder's impulsive redirection of Liddy's derring-do occurred after the Bailley bust. As I've mentioned, Dean subordinate and former N.Y.P.D. detective John Caulfield said that Dean initially showed an interest in the Watergate in November of 1971 – seven months before the break-ins.[45] I noted earlier in the chapter that Magruder told the authors of *Silent Coup* that Dean had targeted the D.N.C.

Also in early May, McCord, in his capacity as the C.R.P. security director, continued making moves to actualize the Watergate break-in by conscripting Alfred Baldwin, III.[46] The corpulent, 36-year-old Baldwin was the scion of an affluent Connecticut clan of prominent lawyers and politicians.[47] After graduating from Connecticut's Fairfield University, Baldwin enlisted in the Marines.[48] As a Marine, Baldwin was stationed at Quantico, Virginia, where the F.B.I. Academy is located, and he came into contact with F.B.I. recruits.[49]

Baldwin said that he was so impressed with the F.B.I. recruits that he aspired to be a G-man, but, at that time, prospective F.B.I. recruits were required to have degrees in either accounting or law.[50] So Baldwin attended and then graduated from the University of Connecticut School of Law.[51] Though Baldwin failed the Connecticut bar exam, he, nonetheless, became an F.B.I. agent in 1963.[52] He resigned from the F.B.I. in 1967.[53] When McCord phoned Baldwin to offer him a job, the latter was divorced and tasting hard times.[54]

The cover story for McCord hiring Baldwin is mired in improbability: McCord, acting as the C.R.P. security director, supposedly phoned Baldwin in Connecticut at 6:15 P.M. and offered him the charge of "bodyguard" for Martha Mitchell, John Mitchell's perpetually drunk and surly wife, who was embarking on a barnstorming campaign the following afternoon.[55] McCord claimed that his sole rationale for hiring Baldwin was that Baldwin's name was in a registry published by the Society of Former Special Agents of the F.B.I., and McCord randomly chose him from the registry.[56]

Though McCord and Baldwin vowed that their first contact was when McCord initially phoned Baldwin and offered him employment, the registry where McCord ostensibly gleaned Baldwin's name and number contained scores of former F.B.I. agents in the Washington, D.C. area.[57] The cover story then asserted that Baldwin jumped on a flight from Hartford, Connecticut to Washington, D.C. two hours later.[58] McCord had also booked a room for him at a D.C. hotel.[59] Since the assignment to serve as a bodyguard for Martha Mitchell was slated for the next day, rudimentary logic dictates that McCord would've conscripted a former F.B.I. agent in the D.C. area who wouldn't be required to travel from Hartford to D.C. and also receive per diem payments for lodging and living expenses.[60]

In a 1997 interview, Baldwin made an implausible cover story even more implausible when he said that he and McCord struck a deal: The F.B.I. would rehire Baldwin if he worked for McCord and the C.R.P.[61] Even if McCord had the juice to ensure that the F.B.I. rehired Baldwin, it's highly improbable that the two would negotiate such a deal if they were talking for the first time.

Baldwin boarded an Amtrak the following afternoon with Mrs. Mitchell, but the trip translated into an inauspicious venture for both Baldwin and Mrs. Mitchell. The train they embarked on collided with a pedestrian, and Baldwin relayed a graphic description of the man's remains to Mrs. Mitchell.[62] She did not appreciate Baldwin's depiction of the misfortune, because she described him "as the gauchest character I've ever met."[63] Mrs. Mitchell also accused him of shuffling about the train in his bare feet, which seemingly exacerbated his gaucheness in her mind.[64] Baldwin was quickly relieved of his bodyguard duties for Mrs. Mitchell.[65] McCord, however, reportedly told Baldwin to retrieve additional clothes in Connecticut and return to D.C. for reassignment.[66]

CHAPTER 11

BREAKING AND LOITERING

After Baldwin returned to D.C. from Connecticut on May 11, McCord provided him with accommodations at the D.C. Howard Johnson's, which was directly across Virginia Avenue from the Watergate: The D.N.C. offices were clearly visible from his hotel room.[1] Baldwin then made a jaunt to Connecticut on Tuesday, May 23, and he returned to the Howard Johnson's on Friday, May 26.[2] Upon Baldwin's return to the Howard Johnson's, he testified to the Watergate Committee that he was greeted by McCord, who had converted the hotel room into an electronics emporium.[3] McCord told Baldwin that after he unpacked, McCord would explain his various tasks to him.[4]

The official narrative of Watergate starts to disintegrate upon Baldwin's return to Howard Johnson's. Baldwin stated to the F.B.I., Congress, and the media that McCord was listening to a bugged conversation in the Howard Johnson's room on May 26 – two days before the Watergate burglars planted bugs in the D.N.C.[5] Baldwin, moreover, told the *Los Angeles Times* that he saw McCord in the D.N.C. on the night of May 26 – two days before the Watergate burglars had successfully broken into the D.N.C.[6] McCord, the super spook, rented the Howard Johnson's hotel room on behalf of McCord and Associates. McCord's decision to rent the room on behalf of McCord and Associates was either the nadir of stupidity or the harbinger of a secret agenda.[7] As the machinations of the two Watergate break-ins unfold, McCord will emerge as the impish ringmaster to a very bizarre circus.

Liddy deployed Cuban anti-Castro mercenaries for the Watergate break-in: In addition to the three Cubans who made a debacle of the Dr. Fielding break-in, Liddy and Hunt also conscripted Ronaldo Pico, Virgilio Gonzalez, and Frank Sturgis.[8] Gonzalez was a locksmith, and he would have been very practical for the Dr. Fielding break-in.[9] Frank Sturgis was a former marine, thug, and American-born soldier-of-fortune who had once been a Castro devotee, but he eventually defected from Castro and united with anti-Castro Cubans in the U.S.[10] To whet the Cubans' eagerness for the break-in, Hunt told them that assassins, waiting in the wings, would murder Castro after the Watergate caper.[11]

The Cuban contingent, using pseudonyms, posed as executives for the "Ameritas" corporation when they checked into the Watergate Hotel on Friday May 26.[12] Liddy and Hunt occupied a Watergate Hotel room that served as the "command post."[13] Liddy, Hunt, and the Cubans attended an "executive dinner" that night in the Watergate's Continental Room, which was in the basement of the office building.[14] McCord didn't attend the executive dinner.[15] The Continental Room granted access to a corridor that led to the building's underground garage and then to a staircase that ascended to the sixth floor of the Watergate, where the D.N.C. was headquartered.[16]

The burglars dined and watched an industrial film.[17] Baldwin or McCord was then slated to radio to Hunt from their lair in the Howard Johnson's when the D.N.C. offices on the 6th floor had been vacated.[18] The events unfolding at the "Ameritas" banquet in the Watergate's Continental Room were patently peculiar, reinforcing the impression that McCord and Hunt had a secret agenda. According to Hunt, the corridor from the Continental Room to the underground garage and staircase that gave the burglars access to the D.N.C. had an alarm that became activated at 11:00 P.M.[19] He wrote that he and McCord had discovered the alarm when they were initially casing the Watergate.[20]

Hunt also wrote that McCord informed him that the D.N.C. was generally vacant after 10:00 P.M., which gave locksmith Gonzalez a one-hour window to proceed through the corridor to pick and tape the locks that would facilitate the break-in.[21] But McCord and/or Hunt was/were lying, because the D.N.C. was generally occupied until after midnight.[22] Jim Hougan also noted in *Secret Agenda* that the corridor proceeding from the Continental Room to the garage did not even have an alarm![23]

The tons of ink spilt on Watergate and the millions of dollars spilt on its government investigations and adjudications have remarkably neglected to impale Hunt and McCord on such a preposterous, blatant lie. Hunt spouted a myriad of additional lies about that night, but, for the sake of simplicity, I've only addressed Hunt and McCord's big lie. (*Secret Agenda* offers a comprehensive overview of Hunt's litany of lies on the night of May 26, 1972.)

Throughout the executive dinner in the Continental Room, Hunt ostensibly remained in walkie-talkie contact with McCord who was ostensibly perched in the Howard Johnson's, surveying the D.N.C. offices. McCord, via Hunt, asserted that the D.N.C. was occupied until after 11:00 P.M., so the first break-in attempt was aborted.[24] McCord and/or Hunt sabotaged the first break-in attempt, and their motives will ultimately be elucidated.

The events surrounding the first attempted break-in into the D.N.C. were patently peculiar, but the events surrounding the second attempted break-in were downright outlandish. McCord and the Little Havana contingent, wearing suits and carrying briefcases, walked into the Watergate office building at 12:30 A.M. on Sunday morning, May 28, and each signed the visitors' log with an alias.[25] The burglars stated that their destination was the Federal Reserve Board on the eighth floor.[26] Astonishingly, the guard, who was perhaps cognitively challenged, granted McCord and his swarthy accomplices access to the elevator.[27] After exiting the elevator on the eighth floor, the would-be burglars then descended the staircase to the D.N.C. on the sixth floor.[28]

The Federal Reserve Board had been burgled earlier that month, and its security had been intensified.[29] In addition to the Watergate guards, a roving guard employed by the Federal Reserve Board checked on the Federal Reserve Board's offices twice nightly.[30] McCord was aware of the fact that a Federal Reserve Board guard was slated to make his Watergate rounds at about the same time that he and the Little Havana contingent were brazenly signing the visitors' log.[31]

If the Federal Reserve Board guard reviewed the visitors' log that night, which was standard protocol, he would have invariably felt compelled to investigate the "visitors" who ventured to the Federal Reserve Board after midnight.[32] If the visitors were not on the eighth floor, then the guard would've likely surmised that McCord & Company had signed in under false pretenses and were elsewhere in the building. After a search of the building, McCord & Company would be detained with their various bugs, cameras, and ancillary spook equipment.

After the burglars' audacious entry into the Watergate, they loitered on the 6th floor while Gonzalez had great difficulties picking the lock to the D.N.C.'s front door.[33] According to burglar Martinez, McCord made a jaunt to the eighth floor as Gonzalez was laboring with the lock.[34] Martinez maintained that he ventured to the eighth floor to apprise McCord of Gonzalez's progress or lack thereof, and McCord was talking to a pair of guards.[35] Martinez did not question McCord about his conversation with the two guards, but, rather, he assumed that they were McCord's inside men.[36] Unfortunately, it's difficult to surmise whether or not Martinez is being truthful or engaging in spook obfuscation.

After expending 45 minutes, Gonzalez was unable to pick the lock. McCord & Company subsequently returned to the Watergate Hotel room where Liddy and Hunt were ensconced.[37] Gonzalez conveyed to Liddy that the lock on the D.N.C.'s door could not be surmounted with his lock picking accessories and said that he needed additional lock picking tools to breach the D.N.C. lock.[38] Liddy cross-examined Gonzalez about the fitness of the lock, because he worried that the Democrats would notify the police about a possible break-in if Gonzalez had damaged the lock.[39] But Liddy and Gonzalez had a linguistic barrier.[40]

Liddy was not assured by Gonzalez's responses, and, ever the man of action, he signed into the Watergate visitors' log at 2:55 A.M.[41] He was en route to the Federal Reserve Board too![42] After descending two flights of stairs to the D.N.C., Liddy experienced a wave of cold comfort when he inspected the D.N.C. lock and realized it wasn't obviously marred.[43] When Liddy returned to the command post, contrary to Hunt's objections, he ordered Gonzalez to book a flight to Miami forthwith and retrieve the requisite tools to infiltrate the D.N.C.[44]

Gonzalez seemingly made an expeditious round-trip to Miami, and he returned to D.C. later in the afternoon.[45] The third break-in attempt commenced at around 11:00 P.M. that night – Sunday, May 28th.[46] McCord & Company proceeded through the Watergate's underground garage to the basement stairwell doors, whose locks McCord had previously taped.[47] They climbed to the sixth floor and Gonzalez picked the D.N.C.'s lock.[48] As two of the Cubans were taking pictures of the documents on the desk of the D.N.C. chairman, McCord inexplicably curtailed the caper before they could photograph documents in the filing cabinets.[49]

McCord and Hunt played Liddy with respect to the bugging target: Liddy directed McCord to bug the phone of the D.N.C. chairman, but their actual target was the phone in a vacant office that was adjacent to the office of Spencer Oliver, the executive director of the Association of State Democratic Chairmen, and Oliver's secretary – Maxie Wells.[50]

McCord and Hunt also played Liddy with regards to the photographic yield of the first burglary. The Cubans expended nearly two cassettes taking pictures of the documents on the D.N.C. chairman's desk.[51] McCord had been given the two film cassettes to develop.[52] After the break-in, when Liddy pressed McCord for the developed prints, McCord told him that the photographer he would normally use to develop the film was on vacation.[53] Hunt took possession of the two film cassettes at Liddy's behest, and he flew to Miami to have the film developed by a "person of confidence."[54]

The thirty-eight developed photos showed various documents being held by hands sporting surgical gloves with a "shag-type" carpeting backdrop.[55] Neither the D.N.C. offices, nor the Watergate Hotel rooms, had such "shag-type" carpeting, but that type of shag carpeting was in Baldwin's room at the Howard Johnson's.[56] McCord and/or Hunt had obviously pulled a switcheroo with the film.[57] Although Liddy was not aware that he had been played, insult was certainly added to injury when Magruder, the "little punk" he so detested, told him the photographed documents were "worthless."[58]

Liddy was also irked that McCord rented a Howard Johnson's room on the fourth floor that did not have line-of-sight transmission to the D.N.C. bug.[59] So the day following the break-in, Monday, Baldwin moved into a Howard Johnson's room on the seventh floor that would optimize the bug's transmission.[60] On Wednesday night, Liddy packed a pistol in his briefcase and called on McCord at the Howard Johnson's.[61] McCord met Liddy at the door of the hotel room and escorted him into the darkened room.[62]

Liddy stood amidst a boutique of electrical gadgets as he caught site of Baldwin.[63] McCord introduced Liddy and Baldwin by their operational pseudonyms.[64] McCord then told Liddy that two bugs had been placed in the D.N.C., but he hadn't found the "signal" for one of the bugs.[65] The following night, Liddy returned to the Howard Johnson Hotel room, and McCord handed Liddy the typed logs that had been gleaned to date from the operational bug.[66] To Liddy's utter astonishment and chagrin, McCord was not recording the conversations.[67]

When Liddy questioned McCord about his rationale for not recording the conversations, McCord offered him disingenuous technological mumbo jumbo, which, in essence, meant that the receiver and the tape recorder had incompatible frequencies.[68] But Liddy continued to press McCord on the absence of the taped conversations.[69] McCord replied that much of the information emanating from the D.N.C. was extraneous.[70] McCord assured Liddy that the extraneous content would be edited out of the logs, and McCord would distill the logs to include only germane content.[71] Liddy declined McCord's offer: He said he wanted the logs in their entirety.[72] At home, that night, he read the logs.[73] Liddy concluded that the tapped phone was being used by multiple people but not the D.N.C. chairman.[74]

McCord ostensibly created a rather slipshod monitoring routine for Baldwin: He would monitor the bug Monday through Friday from 8:00 A.M. to 6:00 P.M.[75] Baldwin also took protracted breaks and visited friends in Connecticut, so the receiver was unattended for extended intervals.[76] Baldwin estimated that he eavesdropped on approximately 200 phone calls from his perch at the Howard Johnson's.[77] He said that several secretaries used the phone in the vacant office that was next to Spencer Oliver's due to the privacy it afforded, and they would stress: "We can talk; I'm on Spencer Oliver's phone."[78] Baldwin described some of the conversations as "explicitly intimate."[79] A federal prosecutor characterized the conversations as "extremely personal, intimate, and potentially embarrassing."[80] In fact, an assistant U.S. attorney told an attorney representing the D.N.C. that he wanted to use the Democrats' conversations to prove that blackmail was indeed the motive for the Watergate burglary.[81]

CHAPTER 12

BREAKING AND LOITERING: THE SEQUEL

T he talented Mr. Bailley now reenters the narrative to play an unsuspecting, but, yet, perhaps, pivotal role in propelling Watergate toward its denouement. The raid on Bailley's business and apartment in April ultimately resulted in a grand jury. The D.C. U.S. attorney's office started investigating Bailley because of the exploited graduate student, and it quickly found other women who were willing to testify against him.[1]

On Friday, June 9, the *Washington Star* published an article, "Capitol Hill Call-Girl Ring," reporting that Bailley was the subject of a 22-count indictment for heading a "high-priced call ring" that was "staffed by secretaries and office workers from Capitol Hill and involving at least one White House secretary."[2]

Dean was, apparently, quite concerned about the article: Within an hour of the article's publication, he phoned the D.C. U.S. attorney's office and talked to the assistant U.S. attorney who was spearheading the Bailley investigation.[3] Dean told the assistant U.S. attorney that he was phoning on behalf of the president.[4] Shortly thereafter, the assistant U.S. attorney who spoke to Dean and his boss were en route to Dean's office in a White House limousine.[5] Dean had requested that the two federal prosecutors bring all the "documentary evidence" pertaining to the Bailley investigation, but they only brought Bailley's address book and the nude photos that had been seized during the F.B.I.'s execution of the search warrant.[6]

Dean, wearing a gray pin-stripe suit and crisp blue shirt, greeted the two federal prosecutors.[7] After obligatory introductions, Dean quickly became preoccupied with Bailley's address book.[8] It contained the numbers of friends, colleagues, clients, former and current girlfriends, prostitutes at the Columbia Plaza, the secretaries and wives of powerful Democrats and Republicans, etc.[9] At least the former seminarian didn't have to be concerned about the cardinal sin of sloth.

Bailley's phonebook also contained the aliases and numbers of Mo and Riken.[10] In *White House Call Girl*, Phil Stanford discussed Dean's possible quandary: "Considering Dean's closeness not just to Mo, but Heidi as well, it is first of all barely conceivable that he isn't already aware of Heidi's Columbia Plaza operation, or for that matter, Bailley's connection to it. But even if he isn't, we can only imagine his distress when he sees the entries for "M.B." or "Clout," along with what must be familiar phone numbers."[11] Dean requested that the federal prosecutors surrender Bailley's address book to him over the weekend.[12] But his request contravened the maintenance of evidence in an active case, and they refused his entreaty.[13] Dean defaulted to requesting that he make copies of the address book and the prosecutors relented.[14] Dean then had a secretary photocopy it.[15] As I mentioned in Chapter 8, Bailley's secretary/sister remembered "Clout" leaving numerous messages for her brother.[16] She also recalled that the same woman left messages as "Ms. Biner" but most often as "Mo."[17]

On the same day that Dean met with the two federal prosecutors, he phoned a Washington attorney and counsel to the Republican National Committee who acted as a "backchannel" between the Nixon administration and the federal judge presiding over Bailley's case.[18] The judge in question just happened to be a Nixon appointee.[19] Bailley and his counsel showed up in U.S. District Court before the aforementioned judge the following week, and the proceedings quickly assumed a surreal scope that was not charitable to the talented Mr. Bailley.[20]

The assistant U.S. attorney prosecuting Bailley, who met with Dean the previous Friday, recommended that the judge independently and preemptively commit Bailley to a psychiatric hospital for a 60-day evaluation, even though he emphasized that such a recommendation was not being made by the government.[21] Bailley's prosecutor then suggested that the matter be discussed in the judge's chambers – sans the public and the press.[22] A procession that consisted of the judge, his clerk, the federal prosecutor, Bailley, Bailley's attorney, two U.S. marshals, and a court reporter then walked to an adjacent, vacant courtroom.[23]

When the hearing reconvened, the federal prosecutor argued that Bailley had taken pictures of various, nude females with "whipped cream" on their bodies, and he would use their photos at a later date for self-gratification, which demonstrated that he was cracked.[24] Bailley's lawyer attempted to instill a modicum of sanity into the insane hearing by contending that Bailley's sexual innovations did not entail insanity, and he adamantly argued that Bailley should not be committed.[25]

(The "Twinkie defense" was successfully deployed as a rationale for insanity for the man who murdered San Francisco's mayor and also a prominent gay politician. The Twinkie defense posited that the murderer suffered from diminished capacity due, in part, to his diet, which included too many Twinkies.[26] The "Twinkie defense" has become infamous in the annals of American jurisprudence, but the whipped cream argument for insanity has been overlooked.)

The deck was stacked against Bailley, because, after the judge listened to the whipped cream rationale for insanity, he ordered that Bailley be committed.[27] The judge also ruled that the evidence in the case – nude pictures, sexual aids, pornography, and, of course, Bailley's address book – not be admitted into the court's evidentiary file.[28] He then imposed a gag order that precluded the federal prosecutors, Bailley, and his attorney from discussing the case publicly.[29]

Bailley was deemed sane after a mere fifteen days in the laughter academy, but the court's duplicity and his time spent among the criminally insane were devastating to him.[30] Bailley was never the paragon of sanity, and he emerged from the psychiatric hospital a seriously muddled, frightened man.[31] After major skullduggery by the government and judge, and an additional wave of indictments, Bailley pled to five years in a federal prison.[32] The assistant U.S. attorney prosecuting Bailley confessed to the authors of *Silent Coup* that Bailley was committed to discredit him.[33]

The June 9 *Washington Star* article had very negative implications for the talented Mr. Bailley, but it had apocalyptic implications for the talented Mr. Nixon. The following Monday, June 12, Jeb Magruder summoned his old pal G. Gordon Liddy to his office.[34] Magruder instructed Liddy to again burgle the D.N.C.[35] Liddy replied that breaking into the Watergate again was feasible, but he did not have the operational budget for a second Watergate break-in.[36] Magruder suddenly became uncharacteristically animated, striking the lower left drawer of his desk.[37] As he struck his desk drawer, he blurted: "Here's what I want to know."[38] Liddy was fully aware that Magruder's lower left desk drawer was a repository for dirt on the Democrats.[39] Magruder wanted the phone of the D.N.C. chairman bugged, and he also instructed Liddy to photograph all the files in the D.N.C. chairman's filing cabinets: "Take all the men, all the cameras you need."[40] Liddy conveyed Magruder's dictate to Hunt, and Hunt rounded up the usual suspects.[41]

Magruder's directive to Liddy came in the wake of Dean's acute interest over the *Washington Star* article, and the authors of *Silent Coup* questioned Magruder about the prime mover of the second break-in.[42] Magruder hemmed and hawed a bit before confessing that Dean was the instigator for the second Watergate break-in.[43]

The Little Havana contingent flew into D.C. on Friday afternoon, June 16, to partake in history's most famous, bungled burglary.[44] At 8:30 on that fateful night, McCord had a last supper of sorts with the Cubans.[45] The break-in was planned for 10:00 P.M.[46] But lights continued to emanate from the D.N.C. at 10:00 P.M. and the break-in was delayed.[47] At 10:50 P.M., McCord signed into the Watergate under a pseudonym, and he took the elevator to the eighth floor.[48] McCord taped the door locks leading to the underground garage, the B-2 and B-3 level door locks, and the 6th and 8th floor stairwell door locks.[49] McCord's taping spree was overkill: He didn't have a cogent reason to tape the lock on the 8th floor stairwell door, because the burglars would access the D.N.C. from the 6th floor. As I've previously mentioned, the Federal Reserve Board, on the 8th floor, had been recently burgled, and McCord was cognizant of the fact that Federal Reserve Board guards inspected the location twice nightly.[50]

When McCord finished up his taping spree at around 11:00 P.M., he walked over to the Watergate Hotel room that was occupied by Liddy and Hunt, and he relayed to them that the requisite locks on the doors leading to the D.N.C. had been taped.[51] After apprising Liddy and Hunt about the locks, McCord walked over to the Howard Johnson's room, where Baldwin awaited him.[52] At 11:30, McCord notified Liddy via walkie-talkie that lights continued to emanate from the D.N.C., and Liddy decided to delay the break-in until after the Watergate guard made his midnight rounds.

At 11:51 P.M., the Watergate guard who worked the graveyard shift reported for duty.[53] During the commencement of his midnight rounds, he discovered the taped locks on the B-2 and B-3 entrances to the office building.[54] He removed the tape from the door locks and returned to his desk to note the taped locks in the security log.[55] Perplexed, the guard left a message concerning the taped locks for his superior with the security firm's answering service.[56] As the security guard awaited word from his superior, his uncertainty mounted, so he phoned his supervisor's supervisor who told him to check the building's other doors to see if additional door locks had been taped.[57]

Just as the guard was about to start checking the building's other doors, the final volunteer to leave the D.N.C. cut the lights and bounced down the stairwell.[58] The security guard and the D.N.C. volunteer decided to walk across Virginia Avenue and grab a bite at the Howard Johnson's.[59] At the Howard Johnson's, the security guard ordered a cheeseburger, French fries, and a shake to go.[60]

Mercenary thug and alcoholic Lou Russell now reprises his role in Watergate. At about the same time the security guard was in Howard Johnson's, Russell was visiting his daughter in Benedict, Maryland; he told her that he had to return to D.C. to carry out "some work for McCord."[61] From McCord's perch on the seventh floor in the Howard Johnson's, he radioed Liddy and deceitfully told him that the D.N.C. lights had yet to be extinguished.[62] In *Secret Agenda,* Jim Hougan speculated that McCord told Liddy a bald-faced lie, because he awaited the arrival of Russell.[63]

As the security guard sat in the lobby, polishing off his dinner, his supervisor phoned him around 12:30 A.M. and directed him to check the building's other doors.[64] The security guard had now received two directives to check the building's doors, but he disregarded both for an hour.[65] McCord phoned Hunt at approximately 12:50 A.M., and, after he hung up, he packed his bag of gadgets and said to Baldwin that he was walking "over there."[66] Before McCord departed, he handed his walkie-talkie to Baldwin.[67]

By 1:05 A.M., McCord arrived at the Watergate Hotel room occupied by Liddy, Hunt, and the Cubans.[68] Though McCord had a gait that was akin to a waddle, he should've been able to amble across Virginia Avenue to the Watergate Hotel in five minutes or less.[69] The burglary was running three hours behind schedule, and McCord explained to the hyped-up team that his 15 minute walk from the Howard Johnson's to the Watergate command center was due to the fact that he had checked to see if the door lock to the office building's B-2 entrance was still taped.[70] He said the tape on the lock was intact.[71] The Watergate security guard had, by then, removed the tape from the door locks on the B-2 and B-3 levels, so that was McCord's second bald-faced lie that night.[72]

At about 1:10 A.M., the team arrived at the Watergate's garage, and they discovered that the tape was missing on the B-2 door lock.[73] The baffled Cubans looked at McCord, and, to conceal his prior lie, he said that the tape had been removed in the past ten minutes.[74] After a brief huddle, McCord and two of the Cubans – Martinez and Barker – walked back to the Watergate Hotel room to consult with Hunt and Liddy.[75] In the meantime, Gonzalez picked and taped the lock to the B-2 entrance, and soldier-of-fortune Sturgis stood nearby, acting as his bodyguard.[76] Gonzalez taped the B-2 horizontally instead of vertically, which was a telltale indication that the lock had been retaped.[77] After scampering to the 6th floor, Gonzalez, once again, found the lock on the D.N.C.'s front door to be impenetrable, so he and Sturgis started to remove the door from its hinges.[78]

McCord and the two Cubans arrived at Liddy and Hunt's Watergate Hotel room by 1:20 A.M., and McCord told Liddy and Hunt about the tape's detection.[79] A disagreement erupted between Hunt and McCord: Hunt lobbied to abort the break-in.[80] But McCord lobbied for the burglary to proceed.[81] Liddy ultimately concurred with McCord, because McCord would be a hands-on participant in burglary, and he would seemingly suffer the greatest consequences if the burglars were busted.[82]

According to burglar Martinez, he and Barker walked back to the garage, but McCord was noticeably absent.[83] In *Secret Agenda,* Jim Hougan theorized that McCord was briefing Russell on the latest developments of the break-in.[84] Barker and Martinez saw that the B-2 entrance had been retaped, and they scaled the staircase to the sixth floor.[85] By 1:40 A.M., McCord reunited with the Little Havana contingent on the sixth floor.[86] Martinez maintains that he asked McCord if he had removed the tape from the B-2 door lock after entering the stairwell, and, once more, McCord lied, replying that he had.[87]

As the burglars were infiltrating the D.N.C., the security guard finally acted on his prior orders, and he found that the lock on the B-2 level had been retaped.[88] The security guard was now in the throes of Hamlet-like ambivalence as to whether or not he should notify the police when he wandered back to the lobby and consulted with a Federal Reserve Board guard who was in the midst of making his Watergate rounds.[89] Though the Federal Reserve Board guard told him to notify the police, the security guard continued to be plagued by ambivalence and phoned his superior.[90] The security guard finally phoned the police at 1:47 A.M.[91] His belated phone call would be the neutron shot into plutonium that started a thermonuclear reaction, reducing the Nixon administration to cinders.

CHAPTER 13

REVENGE OF THE KEY

At 1:52 A.M., a D.C. police dispatcher requested that a unit respond to a possible burglary at the Watergate.[1] An unmarked car, accommodating three plainclothes cops, was parked within two blocks of the Watergate.[2] A vice squad cop by the name of Carl Shoffler snatched the handset and replied, "We got it."[3] Shoffler was the least senior of the three police officers, and his zeal to reply to the dispatcher contravened a customary protocol prescribing that the officer with the most seniority generally replied to the dispatcher.[4]

Within minutes of being notified by the dispatcher, Shoffler and his fellow officers were in the Watergate's lobby.[5] The security guard attempted to edify the officers about the circumstances precipitating his call to the police.[6] But the police had difficulties comprehending him, so the security guard ushered the officers to the B-2 entrance and showed them the taped door.[7] The three police officers rendezvoused with the Federal Reserve Board's roving guard in the lobby, and he informed them about the recent burglary at the Federal Reserve Board.[8] The Federal Reserve Board guard and the police officers then climbed the staircase to the 8th floor, and they discovered that the stairwell's door lock had been taped.[9]

The police officers then descended the stairwell to the 7th floor.[10] They did not find tape on the seventh floor's stairwell door lock, so they descended to the sixth floor, where they discovered the stairwell door lock had been taped.[11] The noise made by the police startled Martinez, who looked to McCord for guidance.[12] McCord assuaged his concerns by telling him that it was the security guard, but, as a precaution, McCord ordered that the burglars' walkie-talkies be switched off, severing their communication with Liddy and Baldwin.[13]

Although Baldwin was presumably the lookout from his perch at the Howard Johnson's, his eyes were ostensibly fixated on the television, watching a 1950s horror flick – *Attack of the Puppet People*.[14] After the plight of the puppet people had been resolved, Baldwin stepped onto the balcony of his Howard Johnson's hotel room, and he watched the 8th floor of the Watergate office building light up.[15] According to Baldwin's Senate testimony, he told Liddy, via walkie-talkie, about the eighth floor lighting up, and he was told that it was the guard making his 2:00 A.M. rounds.[16] Baldwin nonchalantly asked Liddy if the burglars were attired like hippies, and Liddy responded that the burglars were dressed in suits.[17] Liddy wrote that Baldwin then barked out a sequence of observations, and he concluded with the following remarks: "They've got guns. It's trouble!"[18]

The D.C. police officers discovered McCord and his cohorts ducked behind a desk in a secretary's cubicle.[19] In McCord's bag, the police found three bugs and also a bug hidden in a smoke detector.[20] The police lined up the burglars in the customary pose after apprehension; their hands were against the wall, their feet were spread.[21] When the burglars were lined up, Martinez flirted with death by stealthily reaching inside his suit coat; police officer Shoffler pushed him in the back and ordered that he not move.[22] Martinez again stealthily reached inside his suit coat, and Shoffler struck him once more and thrust him against the wall.[23] Martinez had twice attempted to discard the key that was in his suit jacket.[24] The key was to the desk drawer of Ida "Maxie" Wells: Martinez deemed it so important that he nearly took a bullet for his efforts to discard the key.[25] The burglars' cameras were set up on Well's desk too.[26]

As the arrests were unfolding in the D.N.C., additional squad cars, with their lights blazing, started screeching to a halt before the Watergate.[27] The cognitively challenged security guard was standing next to an "unidentified white male," when he unlocked the lobby door for the arriving police officers, directing them to the sixth floor.[28] The security guard then unlocked the doors for an "unidentified white male" who quickly melted into the night.[29] The police officers remaining in the lobby asked the security guard about the man who had just skirted out of the front door, and the security guard replied that he did not recognize him.[30] The F.B.I. later concluded that the security guard allowed "the sixth man" on the burglary crew to leave unscathed.[31]

Hunt then excitedly disclosed to Liddy that one of the Cubans had a key to their room.[32] Hunt's revelations were quite perplexing, because the Cubans had been instructed to leave their room keys with Liddy and Hunt.[33] Hunt and Liddy then departed the Watergate Hotel so quickly that they did not sanitize the second hotel room that had been used by the Cubans.[34] They abandoned electronic equipment, and $100 bills that sequentially corresponded to the $100 bills carried by the burglars.[35] The room also contained an address book that had Hunt's White House telephone number, and, strangely enough, a check Hunt had written to his country club.[36]

After Hunt gave Liddy a ride to his Jeep, he circled back to the Howard Johnson's to check on Baldwin who was in the midst of watching the burglars being hauled away.[37] Hunt claims that he told Baldwin to load the electronic equipment in the van and "get out of town."[38] Conversely, Baldwin recalled Hunt instructing him to deliver the electronic equipment to McCord's home.[39] Baldwin packed the van full of McCord's various electrical gadgets and sped to McCord's home in Maryland, where he deposited McCord's sundry gadgets with McCord's wife in the wee hours before barreling to his mother's house in Connecticut.[40]

Baldwin, McCord's highly unusual selection to serve as a bodyguard for John Mitchell's wife, had repeatedly phoned his mother from his Howard Johnson's room.[41] The F.B.I. quickly tracked him down via his mother's phone number.[42] By July 5, two weeks after the second break-in, Baldwin entered into an immunity agreement with D.C.'s U.S. attorney, and he sang a protracted aria about the Watergate caper shortly thereafter.[43] But news of Baldwin's aria did not pierce the public until early September.[44]

Liddy made it home at about 3:00 A.M.[45] He was fully cognizant that McCord's fingerprints were on file, because he had been an F.B.I. agent – McCord would be identified within twenty-four hours.[46] Liddy was rather fatalistic about the outcome of the Watergate burglary: As he crawled into bed, he said to his wife: "There was trouble. Some people got caught. I'll probably be going to jail."[47]

The progenitors of the official Watergate narrative have made a diligent effort to vaporize the "call-girl theory" as a motive for the Watergate burglaries. But, despite their efforts, the "call-girl theory" refuses to go gently into that good night. Though Bailley has been disbarred, and he has a history of psychiatric troubles, he is extensively corroborated about the Columbia Plaza brothel and the D.N.C. serving as a conduit. Lou Russell regaled a prominent attorney and others with anecdotes about taping call girls at the Columbia Plaza whose clients were gleaned from the D.N.C.[48] In a civil lawsuit, a former federal prosecutor revealed that a federal investigation discovered D.N.C. employees at the Watergate acted as a conduit to the Columbia Plaza brothel, and his superiors ordered him to "shut down" the investigation.[49]

The phone used by the D.N.C.'s Spencer Oliver and Maxie Wells has played an integral role in the "call-girl theory," because it was the target of the first burglary. The key possessed by burglar Martinez is a telltale indication that Maxie Wells' desk was a target during the second Watergate break-in: Martinez said that Hunt gave him the key to Wells' desk and showed him a floor plan to target it.[50] Although Hunt denied giving Martinez the key, he, nonetheless, admitted to the authors of *Silent Coup* that the target of the first break-in was a phone used by Wells and her boss Spencer Oliver.[51] Two of the burglars also confessed that the phone used by Wells and Oliver was the target of the first break-in.[52] Moreover, the burglars' photographic equipment was set up on Wells' desk during the second break-in.[53] An F.B.I. agent also told a source in the D.N.C. that the burglars' bugging target had been the phone in the usually vacant office used by Oliver.[54]

The belief that Wells and Oliver were the bugging targets of the burglars received additional validation from the courts when Maxie Wells filed a $5.1 million defamation suit against G. Gordon Liddy.[55] Liddy had publicly declared that Mo Dean had been a prostitute, and her scantily clad picture was in Wells' desk.[56] Strangely enough, the Deans dropped a libel lawsuit against Liddy, but their attorneys encouraged Wells to sue Liddy for libel.[57] *Wells vs. Liddy* was ultimately adjudicated in a Baltimore federal court, and the first trial ended in a hung jury – 7 to 2 – in Liddy's favor.[58] Wells' lawyers appealed the decision and were granted a second trial, which Liddy won unanimously.[59] Consequently, two juries have opted not to find Liddy guilty of defamation for saying that Wells' desk contained information on the Columbia Plaza prostitution ring. The depositions and trial testimony generated by the *Wells vs. Liddy* trials further validated the "call girl theory." A Fox reporter testified that a former D.N.C. treasurer confessed to him that D.N.C. personnel arranged amorous liaisons for visiting Democratic dignitaries when they visited Washington.[60]

The government and mainstream media have assiduously disavowed the "call-girl theory" of Watergate, but overwhelming evidence confirms that it's a bona fide reality. Indeed, at this point, the overkill of evidence should conclusively force the "call-girl theory" of Watergate as a "conspiracy theory" into mandatory retirement.

Heidi Rikan and Phillip Bailley have played their unsuspecting, respective roles in Watergate, and they will now recede into historical anonymity. Unfortunately, Lou Russell's exact role, if he played one, on the night of the second Watergate break-in may remain an everlasting enigma. Russell, however, experienced a dramatic surge of upward mobility after the second burglary.

Within 24 hours of the Watergate bust, Russell reportedly received a rather odd phone call from a former F.B.I. agent who would ultimately be appointed the chief investigator of the Watergate Committee, which was about eight months from forming.[61] The two had become acquainted with each other when Russell was an investigator for the House Committee on Un-American Activities years earlier.[62] The former F.B.I. agent who phoned Russell was a friend of the Kennedys, and he had also served as a special assistant for President John Kennedy.[63,64]

Shortly after Russell received the phone call from his bygone acquaintance, he received a phone call from a friend of the acquaintance.[65] The friend was an affluent stockbroker and hardcore Republican.[66] The stockbroker quickly transmuted himself into a "Good Samaritan" for Russell: His largesse included an apartment in upscale Silver Spring, Maryland, a new car, and he provided Russell with "walking around money."[67] The stockbroker told Jim Hougan that he provided these amenities to Russell "out of the goodness of my heart."[68] Russell would also accommodate Heidi Rikan in his new, upmarket digs.[69] Rikan moving in with Russell indicates that they, at the very least, had an association, which, in part, further corroborates Bailley.

The stockbroker could have bestowed his largesse on Russell from a bountiful heart or, perhaps, because Russell was mum's the word about his extracurricular Watergate activities? Russell was an employee of McCord, so the F.B.I. called on Russell two weeks after the Watergate bust.[70] The F.B.I. agents questioned him about his Watergate involvement and also about his alibi during the break-in.[71] Russell informed the F.B.I. agents that he was dining at the Howard Johnson's restaurant from 8:30 P.M. to 10:30 P.M. on the night in question.[72] He claimed that during those two hours he sat by himself, strolling "down memory lane."[73]

Russell said that earlier in his life he dated a woman who had her hair coiffed at the Watergate, and on those occasions they would lunch at Howard Johnson's.[74] Russell asserted that he sat by himself in the Howard Johnson's for two hours fondly ruminating about his long lost love.[75] He also conveyed to the F.B.I. agents that he did not see McCord on that fateful night.[76] The F.B.I. agents were incredulous, but Russell wasn't budging an inch.[77] When Russell's bygone friend became the chief investigator for the Watergate Committee, he inexplicably neglected to pursue the Russell-Rikan Watergate nexus.[78]

CHAPTER 14

PANDORA'S BOX

One of the ultimate Watergate questions is who was the prime mover of the break-ins? According to Magruder, testifying before the Watergate Committee, John Mitchell sanctioned the Watergate break-in.[1] But when the authors of *Silent Coup* interviewed Magruder, he implicated John Dean – not John Mitchell – as the prime mover of the second burglary.[2] In a civil lawsuit deposition, Magruder also confessed that John Dean had prior knowledge of the Watergate break-in.[3] Mitchell, moreover, adamantly denied that he sanctioned the Watergate burglaries.[4]

A Mitchell aide who attended the Key Biscayne meeting stated that Magruder lied before the Watergate Committee, because Mitchell did not order the break-in at the meeting.[5] After the initial break-in, Magruder maintained that he had a meeting with Mitchell, who complained about the intelligence yield of the first break-in.[6] Magruder then claimed that Mitchell summoned Liddy to excoriate him about the useless yield of the first burglary.[7] Both Mitchell and Liddy deny that such a meeting ever occurred.[8] On two occasions, Mitchell and two different sources refute Magruder when he implicated Mitchell as a conspirator in the Watergate break-ins. In contrast, he implicated Dean as being the prime mover of the second burglary, and he testified that Dean had prior knowledge.

After Magruder became a witness against all the president's men, he was incarcerated for six months for his role in Watergate.[9] He then earned a master's degree from Princeton Theological Seminary and served as a Presbyterian pastor.[10] He and his wife divorced in 1984, and he also had a second marriage end in divorce.[11] As Magruder skidded into alcoholism, his life started to unravel: He was charged with public intoxication, and he was also arrested for a D.W.I.[12] Magruder ended up a broken man, living with his daughter.[13] He died in 2014 as the result of a stroke.[14]

In 2003, Magruder inexplicably told a whopper to PBS and the Associated Press: He said at the Key Biscayne meeting he overheard Nixon's distinct voice sanctioning Watergate as John Mitchell talked to Nixon on the phone.[15] The Mitchell aide who was at that meeting called Magruder a "congenital liar."[16] The Nixon library also confirmed that the White House "Daily Diary" did not log a call to Key Biscayne that day.[17]

When the Watergate cover-up ultimately collapsed on the Nixon administration and Magruder flipped, a federal prosecutor reportedly conceded that Magruder was so utterly obsequious to federal prosecutors that he told multiple variations of his story in an effort to please the prosecutors and minimize his prison stint.[18] Magruder's differing accounts were so contradictory that federal prosecutors debated whether or not they could call him as a witness in good faith, because his testimony was littered with four-dozen discrepancies.[19]

Magruder's Monday, June 12 directive to Liddy for the second burglary came in the aftermath of Dean's acute interest in the *Washington Star* article the preceding Friday. In addition to Dean meeting with the assistant U.S. attorney and his boss who were prosecuting the Bailley case, he phoned an attorney who acted as the Nixon administration's "backchannel" to the judge overseeing Bailley's case: A judge who neutralized Bailley by ruling that he receive a psychiatric evaluation, in part, based on the whipped cream rationale for insanity. Dean also exhibited an interest in the Watergate months before the first break-in, when he directed a subordinate to reconnoiter the D.N.C.

Although *Silent Coup* implicated John Dean as the prime mover of the Watergate break-ins, McCord and Hunt had their own agenda during the Watergate burglaries that was seemingly divorced from Magruder and/ or Dean and ultimately Liddy. Earlier in the book, I established that Hunt and McCord's retirements were, most likely, bogus covers, and they remained in contact with the C.I.A. Moreover, a few days prior to McCord's arrest at the Watergate, he was seen visiting the C.I.A.'s headquarters in Langley, Virginia.[20]

By engaging Hunt and McCord in the burglaries, Liddy was opening a Pandora's Box that became a fountainhead of misdirection, chaos, and great misfortune for himself and the Nixon administration. The first indication that McCord and Hunt had a different agenda from Liddy's was their pretense of meeting for the first time after they were ostensibly introduced by Liddy, even though their working relationship probably dated back to at least 1963. A second indication that McCord and Hunt had a divergent agenda was their lie that the corridor leading from the Continental Room to Watergate's underground garage had an alarm that became activated at 11:00 P.M. Hunt and McCord also colluded to give Liddy faux pictures supposedly taken by the burglars during the first break-in.

Though Baldwin's veracity is problematic, he told the F.B.I., *Los Angeles Times,* and Congress that McCord was listening to a bugged conversation in the Howard Johnson's room on May 26 – two days before the Watergate burglars had planted bugs in the D.N.C. According to Baldwin, McCord could seemingly gain entry to the D.N.C. at will. McCord's expertise in covert surveillance and also his years in the shadowy milieus of the C.I.A.'s Office of Security lends credence to Baldwin's assertions.

So, the various machinations McCord underwent with the Cubans during the first and second Watergate break-ins, and also his vanishing acts during the second break-in were essentially a theater of the absurd. Plus, a seasoned F.B.I. and C.I.A. agent like McCord would immediately discern that the discovery of the tape on the door locks jeopardized the fidelity of the break-in. His lie about checking the tape in the garage, while he was perhaps meeting with Lou Russell, ensured the burglars' arrest.

The next logical question is whether or not Hunt completely shared McCord's agenda? Hunt started recruiting Cubans even before the formation of the Plumbers. Hunt also colluded with McCord in a lie when they asserted that the door outside the Watergate's Continental Room had an alarm that became activated at 11:00 P.M.

Though McCord and Hunt colluded in lies to deceive Liddy, they had very different reactions when the team arrived at the Watergate's garage and found the tape removed from the B-2 door lock. Hunt said he wanted to abort the burglary at once, but McCord insisted that the burglary proceed and McCord ultimately lobbied Liddy to authorize the burglary. If Hunt's response about aborting the burglary was genuine, then he and McCord had different agendas, or, possibly, they shared agendas but Hunt's response was an example of C.I.A. misdirection?

An indication that the Watergate arrests were premeditated was the arrival of D.C. police officer Carl Shoffler. Shoffler was a burly 5'11", and, as an undercover officer, he dressed like a "hippie" with shoulder-length blond hair. But like McCord, Shoffler was a frothing-at-the-mouth right-winger. Shoffler quickly skipped from the Army Security Agency into the D.C. police department in 1969. When Shoffler was in the Army Security Agency, he served at one of the National Security Agency's eavesdropping nerve centers in Virginia, which reportedly intercepted communications emanating from Embassy Row in D.C.[21] Shoffler also had a history of aiding and abetting the C.I.A. in various operations.[22]

In addition to Shoffler's background in intelligence, his chance whereabouts on the morning of June 17 – within two blocks of the Watergate – are highly improbable. Shoffler was assigned to desk duty on the evening of June 16 due to an on-duty injury.[23] His shift ended at 10:00 P.M., but he voluntarily undertook a second shift with a plainclothes unit into the morning of June 17.[24] Shoffler's birthday just happened to fall on June 17, and his wife and children drove to Shoffler's parents' home in Pennsylvania on June 16 to celebrate Shoffler's birthday.[25] The plan was for Shoffler to drive to Pennsylvania and be with his family on June 17, yet, he inexplicably opted to work a second shift.[26]

In fact, Shoffler reportedly informed his former superior at the Army Security Agency that the arrests were the result of a tip he received from McCord lackey Alfred Baldwin.[27] Shoffler also reportedly told his former superior that his "life wouldn't be worth a nickel" if his actual role in Watergate were exposed.[28] Shoffler, however, adamantly denied making such a statement.[29] The two police officers who participated in the Watergate bust with Shoffler repeatedly questioned him about his timing on that fateful night, and he never diverted from merely a wink and a smile.[30] A clerk for the D.C. police's intelligence squad, who was a very close friend of Shoffler, has also been questioned about Shoffler's extraordinary timing on June 17, 1972, and she responded: "There are no coincidences."[31]

Forgoing his birthday festivities, Shoffler logged his seventeenth hour of overtime when he and F.B.I. agents executed search warrants on the burglars' Watergate Hotel rooms.[32] The law enforcement officers found surgical gloves, electronic equipment, $3,200 in sequentially marked $100 bills, but the pièce de résistance of their search was a Cuban's address book containing "H.H.-W.H." and a check of Hunt's made out to his country club.[33] By allowing one of the Cubans to have a key to the Watergate "command center," Hunt provided a hyperlink that led directly to him, which was certainly counterintuitive for a highly intelligent, experienced spook.

I've come to believe that McCord, and perhaps Hunt, had two primary agendas during the Watergate burglaries. The first agenda was to protect the D.N.C.-Columbia Plaza honey trap from detection, and the second agenda was to damage the Nixon administration. McCord hated Nixon and Kissinger for their friendly posturing towards both the Soviet Union and China: He didn't think that Nixon even deserved to be called an

American.[34] Indeed, the deluded and alcoholic chief of the C.I.A.'s counterintelligence thought Kissinger was a Soviet spy, and it wouldn't be irrational to infer that McCord shared his beliefs.[35] To protect the Columbia Plaza brothel, McCord lied to Liddy about the incompatibility of the receiver and recorder. He also had strict control over the logs given to Liddy, and his forthcoming lies to the Department of Justice helped to ensure that Rikan et al. was unscathed throughout the Watergate investigation.

McCord, accompanied by the Cubans, signed into the Watergate logbook at 12:30 A.M. on a Sunday, stating that their destination was the Federal Reserve Board, which had been burgled the prior month. If the Watergate's graveyard shift security guard hadn't been cognitively challenged, he would've confronted McCord & Company or phoned the police, so it appears that McCord was willing to risk arrest that night. McCord's proceeding with the second break-in after the tape had been discovered and removed from the B-2 door lock further demonstrates that he was willing to risk arrest.

Moreover, McCord's bizarre behavior and frequent lies throughout the Watergate caper, and Shoffler's disclosure that he received a tip from Baldwin, if true, provide additional evidence that McCord was definitely willing to fall on his sword. For McCord's participation in Watergate, he was incarcerated for a mere three months and 21 days: He may have been willing to fall on his sword, but he incurred only a minor abrasion.[36] Baldwin became a government witness and was given immunity from prosecution.[37]

CHAPTER 15

THE BURNING MAN

B right and early, the morning after the Watergate bust, Liddy, ever the man of action, was at his C.R.P. office, shredding Gemstone and other incriminating documents.[1] He phoned Magruder at about 11:00 A.M. E.S.T.[2] He would have phoned Magruder much earlier, but Magruder was in Los Angles traveling with John Mitchell on a C.R.P. fundraising junket.[3] Liddy phoned Magruder from a secure phone in the White House's Situation Room, and he insisted that Magruder scurry to the nearest military base and return his call from a secure phone.[4]

But Magruder did not have Liddy's "Spy vs. Spy" dedication: He was in the midst of eating breakfast, and he ambled to a nearby pay phone and phoned the White House.[5] Liddy had very, very, very bad news for Magruder: James McCord, the C.R.P.'s security chief, had been apprehended burglarizing the Watergate with four other men.[6] Magruder, probably nearing spontaneous combustion, excoriated Liddy for deploying McCord.[7] Liddy accepted full responsibility for his gaping gaffe, but he insisted they needed to focus on problem solving.[8]

After Liddy's phone call, Magruder maintained that he told a Mitchell aide about the arrests of McCord and the Cubans in the hotel where the Mitchell entourage was encamped.[9] Magruder asserted that the conversation unfolded in a hotel room that was across the hall from where Mitchell was holding a meeting.[10] The Mitchell aide, in turn, informed Mitchell who summoned Magruder.[11] Magruder then described a huddle among Mitchell, two of Mitchell's aides, and himself where the four collectively decided that Attorney General Richard Kleindienst, who replaced Mitchell when the latter became Nixon's 1972 campaign manager, should spring McCord from jail.[12] Magruder testified before the Watergate Committee that Mitchell then dispatched one of his aides to phone Liddy and direct him to talk to the attorney general.[13]

Liddy despised rats – at least, in a non-culinary context – and refused to cooperate with prosecutors due to his loyalty to Nixon. So Liddy's version of that fateful morning was only made public when his autobiography, *Will,* was published in 1980, after the statute of limitations for the Watergate crimes had expired. In *Will,* Liddy wrote that Magruder, not the Mitchell aide in question, phoned him around noon E.S.T. and directed him to have a tête-à-tête with the attorney general to liberate Mc-Cord.[14] Liddy expected a torrent of "sniveling" from Magruder, so he was pleasantly surprised when Magruder directed him to contact Attorney General Kleindienst.[15] Magruder told Liddy that Mitchell was the genesis of the directive.[16]

Liddy and a White House aide then ventured to a golf course in Maryland, where he found Kleindienst eating lunch.[17] Liddy invoked Mitchell's name and requested that the attorney general spring McCord.[18] After Kleindienst fielded Liddy's request, he responded to Liddy with an "instantaneous and rather abrupt" rebuff.[19] The attorney general and Mitchell were friends, and he did not believe that Mitchell would send Liddy on such a fool's errand.[20]

Magruder's account of Mitchell commencing the Watergate cover-up on the morning of June 17 would, astonishingly, become the government gospel.[21] Mitchell, however, testified that he never authorized Liddy to visit Attorney General Kleindienst.[22] Moreover, the Mitchell aide Magruder fingered for the phone call to Liddy adamantly denied that he placed the call.[23] In fact, when the aide in question heard about Liddy's jaunt to the golf course the following day, he phoned Liddy and reprimanded him for invoking Mitchell's name.[24]

If Liddy's account is accurate, the official Watergate narrative contravenes the space-time continuum that govern the inhabitants of Earth. According to Liddy, he received the phone call from Magruder at about noon, and then he undertook the task of finding the attorney general at the golf course.[25] Liddy rendezvoused with Attorney General Kleindienst at about 12:30 EST.[26] However, Mitchell's security log showed that Magruder and the Mitchell aide, who ostensibly phoned Liddy, entered the hotel room across the hall from Mitchell at 9:55 W.S.T. or 12:55 E.S.T.[27]

So, Liddy's rendezvous with the attorney general occurred about half an hour before Mitchell was even apprised of McCord's status. As I've mentioned, Magruder was a pusillanimous individual, and he wouldn't have had the moxie to preemptively launch the Watergate cover-up. He admitted as much to the authors of *Silent Coup*: He confessed his commencement of the cover-up was the result of a conversation that he had with Dean, who was in the Philippines.[28]

Haldeman phoned Magruder at the Beverly Hills Hotel and inquired about the Watergate break-in.[29] A very anxious Magruder told Haldeman that a rogue element of the C.R.P., namely James McCord, who worked with G. Gordon Liddy, had burglarized the D.N.C.[30] Haldeman had never heard of McCord and was only vaguely familiar with Liddy.[31] Haldeman then phoned Ehrlichman.[32] Ehrlichman had already received a call from a Secret Service agent who said that the police report stated one of the burglars possessed a check written by E. Howard Hunt and also Hunt's White House phone number.[33]

Ehrlichman knew that Hunt and Nixon's special counsel Chuck Colson were Brown University alumni and friends.[34] He hastily phoned Colson, and Colson told him that Hunt had been discharged by the White House.[35] Colson, however, had erred, because the White House was still compensating Hunt.[36] After Ehrlichman phoned Colson, Haldeman phoned Colson, who adamantly insisted that he was clueless about the break-in.[37]

In the aftershocks of the Watergate bust, when Magruder returned from his Los Angeles sojourn, he tossed his Gemstone documentation into his fireplace.[38] In his autobiography, Magruder wrote that he chuckled at "…the graphic details of the social lives of some of the Democratic staff."[39] Hunt, too, burned various incriminating documents at his home in Maryland.[40]

The burn-fest of Magruder and Hunt was merely playing with matches compared to the pyromania extravaganza at McCord's home. Mrs. McCord, McCord's secretary, and the secretary's husband, who had been on the staff of the House on Un-American Activities, tossed everything that was made of paper from McCord's home office into the fireplace.[41] A rightwing C.I.A. asset and friend of McCord's also accompanied the trio in their pyromania.[42]

The burning frenzy was so industrious that McCord's home became immersed in smoke: The walls of the house were encased in soot, necessitating a repainting.[43] According to Mrs. McCord, the rationale for the blaze was an anonymous bomb threat that she received over the phone from Houston, Texas.[44] After she talked to her jailed husband about the threat, he told her that his office was filled with papers that should be burned to preempt them from becoming incendiary in the event of a bomb detonation.[45] In *Secret Agenda,* Jim Hougan wondered if the anonymous phone call received by Mrs. McCord had been collect, because she was aware of the bomber's whereabouts.[46]

Monday, June 19, was particularly vexing for the hierarchy of the Nixon administration. Nixon's Machiavellian management tactics had fostered various tectonic plates of power within his administration, and each had its secrets and competing agendas.[47] Nixon's strategy of tension was particularly salient between the White House staff and the C.R.P. staff.[48] Both camps were fumbling about for answers, and scratching their heads as they attempted to determine who had sanctioned the Watergate burglary.

On that Monday morning, Liddy showed up at the C.R.P. headquarters, and he had a chat with Magruder.[49] For some inexplicable reason, Magruder was not grateful for Liddy's marathon shredding session over the weekend: "Gordon, let's face it, you and I can't work together," Magruder said. "Why don't you talk to Dean. He's going to help us on this problem."[50] Magruder told Liddy that Dean would be in touch with him.[51] And lo and behold, Liddy received a phone call from Dean that morning.[52] Dean and Liddy rendezvoused at the Executive Office Building, and, at Dean's request, they took a walk in the nearby park and sat on a park bench.[53]

Dean's *Blind Ambition* and Liddy's *Will* conveyed diametric tales about their walk in the park. In *Blind Ambition*, Dean described Liddy as unshaven and slovenly.[54] Dean's description of Liddy paints a picture of the latter as being maniacally unhinged, which wasn't a major feat. But, according to *Will*, Liddy was calm and well rested.[55] Liddy wrote that he inquired if Dean was, in fact, the "damage control action officer," and Dean responded in the affirmative.[56] Both Liddy and Dean concur that Dean inquired if anybody affiliated with the White House was enmeshed in the Watergate burglary.[57,58] Liddy named a Haldeman aide who may have been aware of the break-in.[59] In *Blind Ambition*, Dean played out a mental progression that was slightly analogous to the song "Dry Bones": "The toe bone connected to the heel bone / The heel bone connected to the foot bone..." In Dean's version of "Dry Bones," the Haldeman aide knew, so Haldeman knew, so Nixon knew.[60]

According to *Will*, Liddy thought Dean was his informatic conduit to the president, and he expressed his concerns about the welfare of the burglars: He sought their bail, attorneys' fees, and support for their families.[61] Liddy wrote that Dean acquiesced to his various requests for the burglars.[62] But Dean wrote that he explicitly told Liddy that he would not accept an iota of financial responsibility for the burglars' welfare.[63] Liddy also wrote that Dean suggested Hunt leave the country.[64] The dramatic apogee of Liddy and Dean's walk in the park occurred when Liddy offered to sacrifice himself for the team.[65] Liddy told Dean to name the street corner, and he would voluntarily await an assassin's bullet.[66]

According to Liddy, Dean's role as a "damage control action officer" had been a fortuitous undertaking – for Dean: He discovered that Liddy was not aware of the role he may have played in the Watergate burglaries, and Liddy would also take a bullet in lieu of folding under questioning. Liddy, however, wrote that Dean quickly eschewed his role as a "damage control action officer."[67] Baffled, Liddy inquired who would now emerge as the administration's fixer, and Dean replied that the individual in question would introduce himself to Liddy.[68]

CHAPTER 16

THE PLAGUE

A fter Dean's walk in the park with Liddy, Ehrlichman summoned him around noon: Haldeman and Ehrlichman had assigned Dean to investigate the break-in, which would prove to be an inauspicious decision.[1] Before the Watergate Committee, Dean testified that he gave Ehrlichman the whole shebang about his chat with Liddy in the park.[2] But Ehrlichman testified to the Watergate Committee that Dean didn't mention his morning walk in the park with Liddy when they met at noon on that fateful Monday.[3]

Ehrlichman and Dean would meet again at 4:00 P.M. that day in the presence of Charles Colson, Nixon's special counsel, a Haldeman aide, and Nixon's deputy director of communications, because Ehrlichman was groping for responses to dispense to the press about the break-in.[4] At the meeting, Dean testified to the Watergate Committee that Ehrlichman instructed him to phone Liddy and have Liddy instruct Hunt to abscond from the country.[5] Dean testified that he phoned Liddy from Ehrlichman's office.[6] But when Ehrlichman testified before the Watergate Committee, he unequivocally denied that he had ordered Hunt to abscond.[7]

Earlier in the day, Dean had relayed to Colson that he had directed Hunt to go on the lam, but Colson maintained that he vetoed Dean's ludicrous idea and told Dean to have Hunt remain stationary.[8] Hunt wrote that he received a call from Liddy at about 11:30 A.M., and Liddy instructed him to leave the country, but, within half an hour, Liddy phoned again and rescinded the directive.[9] Ehrlichman provided the Watergate Committee with synopses of the conversations gleaned from Nixon's deputy director of communications and Colson about the meeting on June 19 at 4:00 P.M., and both stated that Ehrlichman did not order Hunt out of the country, even though Colson could not recall his participation in that specific meeting.[10,11]

The meeting attendees also discussed their next move regarding the contents of Hunt's safe. Colson proposed that Dean, as counsel to the president, take possession of the safe's contents.[12] Ehrlichman concurred with Colson.[13] Though Ehrlichman directed Dean to be present when

Hunt's safe was opened that night, Dean was missing in action: The Haldeman aide who attended the 4:00 P.M. meeting in Ehrlichman's office, and a Dean subordinate were present when technicians drilled open the safe.[14] The next morning, General Services Administration personnel delivered "several cartons" that contained the contents of Hunt's safe to Dean.[15] Before the Watergate Committee, Dean testified that Ehrlichman told him to shred the safe's documents and "deep six" the briefcase that contained various electrical gadgets.[16] Ehrlichman categorically denied that he issued those instructions to Dean.[17]

Dean then proceeded to hoodwink all concerned parties: He pinched two of Hunt's notebooks, and he didn't tell a soul about his theft.[18] Dean ultimately destroyed the notebooks, but he withheld that inconvenient truth from the Watergate Committee.[19] Hunt wrote that the two notebooks elucidated Dean's role as one of the "principals" of Gemstone.[20] I'm disinclined to look upon Hunt as a beacon of veracity, but, if Hunt's notebooks implicated Dean in Gemstone, Dean certainly had a powerful motive to destroy the notebooks and lie about it.

As the White House was attempting to untangle the Watergate bust on Monday, Mitchell returned from his Los Angeles junket.[21] Upon Mitchell's arrival in D.C., Magruder ironically suggested that Mitchell convene a meeting at his Watergate apartment to discuss the D.N.C. break-in.[22] The two aides who had accompanied Mitchell to Los Angeles attended the meeting, and, at Magruder's behest, Dean was invited, too.[23] Before the meeting commenced, the F.B.I. had discovered McCord's identity and his C.R.P. affiliation, and it also connected Hunt to the Cubans.[24]

Puzzlement, melancholia, and jet lag enveloped the meeting as the attendees discussed who was responsible for the Watergate break-in and their response.[25] Magruder and Dean disclosed nary a word of substance.[26] Fate often seems fickle: If Magruder and Dean had come clean that night, Richard Nixon probably would have sailed into history as a great president and statesman.

The following morning, Tuesday June 20, the *Washington Post* published an article, co-authored by cub reporter Bob Woodward, about the arrested burglars' connection to Hunt and the White House via their address books.[27] In *All the President's Men*, the best seller authored by Bob Woodward and Carl Bernstein, Woodward contended that he talked with his sagacious secret source, "Deep Throat," the preceding day, and Deep Throat imparted to him that Hunt was "definitely involved" in Watergate.[28] Deep Throat, as delineated by Woodward, was a fabrication, which will be demonstrated in subsequent chapters. But the article, nonetheless, sparked the ire of Nixon, because it linked the Watergate burglary to the White House.[29]

In the aftermath of the Woodward article on Tuesday, the Nixon administration continued to grope for answers about the Watergate break-in's prime mover. Haldeman, Mitchell, Dean, and Attorney General Richard Kleindienst converged in Ehrlichman's office.[30] The discussion initially revolved around leaks, and Kleindienst assured the meeting attendees that the leaks about McCord and Hunt hadn't emanated from the Justice Department.[31] Mitchell was light-hearted as he disavowed prior knowledge of the break-in.[32] Mitchell's utter lack of apprehension slightly assuaged the concerns of Haldeman that he was enmeshed in the break-in.[33] Dean held his cards close to his vest, so the meeting generated more questions than answers.[34]

Dean then accompanied Attorney General Kleindienst to the Justice Department after the morning meeting.[35] According to Kleindienst, Dean invoked Nixon's name when he requested that Kleindienst surrender the F.B.I. reports that the Watergate burglary had generated.[36] But Kleindienst refused to surrender the reports to him.[37]

In *Blind Ambition*, Tuesday was a very busy day for Dean. After his meeting with the attorney general, he returned to his office and continued sifting through the contents of Hunt's safe.[38] He and Magruder then rendezvoused at his office and strolled to the C.R.P. headquarters.[39] In the Gospel of Watergate According to John, otherwise known as *Blind Ambition,* Magruder then supposedly confessed to Dean that Mitchell had sanctioned the Watergate break-ins during their Key Biscayne meeting.[40]

Also on Tuesday, Liddy was contacted by one of Mitchell's principal aides.[41] The Mitchell aide who contacted Liddy and a second Mitchell aide met with Liddy in the former's Watergate apartment.[42] Liddy convened the meeting with his spook mojo: He inquired if there was a radio in the apartment, and, after a radio was pointed out, he switched it on, because, he explained, their conversation should absolutely not be recorded.[43]

The Mitchell aides were nearly speechless as Liddy described the scope of his activities, including the break-in into the office of Daniel Ellsberg's psychiatrist.[44] Liddy implored Mitchell's aides to provide remuneration for the incarcerated burglars' bail.[45] Liddy also named Magruder as the prime mover of the Watergate break-ins.[46]

In Mitchell's presence, the Mitchell aides who had the meeting with Liddy confronted Magruder, and he adamantly refuted Liddy's contention that he sanctioned the Watergate burglary.[47] Mitchell faced a major quandary: Should he believe Magruder, who seemed to be an upstanding, rational individual, or Liddy who appeared to be maniacal? Plus, Mitchell had an additional quandary: The presidential election was less than five months away, and if heads started to roll at the C.R.P., Nixon's reelection bid might be irrevocably damaged.

In Edgar Allan Poe's short story "The Masque of the Red Death," a prince and wealthy nobles sequester themselves in a medieval abbey to escape the plague that is ravaging the prince's fiefdom. But the plague, nonetheless, seeps into the abbey and decimates the prince and his nobles. Like the prince in "The Masque of the Red Death," King Richard thought he was safely sequestered in the White House, even though an unseen and odorless pestilence that was politically lethal had thoroughly tainted the White House within days of the burglars' arrest.

CHAPTER 17

THE WHOLE BAY OF PIGS THING

On Wednesday, June 21, Haldeman met with Nixon and relayed to him that Liddy had spearheaded the Watergate fiasco.[1] The C.R.P. employed Liddy, so Nixon's mental gymnastics vaulted to Mitchell's complicity in the Watergate break-ins.[2] Though Nixon and Haldeman inconclusively discussed whether or not they felt Mitchell was involved in the Watergate hijinks, their discussion quickly shifted to collateral matters that were potentially catastrophic: For example, if a light were shone on Watergate, they rightfully feared "other involvements" might be illuminated.[3]

J. Edgar Hoover, who had headed the F.B.I. since the Jurassic period, died a month before the Watergate bust.[4] Nixon then appointed an acting director of the F.B.I., L. Patrick Gray, and Ehrlichman informed him that Dean would be the administration's point man for the F.B.I.'s Watergate investigation.[5] On that Wednesday morning, Dean met with Gray, and Dean disclosed to him that he would attend the F.B.I.'s Watergate interviews of White House personnel, because Dean, acting in an official capacity, would report the interviews' content directly to the president.[6]

The following day, Thursday June 22, Gray again rendezvoused with Dean.[7] He imparted to Dean that the F.B.I. had uncovered irregularities in a Watergate burglar's bank account: The burglar had deposited five checks in his bank account, and four of the checks had been drawn from an account in Mexico.[8] Gray surmised that the Watergate burglary was a C.I.A. operation, because the burglars had been affiliated with the Agency and also because of the international "money chain."[9] But, in actuality, the assets in the Watergate burglar's bank account were campaign contributions from C.R.P. donors who wished to retain their anonymity.[10] The laundered money was ultimately converted into the $100 bills that had subsidized the Watergate burglary.[11]

Gray divulged to Dean that the F.B.I. would "pursue all leads aggressively" unless the C.I.A. notified the F.B.I. that "there was C.I.A. interest or involvement" in Watergate.[12] Amazingly, the C.I.A. has the ability to quash investigations into its domestic crimes by invoking national security or by declaring the crime was a C.I.A. internal matter, giving the C.I.A. a ubiquitous get-out-of-jail-free card.[13]

On Friday, June 23, Haldeman wrote that he received a morning phone call from Dean.[14] Dean told Haldeman that an "out of control" F.B.I. had traced laundered C.R.P. funds to a Mexican bank account.[15] Dean also told Haldeman that Mitchell was very concerned about the F.B.I. investigation.[16] Haldeman wrote that Dean then offered Haldeman a flickering light at the end of a potentially dark tunnel: He conveyed to Haldeman that Mitchell suggested the C.I.A. should be deployed to "turn off" the F.B.I.'s investigation of the C.R.P.'s Mexican money laundering.[17]

Interviewed by the authors of Silent Coup, Mitchell denied that he instructed Dean to utilize the C.I.A. to stymie the F.B.I.'s investigation into the laundered C.R.P. funds. Mitchell said that Dean's tactics were, in essence, Dean's "gambit," which entailed invoking Mitchell's name when he thought it would be advantageous to his ends.[18] Dean's gambit that Friday morning buttressed Nixon and Haldeman's suspicions that Mitchell had been integral to the Watergate break-in.[19] Dean's gambit-yielding dividends was significantly enhanced by the fissure between the administration's Mitchell and Haldeman factions.[20] Moreover, Nixon's phobic aversion to personal confrontations prevented him from challenging Mitchell face-to-face and inquiring if Mitchell were integral to the Watergate break-in and if he had suggested playing the C.I.A.'s get-out-of-jail-free card. So, Nixon never relinquished the idea that Mitchell had colluded in Watergate.

Haldeman met with Nixon that Friday morning, and he apprised Nixon that Mitchell suggested using the C.I.A. to terminate the F.B.I.'s investigation into the C.R.P.'s Mexican money laundering and Dean concurred.[21] After their conversation quickly cycled through various Tricky Dick machinations, like the spinning reels of a slot machine, Nixon concluded that the C.I.A.'s get-out-of-jail-free card was their consummate play.[22]

Nixon said: "We protected Helms from one hell of a lot of things."[23] Nixon felt that using the C.I.A. to impede the F.B.I.'s investigation of the C.R.P.'s Mexican money laundering was simply one of many political quid pro quos he had engineered over the course of his career: He instructed Haldeman to phone the C.I.A. and "play it tough."[24] He also articulated to Haldeman exactly what to impart to the C.I.A. "people": "The President believes that it is going to open the whole Bay of Pigs thing up again.... That we wish for the good of the country don't go any further into this case. Period!"[25] Nixon's allusion to the "Bay of Pigs" actually referenced the Kennedy assassination; Nixon and Helms had a prior conversation about the Kennedy assassination, and Helms knew exactly what Nixon meant by the "Bay of Pigs."[26]

On Friday afternoon, Haldeman arranged for a meeting among himself, Ehrlichman, C.I.A. Director Helms, and the C.I.A. Deputy Director General Vernon Walters.[27] Shortly before Haldeman attended the meeting, he made a pit stop in the Oval Office and spoke to Nixon, who stressed that he broach the "Bay of Pigs" with Helms and Walters.[28] Helms started the meeting by stating that he had spoken to the F.B.I.'s acting director, L. Patrick Gray, and he told him that the C.I.A. was not involved in Watergate.[29] After Helms disavowed the C.I.A.'s involvement in Watergate, he said that none of the burglars had worked for the C.I.A. in two years.[30] As I've previously demonstrated, Helms' statement was a bald-faced lie.

Haldeman then said to Helms that Watergate might be related to the "Bay of Pigs."[31] When Haldeman mentioned the Bay of Pigs, 5,000 volts of electricity seemingly infused the formerly relaxed atmosphere of the meeting.[32] Helms suddenly clasped the arms of his chair, lunged forward, and shouted: "The Bay of Pigs had nothing to do with this! I have no concern about the Bay of Pigs!"[33] After Helms' outburst, he declared that the C.I.A. would help the administration with the F.B.I.'s investigation.[34] Ehrlichman, however, had made the grave mistake of notifying C.I.A. Deputy Director Walters that Dean would be the administration's point man with the C.I.A. regarding Watergate.[35]

After Haldeman's brief melee with Helms, he reported to Nixon that Helms would comply with Nixon's wishes and call off the F.B.I.[36] In subsequent chapters, I will demonstrate that Nixon's conversation with Haldeman about the "whole Bay of Pigs thing" on the morning of Friday June 23, 1972, created a seismic ripple effect that significantly altered the trajectory of history.

According to Haldeman, Dean gave him the idea of deploying the C.I.A. to checkmate the F.B.I.'s investigation. But Dean eschewed the credit for the scheme before the Watergate Committee: He testified that he had "no idea" about the upcoming meeting among Haldeman, Ehrlichman, Helms, and Walters.[37] Dean further testified that Ehrlichman later informed him of the meeting but not of the "substance of the meeting."[38]

Dean was possibly suffering from memory lapses that day when he testified before the Watergate Committee, because acting F.B.I. Director Gray testified to the Watergate Committee that Dean phoned him shortly after the meeting among Haldeman, Ehrlichman, Helms and the C.I.A.'s deputy director had commenced and alerted him to expect a call from the

C.I.A.'s deputy director.[39] He also testified that Dean advised him to carve out time that afternoon to meet with the C.I.A.'s deputy director.[40]

Acting F.B.I. Director Gray did, in fact, receive a phone call from the secretary of the C.I.A.'s deputy director after the bellicose "Bay of Pigs" meeting, and the two scheduled a meeting for 2:30 P.M. that afternoon.[41] According to Gray, Dean phoned him and inquired if he had arranged a meeting with the C.I.A.'s deputy director.[42] Gray testified to the Watergate Committee that he relayed to Dean that a meeting had been arranged for later in the afternoon. At that meeting, C.I.A. Deputy Director Walters disclosed that the C.I.A. had been involved with the Mexican monies.[43] The following week, Gray talked to C.I.A. Director Helms, who double crossed Nixon: He said that the C.I.A. "had no interest" in the money run through the Mexican account.[44]

CHAPTER 18

PAY THE PIPER

L iddy implored Dean and then two of Mitchell's aides to establish a Widows and Orphans Fund for the burglars' bail, legal aide, and sundry expenses. But Mitchell quickly quashed the idea of compensation for the burglars.[1] Before the Watergate Committee, one of Mitchell's principal aides testified that Mitchell had indeed nixed the idea of compensation for the burglars.[2] Though Mitchell steadfastly denied that he authorized funds for the Watergate burglars, the official Watergate narrative belies his contentions.

On Saturday morning, June 24, at the C.R.P. headquarters, Mitchell had a meeting with the two aides who had met with Liddy and also Dean and Magruder.[3] When Dean testified before the Watergate Committee, he said that Mitchell and one of his aides proffered the idea that the C.I.A. should be used to provide funds for the burglars' expenses.[4] Testifying to the Watergate Committee, Mitchell adamantly rejected Dean's contention.[5] Before the Watergate Committee, the Mitchell aide in question also adamantly denied that such a proposal had been proffered.[6]

The following Monday, June 26, Dean testified that he phoned Ehrlichman and informed him about Mitchell's proposal for prompting the C.I.A. to spring for the burglars' various expenses and that Ehrlichman consented.[7] Dean, then, had three meetings with C.I.A. Deputy Director General Vernon Walters, who was a wily, former lieutenant general in the Army.[8] Dean summoned Walters to his office that Monday.[9] According to Walters, at the first meeting, Dean "pressed" him on whether or not the C.I.A. was involved in the Watergate break-in, and the deputy director emphatically denied the C.I.A.'s involvement.[10]

Dean testified that he reported this unproductive encounter to Ehrlichman, and Ehrlichman instructed Dean to continue pressuring the C.I.A.[11] Dean summoned Walters the next day for a second meeting.[12] He told Walters that "some of the suspects were wobbling and might talk," and he requested that the C.I.A. subsidize them.[13] Walters responded that the C.I.A. would disburse zero funds to the burglars.[14] Dean summoned Walters the following day for a third meeting and requested that the C.I.A. limit the F.B.I.'s Watergate investigation to the five burglars, but, once more, Walters was recalcitrant.[15] C.I.A. Director Helms must have been delighted to have the Nixon administration groveling before the C.I.A. The C.I.A. was, in effect, readying a fatted calf for slaughter.

The Watergate Committee's *Final Report* stated that Dean testified his three meetings with Walters were at Ehrlichman's behest.[16] The *Final Report* neglected to mention that Ehrlichman testified he wasn't even aware of the three meetings.[17] Though Dean's attempt to have the C.I.A. underwrite the burglars' hush money had perished in flames, he, nonetheless, continued to assiduously panhandle for them – despite his swift relinquishment of "damage control action officer." The day of Dean's final, futile meeting with the C.I.A.'s deputy director he, once more, invoked Mitchell's name: In Dean's Watergate Committee testimony, he discussed a meeting that Wednesday with Mitchell and two of Mitchell's aides, where Mitchell proposed that Nixon's personal attorney, a fundraiser *par excellence,* cobble together a Widow and Orphans Fund for the burglars.[18]

Before the Watergate Committee, Dean testified that Mitchell told him to present his fund raising proposal to Ehrlichman and Haldeman.[19] Dean even embellished his testimony with a picturesque, seemingly insignificant anecdote: Dean testified that Mitchell took him aside and whispered to him that Ehrlichman should be keen about placating the burglars, because of their prior shenanigans, which included demolishing the office of Daniel Ellsberg's psychiatrist.[20] The scheme of deploying Nixon's private attorney to raise funds for the burglars' Widow and Orphans Fund ostensibly had Mitchell's imprimatur, so Haldeman and Ehrlichman stamped it with their imprimaturs, and it became a fait accompli.[21]

Testifying before the Watergate Committee, Mitchell vigorously refuted Dean's contention that he suggested using Nixon's personal attorney to solicit money for the burglars.[22] Mitchell had a very sound justification for disputing Dean's account of their meeting in D.C.: Mitchell's logs show that he was in New York when Dean testified that he whispered in his ear and directed him to deploy Nixon's personal attorney to raise funds for the burglars.[23] The *Washington Post* also reported that Mitchell was in New York on that day.[24] Yet again, the Watergate Committee did not question testimony that contravened the rudimentary laws of physics.

Dean phoned Nixon's personal attorney who lived in California.[25] His "Siren song" included the catchwords of Mitchell, Haldeman, and Ehrlichman, and he exhorted Nixon's personal attorney to jump on a D.C.-bound plane.[26] The next day, Dean met with Nixon's personal attorney in

Washington, D.C.[27] He told the attorney that the Watergate break-in could possibly involve the president, and he was being tapped to raise funds for the burglars' defense and their ancillary expenses.[28] Nixon's personal attorney was a fund raising dynamo and not a bagman, but he reluctantly acquiesced to Dean's scheme.[29]

The former N.Y.P.D. gumshoe whom Dean had inherited from Ehrlichman when he became counsel to the president became the bagman for the hush money.[30] The payoffs quickly morphed into a secret agent man escapade replete with codenames, cross-country flights, and clandestine drops.[31] The president's personal attorney raised approximately $220,000 that the gumshoe dispensed.[32] The vast majority of the hush money was delivered to Howard Hunt's wife – $154,000.[33] Hunt's wife was supposed to spread the funds among the Cubans, but the Hunts garnered the lion's share of the hush money.[34]

As Dean engineered hush money payoffs, Nixon felt the jungle encroaching. His psychological foibles, apparently, engendered an interpersonal paralysis that prevented him from confronting his long-standing friend John Mitchell on whether or not Mitchell was culpable in the Watergate break-in, and also if Mitchell had proposed that the C.I.A. be deployed to quash the F.B.I.'s Watergate investigation. Nixon's peculiar psychological matrix of surviving the jungle of American politics at all costs and his bête noire of face-to-face confrontations made Mitchell the first of the president's men for whom the bell tolled.

On June 30, 13 days after the Watergate bust, Nixon summoned John Mitchell to lunch and Haldeman joined them.[35] Nixon's rationale for Mitchell's resignation as C.R.P. chairman was the health of Mitchell's wife, whose alcoholic meltdowns and diatribes were receiving substantial ink from the media.[36] Mitchell's political euthanasia had the bedside manner of Dr. Kevorkian. Strangely enough, Nixon and Haldeman never directly asked Mitchell about his role in Watergate or lack thereof.[37] Mitchell would discover that his political euthanasia had a trap door, which would plunge him into an unimaginable nightmare.

CHAPTER 19

DEFORESTATION

As Dean et al. were groping for sources of hush money, and John Mitchell was being politically euthanized, the machinations to impanel a federal grand jury to investigate the Watergate break-in had commenced. The phrase "grand jury" has commanding connotations – as if the gods of jurisprudence have sent down a decree. A grand jury makes the initial decision to indict (formally accuse) a criminal defendant to stand trial. The special prosecutor of a grand jury selects the witnesses, questions the witnesses, and chooses the evidence that is shown to the grand jurors.

Grand jurors are everyday citizens who have been summoned for jury duty and then are funneled to a grand jury. Unlike a customary trial, a grand jury is cloaked in secrecy: Grand juries are not open to the public, and the identity of the witnesses who testify and their testimony are almost never disclosed. In the case of Washington, D.C., the executive branch appoints the U.S. Attorney for D.C., who prosecutes all D.C. crimes and impanels all grand juries. An assistant U.S. attorney was appointed to be the special prosecutor of the grand jury probing the bungled Watergate burglary.

Former G-man and McCord lackey Alfred Baldwin who coughed up the particulars of the Watergate caper to the F.B.I. in early July was the grand jury's star witness.[1] He implicated Hunt and Liddy, but he could not implicate the Nixon administration or C.R.P. officials higher on the food chain.[2] Though the Nixon administration and C.R.P. minions had a myriad of worries and anxieties throughout the grand jury, they did not lose sleep over a crooning G. Gordon Liddy.[3] F.B.I. agents had attempted to interview him about Watergate within two weeks of the Watergate bust, but he uttered nary a word, which resulted in his summary termination from the C.R.P.[4]

Dean was a whirlwind of hustle and bustle throughout the grand jury. Although the attorney general blocked Dean from the F.B.I.'s investigative reports on Watergate, he persuaded the acting F.B.I. Director Gray to cough up the reports.[5] Gray thought that the information Dean gleaned from the reports would be earmarked for Nixon, but, according to White

House tapes and documents, Dean did not share the F.B.I.'s investigative intelligence with Nixon, Haldeman, or Ehrlichman.[6] In addition to being up-to-date on the F.B.I. investigation, Dean was able to lodge himself into the F.B.I.'s interviews of White House personnel.[7] The F.B.I. agents found Dean to be belligerent and brash, and an F.B.I. agent told the authors of *Silent Coup* that Dean had an understanding of the Watergate investigation that even eclipsed the grand jury's prosecutor.[8]

Dean's *au fait* understanding of the investigation came to Magruder's rescue before Magruder made his second grand jury appearance in August.[9] During Magruder's first grand jury appearance, the federal prosecutors' questioning of him had been brief and cursory.[10] However, Magruder's second appearance would be onerous: The prosecutors had learned that substantial C.R.P. funds sanctioned by Magruder had fueled the Watergate burglars.[11]

The grand jury's prosecutors scheduled an interview with Magruder the day before his second grand jury appearance.[12] Magruder, ever the "nervous Nellie," had the potential to fold when the grand jury prosecutors assailed him with a blistering grilling. But Dean cross-examined him for two hours on questions that the grand jury's prosecutors might fire at him during their interview and also during his second grand jury appearance.[13]

Magruder told the prosecutors that the C.R.P. funds given to Liddy were earmarked for strictly legitimate intelligence assignments and a myriad of additional fabrications.[14] The prosecutors tentatively ingested his banquet of perjury.[15] In fact, Magruder felt his second grand jury appearance was "anticlimactic" compared to the prosecutors' interrogation of the previous day.[16] The day after Magruder's second grand jury appearance, Dean had a tête-à-tête with the assistant attorney general and relayed to Magruder that he would not be indicted.[17]

Before the Watergate Committee, Magruder testified that Mitchell helped him rehearse his perjured statements for half-an-hour prior to his second grand jury appearance.[18] Mitchell also confessed to the Watergate Committee that he had prior knowledge of Magruder's upcoming perjury during his second grand jury appearance.[19] Obviously, Mitchell was not aware that Magruder's lies would translate into his near ubiquitous complicity in Watergate, but he was extremely concerned about the Gemstone meetings being made public, even though he repeatedly put the kibosh on Gemstone and its incarnations.[20]

Magruder made a third stand before the grand jury in early September.[21] The F.B.I. subpoenaed Magruder's diary, which reflected the January and February Gemstone meetings in Mitchell's office among Mitchell, Dean, Magruder, and Liddy.[22] Magruder conscripted both Dean and Mitchell to help craft his perjured statements about the Gemstone meetings.[23] The trio agreed that Magruder would testify that the first meeting had been cancelled and the second meeting entailed the discussion of a new election law.[24]

In the middle of September, the Watergate grand jury concluded its probe.[25] Hunt, Liddy, McCord and the Cubans were walloped by multiple indictments.[26] The federal prosecutors declared that the indictments of the Watergate burglars ended its investigation: "We have absolutely no evidence to indicate that any others should be charged."[27] The day the indictments were returned against the Watergate burglars, a grateful Nixon summoned Dean to the Oval Office and, in the presence of Haldeman, showered him with accolades.[28] Dean told Nixon that three months earlier he would have had difficulties imagining such a joyous day.[29]

Ironically, as Nixon deluged Dean with accolades, John Mitchell phoned to congratulate Nixon on the narrow scope of the Watergate indictments.[30] Nixon's closing comments to Mitchell were jocular, but they demonstrate that Nixon's suspicions about Mitchell ordering the Watergate break-in had not dimmed: "…anyway get a good night's sleep. And don't … don't bug anybody without asking me. Okay?"[31] Nixon wrote in his diary that Dean had "enormously impressed" him.[32] He also wrote that Dean had the "the steel and mean instinct" that would be required to "clean house" after the election.[33] Nixon's diary entry demonstrated that Dean was now imbedded in Nixon's inner circle, and he could breathe the sweet, rarefied air of Mount Olympus. The diary entry also demonstrated that in addition to being a meritocracy, the Nixon administration was a cold-blooded reptilianocracy.

In October, the *Washington Post* team of Bob Woodward and Carl Bernstein published a front-page article, "F.B.I. Finds Nixon Aides Sabotaged Democrats," which discussed the dirty tricks of a C.R.P. operative who had an affinity for sowing chaos in the Democratic ranks.[34] The article listed the various transgressions of the operative: "Following members of Democratic candidates' families and assembling dossiers on their personal lives; forging letters and distributing them under the candidates' letterheads; leaking false and manufactured items to the press; throwing campaign schedules into disarray; seizing confidential campaign files; and investigating the lives of dozens of Democratic campaign workers."[35]

Woodward and Bernstein wrote that the dirty tricks against the Democrats were underwritten by a "secret" fund controlled by John Mitchell, which fluctuated between $350,000 and $700,000.[36] Woodward's legendary, surreptitious, and omniscient source – "Deep Throat" – ostensibly provided Woodward with information for the article.[37] Though the article contained various gaffes, its most egregious error concerned Mitchell as the curator of the "secret" fund, because Mitchell never controlled a secret fund that was used to bankroll "intelligence operations."[38]

Despite assaults from Woodward and Bernstein articles, Nixon easily crushed his Democratic opponent, George McGovern, in the November 1972 election. But after Nixon sailed through the election, an additional obstacle to ensuring that the Watergate cover-up remained hermetically sealed confronted Dean et al.: feeding the monkey. Hunt increasingly clamored for additional hush money.[39]

When Nixon's personal attorney decided to disengage from the hush money biz, a former Mitchell aide became the primary bagman for the hush money.[40] After the hush money baton had been passed to the former Mitchell aide, Hunt started to vociferously bellyache about the precipitous decline in hush money that he was reaping.[41] A vociferous Hunt potentially translated into major difficulties for the second Nixon administration due to his nuanced understanding of the Watergate break-ins and also the break-in into Ellsberg's psychiatrist's office.

In the middle of November, after Nixon's reelection, Hunt phoned his old buddy and fellow Brown alumni Charles Colson to complain that the Nixon administration was not honoring its prior "commitments."[42] In fact, Hunt's complaints quickly escalated into extortion.[43] He demanded the "liquidation of everything that's outstanding."[44] Colson recorded his conversation with Hunt and gave the tape to Dean.[45] Dean testified that he played the tape of Hunt's threat to Haldeman and Ehrlichman.[46] In Ehrlichman's testimony before the Watergate Committee, he denied that Dean had played the tape for him.[47] Dean also testified that after playing the tape to Haldeman and Ehrlichman, he made a jaunt to New York City, because John Mitchell summoned him to discuss the hush money.[48]

Mitchell may have thought that Watergate was in his rearview mirror, but, in actuality, he was en route to a high-speed collision with it. Mitchell maintained that Dean played the Hunt-Colson tape for him at New York City's Metropolitan Club.[49] The tape included an excerpt of Hunt accusing Mitchell of committing perjury.[50] But, before listening to the entire tape, Mitchell told Dean to hit the stop button.[51] He then stormed out of the Metropolitan Club.[52] Dean's trek to New York City marked the first time Mitchell had been conscripted to resolve the burglars' financial entreaties since he had originally quashed the idea shortly after their arrests.[53] Testifying before the Watergate Committee, Dean even conceded that Mitchell imparted "no instruction or any indication at all ... regarding the matters Hunt had raised" at the Metropolitan Club.[54]

Though John Mitchell didn't co-sign hush money for the burglars at the Metropolitan Club, Dean testified to the Watergate Committee that Mitchell suddenly grasped the gravitas of the hush money about two weeks after their brief chat in New York City.[55] After Mitchell ostensibly beheld the burning bush, he subsequently phoned Dean and directed him to tap into a $350,000 slush fund controlled by Haldeman.[56] Dean invoked Mitchell's name and Haldeman earmarked the slush fund for hush money.[57]

Although Dean was a wunderkind of sorts, he once more had major memory difficulties recalling exactly when Mitchell sanctioned the hush money. Testifying to the Watergate Committee, Dean said that Mitchell green-lighted the hush money in the first week of December.[58] But before the House's Judiciary Committee, Dean recalled that the payola was initially delivered on or before November 28, which means Mitchell endorsed Hunt's hush money on November 28 or before.[59] In *Blind Ambition,* Dean wrote that Mitchell's call, sanctioning the hush money, came on Thanksgiving, which was November 23.[60] In *Blind Ambition,* Dean even provided a touching anecdote about having Thanksgiving with his family when his sister answered the phone: "'John!' she exclaimed. "It's the White House. John Mitchell wants you."[61]

The House's Judiciary Committee concluded that Hunt's attorney handed the C.R.P. counsel a list of his extortionate demands on or about December 1.[62] Dean, however, testified to the Judiciary Committee that Hunt's hush money was delivered on or before November 28. In Dean's account before the House's Judiciary Committee, Hunt's demands were addressed before they were even made. Once again we have government officials embracing accounts that circumvent the laws of physics.

As Hunt's demands were being addressed with payola, McCord started becoming obstreperous, because his attorney reportedly suggested to him that he pin Watergate on the C.I.A.[63] In response to his attorney's continued pressure on the matter, McCord replied: "... even if it meant my freedom I would not turn on the organization that had employed me for nineteen years, and wrongfully deal such a damaging blow that it would take years to recover from it."[64]

Before the start of McCord's trial, he wrote repeated letters to C.I.A. officials warning that the Nixon administration planned to frame the C.I.A. for Watergate.[65] McCord also wrote a letter to one of the retired N.Y.P.D. officers who had served as a Dean minion, and the letter was destined for Dean.[66] McCord was adamant that the Nixon administration would be walking through the valley of the shadow of death if it attempted to frame the C.I.A. for Watergate. "If Helms goes and the Watergate operation is laid at the C.I.A.'s feet, where it does not belong, every tree in the forest will fall. It will be a scorched desert."[67] Nixon announced in December of 1972 that Helms would be leaving the C.I.A.[68] Accordingly, deforestation would become the fate of the Nixon administration.

An argument could be made that Hunt's repeated shake downs of the Nixon administration were exclusively in his self-interest, but, conversely, an argument could also be made that whenever the administration minions acquiesced to a Hunt shake down they were committing additional criminal acts of obstruction. McCord, too, made threats. Ergo, the primary moral of this chapter is never become blackmail fodder for C.I.A. agents who have a proclivity for blackmail.

CHAPTER 20

THE PUGILIST AT WREST

The Watergate burglars' case was adjudicated before 69-year-old U.S. District Court Judge John Sirica.[1] Sirica, a former boxer, was short and stocky. Boxing is a sport of give and take, and his flattened nose suggested that his taking may have exceeded his giving. He had thick, jet-black hair that was sprinkled with silvery filaments. Sirica earned the nickname of "Maximum John," because he was fond of imposing the maximum sentences on defendants who were found guilty in the cases he arbitrated.[2] If Sirica had been a judge in the Wild West, he would have reaped the reputation of a hanging judge.

Sirica's father was an Italian immigrant, and his mother was second generation Italian.[3] Though Sirica and his brother were born in Connecticut, his family made a nomadic odyssey in search of the American dream, living in Ohio, Florida, Louisiana, and Virginia.[4] When Maximum John was a teenager, his family landed in Washington, D.C., where the family moved into a two room flat above a shoemaker's shop.[5] His father eked out a living as a barber.[6] The Siricas treaded the same hardscrabble existence as the Nixon family during the Great Depression.

As a 17-year-old, Sirica sidestepped college and enrolled at George Washington University Law School, which was permissible back in the day.[7] But he found the law school paper chase too daunting, and he dropped out of law school twice.[8] Between stints at law school, Sirica started boxing.[9] But he eventually graduated from Georgetown Law School.[10] After taking the bar exam, Sirica ventured to Miami, where his father and mother had relocated, and he became a sparring partner for a former welterweight champ attempting a comeback.[11] He also had one professional fight.[12] While Sirica was practicing the sweet science, lo and behold, and much to his utter astonishment, the young pugilist was notified that he had passed the bar exam.[13]

Sirica eventually ventured back to D.C., where he started to practice law.[14] He lost his first 13 cases, but, arrogant and stubborn, he doggedly pried himself from the canvas and answered the bell for his next case.[15] Sirica was eventually appointed an assistant U.S. attorney for Washing-

THE PUGILIST AT WREST

ton, D.C. during Prohibition.[16] As he imprisoned his fellow Americans for contravening Prohibition, his father was bootlegging booze from his barbershop.[17] After the repeal of Prohibition, Sirica segued into private practice.[18] Like Phillip Bailey, he scavenged cases in D.C. and narrowly scraped out a living.[19]

Although Sirica was an avowed Republican, he ultimately forged a mentorship with a Democratic high-flyer and prominent trial attorney who enabled him to transition to an esteemed D.C. law firm.[20] During the Eisenhower administration, he was appointed a federal judge for the District of Columbia, which entailed a lifetime appointment.[21] Sirica's proclivity for harsh sentencing and trampling on defendants' rights translated into the appellate court frequently reversing his cases.[22] As Sirica was meting out draconian sentences, he married a woman twenty years his junior, and the couple had three children.[23]

In 1971, as Sirica was raising his brood and depriving defendants of their Constitutional rights, he became D.C.'s chief judge due to sheer attrition: His duration on D.C.'s bench surpassed his fellow D.C. judges.[24] Sirica's seniority allowed him to handpick the cases that were on the D.C. federal court docket, and he eagerly plucked the case of the Watergate burglars.[25] He was determined to thwart the cover-up protecting Nixon, even if it meant disfiguring the rule of law.[26]

A month prior to the onset of the Watergate burglars' trial – December 8, 1972 – Dorothy Hunt, E. Howard Hunt's wife, boarded a United Airlines flight in Washington, D.C. en route to Chicago's Midway Airport.[27] As the plane neared Midway Airport in dense fog and drizzle, air traffic controllers instructed the pilot to make a second approach.[28] Shortly thereafter, the plane abruptly plummeted to terra firma in a residential neighborhood.[29] Forty-one of the plane's 59 passengers and crew died in the subsequent fireball.[30] One of the fatalities was the wife of E. Howard Hunt: Her purse was stocked with $10,000, primarily in $100 bills.[31]

E. Howard Hunt was not a practitioner of matrimonial fidelity, but he was nonetheless devastated by the untimely death of his wife: He wrote that he plunged into a relentless, unforgiving depression in the aftermath of her death.[32] One of the Little Havana contingent described Hunt as a "broken man" and felt that he "looked eighty years old."[33]

Hunt thought that the two "operational notebooks" in his safe that elucidated Gemstone from its inception would be his get-out-of-jail free card.[34] Hunt and his attorney assumed the F.B.I. or Justice Department had confiscated the notebooks without a warrant, which would enable

Hunt's lawyer to file a motion to suppress the contents of the notebooks and demolish the case against Hunt.[35] But when Hunt was permitted to examine the contents of his safe, the two notebooks were nowhere to be found.[36] As mentioned, Hunt wrote that the two notebooks described Dean's role as one of the "principals" of Gemstone, and Dean had pilfered and destroyed the notebooks.[37]

After Hunt's notebooks disappeared, his utter despondency compelled him to plead guilty before Judge Sirica and hope for leniency at the onset of the burglars' trial.[38] The Cubans followed suit and capitulated to guilty pleas the following week.[39] Prior to the trial of Liddy and McCord, Sirica was convinced that Nixon officials higher than Liddy sanctioned the Watergate break-in.[40] He grilled the four Cubans about whether or not "higher ups" had pressured them to plead guilty or if they had been offered money to plead guilty.[41] The four Cubans rejected Sirica's contentions as they attempted to take shelter in the linguistic barrier: Their replies narrowly eclipsed "No hablo Inglés."[42]

Sirica inquired if the Little Havana contingent had ever worked for the C.I.A., and C.I.A. asset Martinez replied: "Not that I know of, your honor."[43] Sirica questioned the Cubans about their surfeit of cash when they were busted, and they responded that they were uncertain of its source, which only served to exacerbate Sirica's incredulity: "Well, I'm sorry, but I don't believe you."[44] A pugnacious Sirica was unable to browbeat the Cubans into folding, so he banished them to the D.C. jail in lieu of $100,000 respective bail bonds.[45] The Cubans confronted maximum sentences of 40 years in prison and fines of $50,000.[46]

At the trial's commencement, seven little indians were cutting up their tricks, but now only two little indians remained to stand trial – Liddy and McCord. According to Liddy, shortly before his trial commenced, Dean phoned him and offered living expenses for his family of $30,000 per annum, his legal expenses covered, a cushy prison, and a presidential pardon after two years.[47] Dean also reportedly sent his former N.Y.P.D. detective underling to assure McCord of clemency.[48] The authors of *Silent Coup* surmise that the entreaties that were made by Dean to both Liddy and McCord were unilateral, because Ehrlichman and/or Haldeman did not discuss them on the White House taping system.[49]

At trial, Liddy and McCord had to contend with Sirica's repeated cross-examination of witnesses, and the judge publicly assailed the prosecution's competence for not aggressively pursuing additional defendants.[50] McCord's attorney became extremely frustrated by Sirica and publicly exclaimed: "Not only does he indicate that the defendants are guilty, but that a lot of other people are guilty. The whole courtroom is permeated with a prejudicial atmosphere."[51] Liddy remarked to his lawyer: "Boy, we drew some judge – a book thrower with the intellect of half a glass of water."[52]

One of the assistant U.S. attorneys prosecuting Liddy and McCord was convinced that sexual blackmail was integral to the Watergate caper, and he planned to aggressively pursue that angle when Alfred Baldwin testified against Liddy and McCord.[53] When Baldwin took the stand, the federal prosecutor pointedly inquired about the conversations that he had overheard from the D.N.C. bug.[54]

The prosecutor's question to Baldwin elicited an extremely bizarre chain reaction: An "objection" echoed in the courtroom.[55] However, the objection did not emanate from Liddy's attorney or McCord's attorney: The objection was launched from the gallery of courtroom onlookers.[56] The source of the objection was an attorney who represented Spencer Oliver and various Democrats, and he had absolutely no connection to Liddy and McCord's criminal trial.[57] Sirica overruled the objection, but then he made a ruling that was very uncharacteristic of his no-nonsense style of jurisprudence: He suspended the trial, so his ruling could be appealed to the U.S. Court of Appeals for the District of Columbia Circuit.[58]

The appellate judge asked the prosecutor of Liddy and McCord about his motives for questioning Baldwin: "Is the government interested in whether this information [overheard by Baldwin] would be used to compromise these people [Oliver and the D.N.C.]?[59] That is a euphemism for blackmail."[60] The prosecutor responded that the conversations overheard by Baldwin were "highly relevant" and the "information goes to the motive and intent."[61] The appellate judge did not seem too concerned about the possibility of blackmail in connection with Watergate, and he overturned Sirica's overruling of the objection.[62]

The ruling of the appellate judge was rather outlandish on two accounts: First, an attorney who was not even affiliated with the case launched the objection. Second, the appellate judge upended an assistant U.S. attorney who deemed Baldwin's testimony regarding blackmail "highly relevant" concerning "intent and motive" for the Watergate break-in. The appellate judge's ruling marked the demise of the prosecution pursuing Watergate's sexual blackmail angle.[63]

On January 30, the jury deliberated a mere 90 minutes to find Liddy and McCord guilty on all counts.[64] Liddy stared at a 35-year prison bid, and McCord faced a 45-year prison bid.[65] Sirica, again, expressed his incredulity that the Watergate break-in was restricted to the septet who appeared in his courtroom: "I am still not satisfied that all the pertinent facts that might be available ... have been produced before an American jury."[66] He set sentencing for March 23.[67]

On Friday March 23, Maximum John Sirica lived up to his billing: The respective maximum sentences he meted out to Liddy, Hunt, and the four Cubans were 20 years, 35 years, and 40 years.[68] Sirica told the defendants that the sentences were "provisional," and their sentences could be reduced if they coughed up their co-conspirators.[69] Sirica, however, did not sentence McCord, because McCord had written a letter that was delivered to the judge: A pall descended over the courtroom as Sirica read the letter aloud.[70]

In the letter, McCord stated that he feared "retaliatory measures" against his family, friends, and himself for summoning the temerity to come forward and tell the actual truth about the Watergate.[71] McCord wrote that the defendants had been subjected to "political pressure to plead guilty and remain silent."[72] McCord's letter, of course, categorically exonerated the C.I.A. from participation in Watergate.[73] The Justice Department then announced that the grand jury would be reconvened.[74] The deforestation process was inevitable, but now it had fully commenced.

As I've demonstrated, McCord's primary objective was to damage the Nixon administration by ensuring that the Watergate burglars were caught in the act. McCord could have delivered the letter to Sirica earlier in the trial. But sentencing was the perfect "cover" for McCord to start deforestation, because it appeared that McCord was merely a C.R.P. apparatchik frightened by a harsh prison sentence – instead of a C.I.A. agent who was zealously devoted to dethroning Nixon.

CHAPTER 21

THE LONG GOODBYE

After Dean's induction into Nixon's inner circle in September, he edified Nixon and Haldeman that the Speaker of the House was marshaling forces for the House's Banking and Currency Committee to conduct an investigation of Watergate.[1] The Speaker had a few scrapes with Johnny Law, presumably due to his excessive drinking, and Haldeman mentioned that he would be ripe for blackmail.[2]

Dean also disclosed to Nixon that "we're" scrutinizing campaign finance reports to determine if the congressmen on the House's Banking and Currency Committee were guilty of contravening campaign finance laws.[3] After Dean, Haldeman, and Nixon discussed the potential blackmailing of U.S. representatives, the administration conscripted allies, like House minority leader and future president, Gerald Ford, to successfully quash a House investigation into Watergate.[4]

Nixon had minimal difficulties turning off a House investigation into Watergate, but he would discover that the Watergate cover-up was analogous to a game of Whac-A-Mole: Every time a threat had been quashed a new threat materialized elsewhere. Though the House investigation had been nullified with relative ease, Nixon found that the collective will of the Senate to organize a Watergate investigation was intransigent. Democratic senators were infuriated over the humiliating presidential election drubbing they had endured in November, and Republican senators were infuriated over Nixon's selfish hoarding of the R.N.C.'s resources for his reelection.[5] In early February of 1973, the senate voted 77-0 to form the "Watergate Committee," which would be comprised of four Democrats and three Republicans.[6]

Sam Dash, a distinguished professor at the Georgetown University Law Center, was appointed to be chief counsel to the Senate Watergate Committee. He became a shining example of democracy as he tenaciously grilled all the president's men during the nationally televised Watergate Committee hearings. Dash would come to symbolize the incorruptible spirit of American democracy, but the Watergate Committee's chief counsel had a scandalous secret: He was in Rikan's black book![7] Rikan possessed both his residential and office numbers.[8] So, perhaps, Dash was a frequent flyer at the Columbia Plaza?

The *New York Times* discussed Dash's state of mind during the Watergate Committee hearings: "Mr. Dash said that he was nervous before the hearings, but that he overcame any jitters with preparation."[9] I, too, would have been extremely "nervous" during nationally televised hearings if my name were in Rikan's black book.

The Watergate Committee also included Senator Lowell Weicker, a Republican from Connecticut.[10] Weicker proved to be particularly bellicose towards all the president's men, and he was the first Republican on the Watergate Committee to call for Nixon's resignation.[11] After Dean became a government turncoat, he and Senator Weicker had a chat at the home of Dean's attorney, where Dean disclosed to the senator that Nixon minions planned to "neutralize," him, if necessary, by coercing him via the illegal campaign contributions he had received.[12] Dean wrote that his conversation with Weicker "perhaps" provoked the senator's acute animus towards the Nixon administration.[13] But maybe the senator from Connecticut harbored a secret? Like Dash, Weicker was in Rikan's black book, too.[14]

As February dragged into March, Nixon frequently summoned Dean, his perceived, trusted sycophant to discuss Watergate.[15] The Oval Office recordings of Nixon and Dean contain a myriad of fascinating exchanges. For example, Nixon was unequivocally baffled about Magruder's rationale for ordering the Watergate break-in, and he pined for an explanation from Dean.[16] Dean responded: "I can't understand why they decided to go in the D.N.C. That absolutely mystifies me..."[17]

At that meeting, Dean also informed Nixon that Ehrlichman had conscripted Liddy and Hunt to burgle the office of Daniel Ellsberg's psychiatrist.[18] Nixon was stunned by that disclosure, and he exclaimed: "What in the world!"[19] As Nixon and Dean were becoming fast friends, a friendship that would prove to have a short half-life, the latter was discovering that March, not April, could be the cruelest month. Dean could not escape the plight of the Watergate Whac-A-Mole as he attempted to ensure that the cover-up remained hermetically sealed. The Watergate burglars had adhered to their omertà throughout the trial, but Hunt's extortion of the administration was escalating as his March 23 sentencing bore down on him.[20]

Hunt met with the C.R.P. attorney who had previously facilitated the hush money, and he demanded an additional $132,000 shakedown before his sentencing.[21] Hunt conveyed his shakedown with an overt blackmail topspin: He told the C.R.P. attorney that in addition to Watergate he had engaged in other "seamy activities" for the White House.[22] The C.R.P. counsel was stunned by Hunt's exorbitant demand and the tight time frame, and he suggested that Hunt write a memo to Colson, who had left the White House and embarked on a career as an attorney in the private sector.[23]

On March 16, seven days before Hunt's sentencing, Hunt's attorney arranged a meeting between Hunt and Colson's law partner, because Colson wanted plausible deniability.[24] Hunt repeated the same threats of prior "seamy activities" he had committed on behalf of the White House to Colson's law partner.[25] One of the "scamy activities" was, of course, the break-in into the office of Daniel Ellsberg's psychiatrist. The former Mitchell aide who had assumed the role of bagman delivered $75,000 to Hunt a few days before his sentencing.[26]

As Nixon minions were actualizing Hunt's latest shakedown, Dean was summoned to the Oval Office on March 21. At the meeting, Dean legendarily proclaimed to Nixon: "We have a cancer, within, close, to the Presidency that's growing."[27] Dean alerted Nixon that the etiology of the cancer was the blackmail of the administration and the proliferating need for administration officials to commit perjury.[28] Dean also told Nixon that the cover-up was susceptible to rupturing.[29]

Dean then came clean with his new pal, Tricky Dick, and gave him the ostensible full-monty on Watergate. Dean said Haldeman conscripted him to create a "perfectly legitimate" campaign intelligence operation.[30] Dean suggested that they use one of the N.Y.P.D. detectives that he had inherited from Ehrlichman, but Haldeman, Ehrlichman, and Mitchell vetoed his recommendation.[31] Dean said that he approached Liddy, because of his F.B.I. and intelligence background and his "extremely sensitive" deeds for the White House.[32] Dean told Nixon that after he and a Haldeman aide talked to Liddy about an intelligence operation, Liddy was introduced to Mitchell.[33] Dean relayed to Nixon that Mitchell "thought highly" of Liddy![34]

As Nixon listened raptly to Dean, Dean said that he received a phone call from Magruder who requested that he join Liddy, Mitchell, and himself in Mitchell's office as Liddy unveiled his intelligence plan.[35] Dean conveyed to Nixon that he and Mitchell thought Liddy's plan was over the top and instructed him to revise it.[36] Dean then informed Nixon that he arrived at the "tail end" of a second meeting, and Liddy was discussing "bugging, kidnapping and the like."[37] Dean said that he abruptly terminated the meeting, because those were illegalities that should never "be discussed in the office of the Attorney General of the United States."[38]

Dean's tale then incorporated a Haldeman aide pushing Magruder for campaign intelligence, and Magruder approaching Mitchell, who probably sanctioned the Watergate caper without being cognizant of "what it was all about."[39] Dean explained to Nixon that he thought Haldeman assumed the C.R.P.'s intelligence machinations were "proper," and Haldeman directed its focus should be on Democratic presidential contender George McGovern.[40] Haldeman's instructions were then transmitted through his aide to Magruder and ultimately to Liddy.[41] Ergo, Watergate. After Dean exculpated himself from playing a premeditated role in Watergate, he punctuated his tale by citing a witness with impeccable credentials: "…as God is my maker, I had no knowledge that they were going to do this."[42]

After Dean implored God to corroborate his tale, the conversation eventually wended to blackmail. Dean said that the cover-up would require $1 million over the next two years, and Nixon, undaunted, replied that cobbling together $1 million would not be "easy," but it was feasible.[43] Haldeman entered the Oval Office after the crescendo of Dean's soliloquy, and the trio discussed contingencies for Watergate damage control.[44]

Later that afternoon, Nixon convened a meeting with Haldeman, Ehrlichman, and Dean.[45] The ultimate conclusion of Nixon, Haldeman, and Ehrlichman was that Dean should write the "Dean Report," which explained the particulars of Watergate and other dirty deeds with, of course, an affable administration spin.[46] The Dean Report would be a Watergate Maginot Line for the White House. Dean fired a number of objections to his authoring the Dean Report but to no avail.[47]

The idea of the Dean Report had been percolating for months: In fact, at the behest of Haldeman and Ehrlichman, Dean had submitted a strategy to draft a Dean Report to Haldeman in early December, but Haldeman had rejected Dean's proposal, because he sought a report that definitively exonerated the Nixon hierarchy from perpetrating the Watergate caper.[48] But Dean countered that all the president's men were privy to the hush money that was ostensibly sanctioned by Mitchell, making all of them highly vulnerable to obstruction charges.[49] Haldeman, Dean wrote, concurred, and he rescinded his directive.[50]

Dean had managed to extricate himself from the Dean Report in December, but now the Dean Report was imbued with considerable gravitas due to the formation of the Senate's Watergate Committee and the impending sentencing of the Watergate burglars. The following day, Thursday March 22, Nixon met with Mitchell, Haldeman, Ehrlichman, and Dean, and the foursome discussed prospective strategies to neutralize the Watergate Committee.[51] Nixon had decided that Dean should sequester himself at Camp David over the weekend and write the Dean Report.[52]

The next day, March 23, the same day Sirica hammered the burglars, the nation's newspapers were not very benevolent to Dean: The preceding day, during the senate confirmation hearings for L. Patrick Gray to become the F.B.I. director, he testified that Dean "probably" lied to F.B.I. agents when he told them that he did not know whether or not E. Howard Hunt had an office at White House.[53] The *New York Times* and *Washington Post* featured front-page stories about Dean's probable lie.[54]

In *Blind Ambition*, Dean expressed his outrage over Gray's prevarication as a "whole army" of reporters descended on his home the morning of March 23.[55] Dean then wrote that the president phoned him and suggested that he embark on a vacation to Camp David, but Dean felt that Nixon had an ulterior motive for prescribing a Camp David retreat.[56] According to *Blind Ambition*, shortly after Dean and Mo arrived at Camp David, Haldeman phoned him and instructed him to commence on the Dean Report.[57] Dean wrote that Haldeman's directive coldcocked him, because Haldeman had not pushed for a Dean Report since Dean had explained the ramifications of such a report to him in their December chat.[58] Dean was having memory difficulties again! The day before in the Oval Office, Nixon had explicitly instructed Dean to cloister himself at Camp David and write the Dean Report.

CHAPTER 22

THE BERLIN WALL CRUMBLES

A
t Camp David, Dean confronted great internal adversity writing the Dean Report, because he "was not going to lie for anybody, even the President."[1] I've come to marvel at Dean's unequivocal moral fiber, and his unconditional willingness to tell the truth! As Dean was locked in an epic struggle with his conscience, he received troubling news from the White House press secretary: *The Los Angeles Times* was running a front-page story that had McCord fingering both Dean and Magruder as having prior knowledge of the Watergate break-in.[2]

Dean wrote that at Camp David he divulged to Mo that Watergate and/or its cover up had tainted Mitchell, Haldeman, and Ehrlichman.[3] And Mo ostensibly responded, literally and figuratively, like a babe in the woods: "That's awful, John. What are you all going to do?"[4] But Mo need not fret. Dean had a plan. In *Blind Ambition*, Dean wrote that Haldeman told him to phone Magruder and lock him into a version of events by surreptitiously recording the conversation: He phoned Magruder, who was quite frantic about *The Los Angeles Times'* article.[5]

Over the course of their conversation, Dean maneuvered Magruder to essentially default to his statements before the grand jury: "I would hope so, John, of course on that meeting, that I have testified that that meeting that we had with Liddy and Mitchell was simply on the general counsel's job and so on."[6] The authors of *Silent Coup* commented on Dean's phone call to Magruder: "That was as far as Dean could get Jeb to go. Nevertheless, Dean would later argue to the Watergate Committee – who were evidentially convinced by his argument and this tape – that Magruder had admitted that Dean had no advance knowledge of the break-ins."[7]

Dean also phoned Liddy's attorney, requesting that Liddy provide a sworn statement that stated Dean was not involved in Watergate. Liddy's attorney, in due course, responded that Liddy would remain mum's the word.[8] The testimony of Magruder and Liddy could potentially prove problematic for Dean, so Magruder's ostensible exoneration and Liddy's obdurate invocation of the Fifth Amendment were precursors to Dean's third phone call: He phoned a friend who was a lawyer and queried him about prospective criminal attorneys.[9] Dean had decided to lawyer up.[10] The house of cards was collapsing on him, and he decided to sing. Government canaries generally sing a song or two to receive their sweetheart deals, but Dean was primed to croon a Wagnerian opera. Magruder drafted on Dean and flipped two weeks later.[11]

Dean had been ensconced in the wooded, bucolic beauty of Camp David for five days when Haldeman summoned him back to Washington.[12] Haldeman had lined up a meeting for Dean, Magruder and Mitchell on the afternoon Dean returned from Camp David.[13] Haldeman thought that they should align themselves via Magruder's perjured grand jury testimony about the two Gemstone meetings with Liddy.[14] The trio had agreed that Magruder would testify about the first meeting being cancelled and the second meeting entailing a discussion of new election laws.[15]

At the meeting among Mitchell, Magruder, and Dean, on March 28, in a vacant West Wing office, Magruder was characteristically a nervous Nelly as he sought assurances from Mitchell and Dean that they would co-sign his perjury before the grand jury: Mitchell indicated to Magruder that he would, but Dean balked at the idea.[16] Testifying before the Watergate Committee, Dean said that Mitchell essentially confessed to sanctioning the Watergate break-in at this meeting.[17]

Astonishingly, Magruder didn't remember Mitchell's startling mea culpa when he testified before the Watergate Committee, even though it would have confirmed his contention that Mitchell sanctioned the Watergate break-in during their 1972 Key Biscayne meeting.[18] Magruder did not include Mitchell's confession in his autobiography either.[19] Magruder only recalled the confession when Mitchell was on trial and taking the fall for the dirty deeds of the Nixon administration.[20]

Two days after Dean met with Mitchell and Magruder, on March 30, he expended five hours telling his tale of blind ambition and woe to his new attorney.[21] Dean had conscripted an adroit and seasoned criminal attorney who had served in Robert Kennedy's Department of Justice, playing an integral role in the prosecution of Jimmy Hoffa.[22] Dean's attorney had also served on the staff of the Warren Commission.[23] Moreover, Dean recruited a co-counsel who was the partner in a law firm whose clientele included a C.I.A. proprietary company.[24] Though the C.I.A. proprietary company shared office space with the law firm, Dean's co-counsel stated he was unaware of the Agency's affiliation with the law firm.[25]

The strategy forged by Dean's legal team was shrewd: They would "shuttle" between the federal prosecutors investigating Watergate and the

Watergate Committee, playing both ends against the middle, seeking immunity for Dean.[26] On April 2, Dean's primary attorney met with federal prosecutors.[27] But the prosecutors were reluctant to play "Let's Make a Deal" and pick Door 1, which entailed immunity for Dean. So Dean and his legal team started enticing federal prosecutors with scintillating illegalities perpetrated by the Nixon administration.[28]

As Dean and his attorneys were in the midst of playing Let's Make a Deal, Dean phoned Haldeman who was in Southern California with Ehrlichman and Nixon and about to embark for D.C. on Air Force One: He confessed to lawyering up, and he disclosed that his lawyer thought he should talk to the prosecutors.[29] Dean testified that Haldeman fired a warning at him: "Once the toothpaste is out of the tube, it's going to be very hard to put it back in."[30] Dean then received a phone call from Air Force One, and a Haldeman assistant told him that he had a meeting in Ehrlichman's office in the late afternoon.[31]

After Dean met with federal prosecutors, he rendezvoused with Haldeman and Ehrlichman in Ehrlichman's office.[32] The Berlin Wall gave Dean an icy reception: Dean testified to the Watergate Committee that Haldeman and Ehrlichman inquired if Dean had met with federal prosecutors, and Dean replied that he "avoided a direct answer to the question" by replying his lawyers were having discussions with the prosecutors.[33]

As Dean was having subsequent meetings with Haldeman, Ehrlichman, and eventually Nixon, he was also in the midst of crooning ariettas to the federal prosecutors.[34] The prosecutors were reluctant to grant Dean immunity, so his ariettas started to up the ante. According to *Blind Ambition,* Dean told federal prosecutors that he had "information pointing to the fact that there was a break-in at the office of Daniel Ellsberg's psychiatrist."[35]

Before the trial of Liddy and McCord began, the C.I.A. provided the Department of Justice with photographs of Liddy and Hunt's Los Angeles' hijinks – one photo featured a smiling G. Gordon Liddy standing in front of the psychiatrist's office building.[36] The Justice Department was initially perplexed about the photographs' significance until Dean crooned an arietta about their relationship to the break-in into Dr. Fielding's office.[37]

Dean's autobiography implies that he provided federal prosecutors with scant details when mentioning the Los Angeles caper: For example, *Blind Ambition* does not indicate that he revealed Liddy and Hunt's involvement in the caper to federal prosecutors.[38] But the day following Dean's disclosure about the Dr. Fielding break-in, the assistant U.S. attorney prosecuting Watergate fired a memo to his boss, an assistant attorney general, delineating Hunt and Liddy's participation in the burglary.[39]

After the assistant attorney general and his underlings engaged in a modicum of excavation, they found the pictures – courtesy of the C.I.A. – of the break-in into Dr. Fielding's office.[40] Shortly after Dean's revelations about the pictures, the assistant attorney general who had become privy to Liddy and Hunt's Los Angeles hijinks discussed the break-in with Nixon.[41] The president ordered him to recoil from the matter.[42]

Ironically, when Justice Department officials realized the significance of the pictures provided by the C.I.A., Daniel Ellsberg was on trial for espionage in Los Angeles.[43] He was staring at 115 years in prison.[44] As Ellsberg's case was wending through federal court, Ehrlichman rendezvoused with Ellsberg's trial judge in Southern California and offered him directorship of the F.B.I.[45] Nixon's acting director of the F.B.I. had become so tainted by Watergate that Nixon withdrew his nomination.[46] Before the Watergate Committee, Ehrlichman testified that Ellsberg's trial judge was hunky dory about becoming the director of the F.B.I.[47] But the judge contended that he told Ehrlichman that he couldn't consider the appointment until the Ellsberg trial had concluded.[48]

When Ellsberg's trial was on its final furlong, the assistant attorney general who was privy to Liddy and Hunt's Los Angeles caper felt rather queasy about maintaining his reticence on such an egregious shredding of Ellsberg's Constitutional rights.[49] So he approached Attorney General Kleindienst, and they collectively decided that the Justice Department had to inform Ellsberg's judge about the break-in.[50]

Kleindienst then met with Nixon and threatened to resign if Ellsberg's trial judge wasn't notified about Liddy and Hunt's break-in into Dr. Fielding's office and Nixon conceded.[51] The Justice Department memo that had been derived from Dean's scintillating arietta, sans Dean's name, was given to Ellsberg's trial judge.[52] The federal prosecutors of Ellsberg had hoped that the judge would be dismissive of the memo, but, instead, he disclosed its existence and demanded further federal investigation.[53]

Publicizing the memo was merely hors d'oeuvres for the peeved judge: For his pièce de résistance, the judge announced that the F.B.I. had illegally taped phone conversations of Daniel Ellsberg, and the Bureau had the audacity to declare that the recordings had been lost![54] The judge then dispensed the following remarks when he dismissed the Ellsberg case: "The totality of the circumstances of this case which I have only briefly sketched offend a sense of justice," he said. "The bizarre events have incurably infected the prosecution of this case."[55]

The Ellsberg trial and the illegalities and malfeasance that it exposed were pyrotechnic media revelations, and Nixon started to feel the implosion of his administration. Nixon took to the airwaves and announced the "resignations" of Haldeman, Ehrlichman, Dean, and Kleindienst.[56] Nixon, Haldeman, and Ehrlichman were at Camp David when Nixon sequentially told Haldeman and then Ehrlichman that they had to be exorcised from his administration.[57] As Nixon broke the news to Ehrlichman, he started to cry uncontrollably.[58] He told Ehrlichman that he and Haldeman would have access to backdoor funding.[59] A choked up Ehrlichman eschewed the largesse and said: "You can do one thing for me, though, sometime. Just explain all this to my kids, will you? Tell them why you had to do this?"[60]

Dean's disclosure to the Watergate prosecutors had caused the previously impenetrable Berlin Wall to crumble, and Nixon scrambled to save his presidency.[61] Nixon announced that he was appointing a new attorney general, who had the authority to appoint an independent special prosecutor to probe Watergate.[62] Nixon replaced Dean with a former partner at the New York law firm where he practiced law prior to his 1968 presidential bid.[63] Nixon now needed to replace the irreplaceable Berlin Wall.

CHAPTER 23

THE ICEMAN COMETH

Haldeman's greatest blunder that endangered Nixon's presidency was recommending that Alexander Haig become Nixon's new chief-of-staff, which Haig assumed on May 4, 1973. Interestingly, the day before Haig assumed the mantle of Nixon's chief-of-staff, the crack investigative team of Bob Woodward and Carl Bernstein reported on the illegal wiretaps that were initially perpetrated by Nixon's minions during and after the Moorer-Radford affair.[1] Haig had played an integral role in the wiretaps, but Woodward and Bernstein didn't mention his complicity: Woodward and Haig shared a little secret that will be elucidated in the next chapter.

Haig was born into an affluent family who lived in a Philadelphia suburb.[2] He was the second of three children.[3] When Haig was ten years old, according to the *Washington Post,* cancer purloined the life of his father, an attorney, and the family was left in dire straits.[4] Fortunately for Haig's family, prosperous relatives prevented the family from vacating their large home and skidding into utter poverty during the Great Depression.[5]

Although Haig was a prankster and an inept high school student, his politically connected uncle enabled him to enroll in West Point near the conclusion of World War II.[6] Haig proved to be an inept student at West Point, too, graduating in the bottom third of his class.[7] A West Point superintendent commented on Haig's military prospects: He was "the last man in his class anyone expected to become the first general."[8] But the West Point superintendent greatly underestimated Haig's ruthless ambition.

After Haig's graduation from West Point, he was stationed in Japan during America's post-WW II occupation of the country.[9] In Japan, he made a superlative career move by marrying a general's daughter, and they had three children.[10] Haig then found himself in the midst of the Korean War.[11] The *Washington Post* reported that Haig claimed he was given the distinguished assignment of carrying General Douglas MacArthur's sleeping bag ashore during an amphibious landing.[12] The *Philadelphia Inquirer,* however, reported that Haig carried the bedroll of a considerably less distinguished general ashore.[13]

After Korea, Haig received a master's degree in international relations from Georgetown University.[14] Haig's crypto-fascist master's thesis endorsed a "new breed" of military officer who would displace "civilian interference" concerning military matters.[15] He envisioned "soldier-scholars" thrusting the levers at the "pinnacle" of power.[16] In Haig's ideal world, his soldier-scholars would probably march Plato's philosopher-kings before a firing squad.

Through sheer nepotism, via his wife's father, Haig landed at the Pentagon, where his ruthless ambition compelled him to routinely work until midnight.[17] Haig also had a shapeshifting, Machiavellian panache that enabled him to ingratiate himself among his superiors and demolish his rivals.[18] Haig joyfully embarked to Vietnam, where he commanded a brigade and received a Purple Heart and a Distinguished Service Cross.[19]

In the summer of 1967, after distinguishing himself in Vietnam, Haig again landed at the Pentagon.[20] Upon Haig's reemergence at the Pentagon, he encountered the peacenik idealism that was blossoming throughout the country.[21] Haig found the surge of doves at the Pentagon to be absolutely repellant, and he segued to a regimental commander at West Point.[22] He was then bumped up to a deputy commandant.[23]

Haig was an alpha male's alpha male, and he terrorized West Point cadets.[24] One cadet challenged West Point's mandatory chapel attendance, and he felt the wrath of Haig: "His fists were clenched. 'You little bastard,' he said. 'I will personally see you out of here one way or the other. You're beyond Communism!'"[25] The terrorized cadet offered insights into Haig's personality: "He can be really charming and buddy-buddy … but then, if you cross him in any way, he just goes bonkers. I'm not saying he's unbalanced; it's just that I think he's a real proud person with some real insecurities."[26]

Nepotism enabled Haig to become a military aide to Harvard scholar Henry Kissinger when the latter became Nixon's National Security Advisor.[27] Though Haig was expected to be a mere courtier for Kissinger, he quickly unleashed his ruthless ambition at the National Security Council.[28] Kissinger was an academic, who had never supervised a staff, and the N.S.C. was in a state of entropy until alpha male Haig instilled it with order.[29] Haig quickly became indispensable to Kissinger and, of course, he demolished his potential N.S.C. rivals.[30]

Through deft manipulation, Haig quickly adapted to Nixon's reptilianocracy, and he became an advisor to Nixon instead of a mere messenger boy of information – to the chagrin of Kissinger.[31] In fact, whenever Nixon was miffed at Kissinger, he would have Haig brief him for five or six days in lieu of Kissinger, invariably plunging Kissinger into an emotional meltdown.[32] Nixon once told Ehrlichman to broach the idea of psychiatric care with Kissinger but Ehrlichman declined.[33]

At the National Security Council, Haig also displayed his panache for shape shifting: Haig would denounce Nixon to Kissinger and Kissinger to Nixon.[34] Haldeman would fall prey to Haig's shapeshifting, too: Haig would morph into Haldeman's man in Kissinger's office and Kissinger's man in Haldeman's office, which translated into secretly sharing secrets about Kissinger to Haldeman and vice versa.[35]

Nixon thought so highly of Haig that over the course of his four-year tenure in the White House he incrementally boosted Haig from a colonel to a four-star general.[36] Though Haig enchanted Nixon, their relationship was not a mutual admiration society. Haig covertly despised Nixon for his attempts at reconciliation with the Red Menace: Haig once screamed that Nixon and Kissinger were "selling us out to the Communists!"[37] He also thought that Nixon was inherently weak and lacked mettle.[38] He joked that Nixon's "limp-wrist manner" meant he was a homosexual.[39] In Chapter 3, I discussed Nixon turning off the Moorer-Bradford affair too quickly, before Haig was fully implicated, and now Haig would become Nixon's trusted, indispensable aide-de-camp.

When Haig became Nixon's chief-of-staff, Nixon's administration and his psyche were imploding with near free-fall acceleration: Nixon had started to prodigiously hit the sauce and also take Dilantin, an antiepileptic drug, that can be highly sedating when mixed with alcohol.[40] And for the coup de grâce with regards to being comfortably numb, Nixon started taking tulenol, a very high-powered barbiturate that has since been banned by the F.D.A.[41] Tulenol aficionados often feel something on their backs only to belatedly realize it's the floor. Nixon's pharmacologically compromised state and his misplaced trust in Haig made him putty in the hands of Haig: Haig quickly had a stranglehold on access to the Oval Office with a zeal that made Haldeman look like an anarchist.[42]

Haig then recruited an old friend from his days at West Point, Fred Buzhardt, to serve as Nixon's special counsel for Watergate.[43] Eugene O'Neil's Iceman acted without accomplices, but Buzhardt will become Haig's accomplice in the demise of Nixon's presidency. Buzhardt, born and raised in South Carolina, was medium height and slender.[44] He had receding brown hair and wore large, gold-rimmed glasses that amplified the purplish pillows under his eyes. Buzhardt's southern hospitality and slow drawl belied that he, like Haig, was a military zealot. After Buzhardt graduated from West Point and served in the Air Force, he earned a law degree from the University of South Carolina, graduating magna cum laude.[45]

Buzhardt eventually had an eight-year stint on the staff of South Carolina's racist and pro-military U.S. Senator Strom Thurmond, who served in the Senate until the ripe old age of 100.[46] As a Senate staffer, Buzhardt worked fanatically to ensure that the Senate passed a bill authorizing an anti-ballistic missile system.[47] He even wrote scathing articles, under a pseudonym, about President Johnson's secretary of defense who opposed the missile system.[48] In fact, Thurmond's wife so feared Buzhardt's ruthless fanaticism that she warned her husband to never be alone with him![49]

Buzhardt segued into to the Department of Defense in 1969, ascending to counsel for the Department of Defense.[50] At the Pentagon, Buzhardt became a superlative janitor: One of his initial assignments was covering up black-market racketeering by military personnel.[51] Buzhardt also conspired to neutralize scandals involving the army's domestic spying program, a massacre of men, women, and children perpetrated by U.S. forces in Vietnam, and the Pentagon Papers, colluding with the White House Plumbers on the latter.[52]

In addition to an unrepentant, fanatical piety to the military and a vehement hatred of the Red Menace, Haig and Buzhardt shared a little secret: Haig's involvement in Moorer-Radford had been treasonous, and Welander's confession was potentially a Damoclean sword suspended over Haig's head. Buzhardt ultimately came to the rescue of his old West Point buddy. In his role as counsel for the Department of Defense, Buzhardt and a Pentagon investigator reinterviewed Welander about Moorer-Radford, and Buzhardt's reinterview exonerated Welander and depicted Haig as an innocent victim of Radford's pilfering.[53] Buzhardt also lied to the Pentagon investigator: He told him that Nixon had ordered the reinterview of Welander.[54] Buzhardt's reinterview of Welander would inevitably become the official narrative on Moorer-Radford.

Haig and Buzhardt wasted little time undermining Nixon's presidency. The C.I.A.'s deputy director, General Vernon Walters, who attended the "Bay of Pigs" meeting and had three meetings with Dean wrote memos about those four interactions.[55] He was slated to testify before the Senate Armed Services Committee about the C.I.A.'s involvement in Watergate, so he collected his memos and generated an affidavit based on the memos.[56] He brought the memos and affidavit to Haig at the White House, and he informed Haig of his impending appearance before the Senate

Armed Services Committee.[57] Walters imparted to Haig that Nixon had the prerogative to quash his testimony and documents under the aegis of executive privilege.[58] After Haig had custody of the memos and affidavit, he dismissed Walters.[59]

When Haig showed Nixon the C.I.A.'s deputy director's memos, affidavit, and discussed his impending Senate testimony, Nixon's immediate instinct was to invoke executive privilege to nullify the memos, affidavit, and testimony.[60] Haig, however, played on Nixon's pettifoggery, like Iago whispering into the ear of Othello: Haig told Nixon that the memos and affidavit heavily incriminated Dean in obstruction.[61] Dean had, by now, become Nixon's chief accuser and, no doubt, his mortal foe in the jungle.[62] The thought of exacting revenge on Dean, most likely, triggered a dopamine burst of pleasure in Nixon's limbic system, but he ultimately declared that Walter's memos, affidavit, and impending senate testimony should be negated by executive privilege.[63]

After Nixon insisted on executive privilege, Haig declared that the C.I.A.'s deputy director's memos, affidavit, and Senate testimony would exonerate Nixon instead of incriminate him, because Ehrlichman and Haldeman would contend that their directive to the C.I.A. director during the Bay of Pigs meeting was made in a strictly legitimate context instead of part and parcel of a cover-up.[64] Though Nixon may have been recovering from a stupor the night before, Haig's strategy was, nonetheless, counter-intuitive to his political instincts.[65] Nixon phoned Haldeman, who arrived at the White House shortly thereafter.[66] When Nixon informed Haldeman about the C.I.A.'s deputy director's memos, affidavit, and impending testimony, Haldeman's initial response was "*Danger Will Robinson!*"[67] Haldeman absolutely insisted that Nixon invoke executive privilege.[68]

After Haldeman's departure, Haig returned to the Oval Office and relayed to Nixon that Buzhardt felt that the memos solely incriminated Haldeman and Ehrlichman in obstruction.[69] Nixon cycled through various mental machinations: He had become so utterly lost that he actually suggested that the C.I.A.'s deputy director rewrite the memos to omit incriminating Haldeman and Ehrlichman.[70] But Haig put the kibosh on Nixon's various schemes as he lobbied for Nixon to provide the Senate Armed Services Committee with the deputy director's memos and affidavit.[71]

An extremely befuddled Nixon finally decided to use executive privilege to quash the memos and affidavit from being given to the senators, but he allowed the C.I.A.'s deputy director to testify.[72] The deputy director testified about the content of the memos, which translated into Haldeman and Ehrlichman metamorphosing from collusion in a minor cover-up to perpetrating an egregious obstruction of justice by deploying the C.I.A. to impede the F.B.I's investigation of Watergate.[73] The next day, a Democratic senator on the Armed Services Committee issued a protracted statement on the C.I.A's deputy director's testimony, and Nixon's credibility was further mutilated.[74] Conveniently, C.I.A Director Richard Helms had ordered his secretary to dispose of all C.I.A. records that might have a bearing on the Watergate investigation.[75]

CHAPTER 24

BALDERDASH BOB AND DEEP THROAT

F amed Watergate reporter Bob Woodward was born in 1943, and he came of age in Wheaton, Illinois, a conservative, prosperous, and pious enclave on the outskirts of Chicago.[1] Wheaton was a W.A.S.P. Xanadu: 94 percent of its denizens were white and Protestant churches were generously sprinkled throughout the hamlet.[2] Republicans also outnumbered Democrats by a margin of four to one.[3] Woodward's father was a talented trial lawyer, who would be awarded a county circuit judgeship.[4]

Outwardly, Woodward grew up in an idyllic environment. "Those who go beneath the surface do so at their peril," Oscar Wilde said of art, and Wilde's statement was equally applicable to the Woodward household: His mother had an affair with a Sears executive that ruptured the family.[5] Twelve-year-old Woodward was the eldest of three siblings when his father was awarded custody of the three children.[6] His father remarried a divorcee who had three children, and the couple eventually had a daughter.[7] So the Woodward household mutated from *Father Knows Best* into *The Brady Bunch.*

Woodward has depicted himself as an outsider of sorts throughout his high school years.[8] But he was elected class president during his sophomore year, and he was one of four commencement speakers for his graduating class.[9] He followed in the conservative wake of his father, and his commencement speech was gleaned from *The Conscience of a Conservative,* a book written by ultra-conservative U.S. Senator Barry Goldwater.[10]

After Woodward graduated from Wheaton Community High School, he skipped into Yale University on a Navy R.O.T.C. scholarship.[11] He doubled down on his dedication to the status quo when he entered Book and Snake, one of Yale's secret societies.[12] At Yale, Woodward majored in English and history.[13] A Yale history professor described his conservative bent as "crypto-fascist."[14]

Though Woodward eschewed the peace, love, and brown rice of the 1960s, he revealed in an interview after his celebrity that he had become disenchanted with the Vietnam War and thought of seeking sanctuary in Canada.[15] But Woodward's recollections about his collegiate misgivings on Vietnam diverge from the memories of his Wheaton Community High

School sweetheart and first wife: When the authors of *Silent Coup* inquired if Woodward had ever talked about evading his R.O.T.C. commitment to the Navy in Canada, she responded with a resounding, "Heavens no!"[16] She also depicted him as "ruthless" and "extremely ambitious."[17]

Following Woodward's graduation from Yale, his R.O.T.C. scholarship mandated a six-year hitch in the Navy – four years of active duty and two years in the Naval Reserve.[18] He was a communications officer who had a "top-secret crypto" security clearance when he served on the *USS Wright* and then the *USS Fox*, which was commanded by Moorer-Radford conspirator Rear Admiral Robert Welander.[19]

After his four-year hitch in the Navy, he was assigned to the Pentagon, where he served a fifth year of active duty, working for the Chief of Naval Operations.[20] His responsibilities included briefing Alexander Haig.[21] The official Watergate narrative, sanctified by the government, ablates Woodward briefing Haig at the White House in 1969 and 1970. And Woodward's "Big Lie" throughout Watergate was that he didn't meet Alexander Haig until 1973.[22] But his Big Lie is trumped by three sources who maintain that he had, indeed, briefed Haig: The Joint Chiefs of Staff Chairman Thomas Moorer, Nixon's Secretary of Defense Melvin Laird, and also an aide to the Secretary of Defense.[23,24] As I mentioned in the Prologue, Woodward's Big Lie has seismic implications.

Woodward was able to forgo serving in the Naval Reserve after his active duty, and he embarked on his civilian incarnation.[25] After his exodus from the Navy, the evolution of his vocational pursuits is extremely perplexing. Though Woodward was accepted to Harvard Law School, he hit the pause button on his legal aspirations and ostensibly worked out a very unconventional arrangement with the *Washington Post*.[26] He didn't have prior newspaper experience, but he offered to work at the *Post* for two weeks sans compensation: Woodward and the *Washington Post* ostensibly agreed that if he had the requisite talent to be a *Washington Post* caliber reporter, the *Post* would hire him. But Woodward had significant troubles fashioning coherent copy, and, after his trial run, the *Washington Post* jettisoned him.[27]

Both accounts of Woodward's brief tenure at the *Post* and his next professional move are mired in improbability: He continued to abandon his legal aspirations, and he landed a job as a reporter for the *Montgomery County Sentinel,* a weekly in suburban Maryland.[28] The *Sentinel* started him out at $110 a week, which was extremely meager when compared to the earning potential of a graduate from Harvard Law School.[29] His career move certainly wasn't on the trajectory of someone who's "ruthless" and "extremely ambitious."

Woodward's hire at the *Montgomery County Sentinel* is also enmeshed in conflicting versions. Woodward has said that an editor at the *Washington Post* furnished him with a laudatory letter that he presented to the editor of the *Sentinel,* but the *Sentinel's* editor disputed Woodward's version.[30] The *Sentinel* editor maintained that Woodward had a laudatory letter, but the genesis of the letter was a "senior officer" in the Navy.[31]

Woodward's dismissal after only weeks at the *Washington Post* lends credence to the *Sentinel* editor's account, because it seems unlikely that a *Washington Post* editor would provide a laudatory letter for a lackluster audition at the newspaper. However, the *Sentinel's* editor changed his tune after Woodward's celebrity, asserting that Woodward, indeed, wielded a laudatory letter from a *Washington Post* editor when he applied to be a reporter for the *Sentinel.*[32]

Woodward puzzled his coworkers at the *Sentinel*: His salary was a paltry $110 per week, but he looked as if he were consistently flush with cash.[33] He never vacated his apartment in Washington, D.C., which perplexed his *Sentinel* coworkers, because it seemed beyond the means of a *Sentinel* reporter.[34] He made daily treks to Rockville, Maryland, where *The Sentinel* was headquartered, in his Karmann Ghia sports car.[35] According to a former *Sentinel* coworker, he even made jaunts to New York City "at least two weekends a month."[36] He also had a mysterious gift of portending revolutions in banana republics.[37]

The *Sentinel* served as Woodward's Triple-A farm team: He was at the *Sentinel* for nearly a year before the *Washington Post* conscripted him as a full-time staff reporter.[38] He had been at the *Post* a mere nine months when the Watergate burglars were busted.[39] According to *All the President's Men,* a phone call from the city editor of the *Washington Post* awakened him the morning after the Watergate bust.[40] After he walked to the *Post,* he learned that the burglars were to appear at the courthouse for a preliminary hearing.[41] Woodward ventured to the courthouse, where the burglars' "attorney of record" supposedly coughed up the names and addresses of his clients.[42]

An ensemble of *Post* reporters hustled and bustled to collectively generate the *Post's* first Watergate article, published a day after the bust – "5 Held in Plot to Bug Democrats' Office Here."[43] The article was bylined by the *Post's* police reporter, but eight reporters, including Woodward and Carl Bernstein, were acknowledged as contributing to the article.[44]

The following morning, Sunday, Woodward and Bernstein were summoned to the *Post.*[45] An Associated Press story had scooped the *Post,* reporting that McCord was the security coordinator for the C.R.P.[46] Accordingly, Woodward and Bernstein focused on McCord.[47] The two reportedly disliked each other: Woodward thought that Bernstein's longish hair and dress evoked the anarchistic counterculture, which Woodward "despised," and Bernstein thought that Woodward evoked Ivy League entitlement.[48]

Despite their reported antipathy towards each other, they began working the phones.[49] Woodward handed the first page of a draft to their editor, and Bernstein perused the draft over the editor's shoulder.[50] Bernstein subsequently rewrote the article.[51] A June 19 *Post* article – "GOP Security Aide is Among the Watergate Burglars" – was bylined by Woodward and Bernstein, launching journalism's preeminent brand.[52]

According to *All the President's Men*, the D.C. police had permitted the *Post's* nocturnal police reporter to examine the address books of burglars Barker and Martinez, and he discovered the "name and phone number of a Howard E. Hunt, with the small notations 'White H.' and 'W.H.'"[53] The reporter's leads were then purportedly shuffled to Woodward.[54] In *All the President's Men*, after the intrepid cub reporter locked onto Hunt, he made a staccato flurry of phones calls to the White House and Robert Mullen Company.[55]

When Woodward purportedly phoned Hunt at the Robert Mullen Company and inquired about Hunt's name being in the burglars' address books, Hunt reportedly shrieked "Good God!" and said that he wouldn't comment on an ongoing case before summarily slamming down the phone.[56] Woodward then reportedly discovered that Hunt had been a consultant to the White House via the deputy director of White House communications who had previously been a *Washington Post* reporter.[57] The president of the Robert Mullen Company allegedly disclosed to Woodward that Hunt had been a C.I.A. officer from 1949 to 1970, and the C.I.A. ostensibly confirmed Hunt's years of employment, which is an absurd lie, because it's extremely unlikely that the C.I.A. would disclose the status of a former or current CIA agent over the phone, especially to a reporter.[58]

Before Woodward's staccato flurry of phone calls, he alleges that he phoned Mark Felt in the guise of Deep Throat who told him that the story was about to "heat up."[59] After further phone calls, he again phoned Felt in the guise of Deep Throat, who told him that the "F.B.I. regarded Hunt as a prime suspect in the Watergate investigation."[60] Woodward then wrote an article that was also bylined by the *Post's* night crime reporter, published on June 20, three days after the bust – "White House Consultant Linked to Bugging Suspects" – elucidating Hunt's links to the White House and Watergate burglars.[61] The fabricated, inextricable legends of Woodward and "Deep Throat" were thus imprinted on the American zeitgeist.

Felt may very well have been a source for Woodward early on, but the unfolding chronology of Watergate largely eliminates Felt from being a later source. In 2005, Woodward rolled out a senile Mark Felt as his sole Deep Throat source throughout Watergate – Felt had been the F.B.I.'s associate director.[62] Woodward has maintained that he initially encountered Felt at the White House when he was a lowly errand boy for the Navy.[63]

According to *All the President's Men*, Woodward set up his meetings with Felt by repositioning a flowerpot with a red flag on his apartment's sixth floor balcony, and Felt made daily treks by Woodward's balcony.[64] When Felt supposedly noticed the repositioned red flag, he and Woodward would have a 2:00 A.M. rendezvous at an underground garage in Arlington, Virginia.[65] On the days that Woodward signaled Deep Throat, the intrepid, young reporter would take "two or more taxis" to the garage to ensure that he wasn't followed to his late night, subterranean encounter with Deep Throat.[66]

Woodward ostensibly started signaling Felt when he lived in an apartment on P Street in D.C.[67] He has reportedly stated that he lived in the P Street apartment until "early 1973."[68] But *Secret Agenda* notes that Woodward lived in the P Street apartment until mid-November of 1972.[69] He then lived in an apartment near the *Washington Post* until January of 1973 before moving into a high-rise in southwest D.C.[70]

Felt was "forced out" of the F.B.I. in June of 1973.[71] But *All the President's Men* specified that he acted in the capacity of Deep Throat into November of 1973.[72] Throughout the 1970s, Felt lived in Virginia.[73] Accordingly, if Woodward's accounts of Felt's treks by his apartment from June of 1973 until November of 1973 are truthful, Felt would've made daily jaunts from Virginia into D.C. An implausible tale indeed!

But his accounts of his meetings with Felt are superimposed on additional absurdities: When Adrian Havill wrote *Deep Truth*, he discovered that Woodward's balcony of his P Street apartment, which faced a sunken courtyard, could be viewed from two vantage points.[74] The first vantage point necessitated Havill exiting his car in an alley, walking "fifty-six steps," and then looking upward at an extremely sharp angle: Havill found that Woodward's balcony was barely visible from this vantage point, and it would've been extremely difficult for Deep Throat to see the flowerpot.[75] Havill also noticed that a myriad of apartments could observe a trespasser in the back of Woodward's apartment building, so daily jaunts to peruse Woodward's balcony without detection would've been virtually impossible.[76] The second vantage point from which to scrutinize Woodward's balcony was from the courtyard behind the apartment building, but access to the courtyard required passing through two locked doors and within view of a reception desk.[77] So, in addition to daily treks from Virginia into D.C., Felt would've had to exit his car and surmount the aforementioned obstacles to view Woodward's balcony.

In *All the President's Men*, Woodward and Bernstein wrote that when Deep Throat sought to contact Woodward, he would etch a clock on page 20 of the *New York Times* that was delivered to Woodward's apartment door every morning before 7:00 A.M. [78] The clock delineated the time of their prospective meeting. However, the *New York Times* wasn't delivered to Woodward's apartment door, but, rather, a stack of newspapers were left at the reception area.[79] The residents of the building then had to retrieve their copies of the *New York Times* from the lobby.[80] So, yet again, the veracity of Woodward and Deep Throat's legendary communication schema is deconstructed by reality.

Although the implausibility of Mark Felt as Deep Throat will be further demonstrated in a subsequent chapter, Deep Throat certainly wasn't the omniscient oracle described by Woodward and Bernstein: In *All the President's Men*, Woodward and Bernstein wrote that Deep Throat never provided erroneous information to them.[81] But, in actuality, *All the President's Men* incorporates various gaffes that were ostensibly courtesy of Deep Throat:

- Deep Throat divulged that E. Howard Hunt was assigned to assist John Mitchell in investigating the Watergate break-ins.[82] As I've demonstrated in previous chapters, Mitchell was never assigned to investigate the break-ins, because Nixon thought that he had been their instigator. Plus, Mitchell had never even met Hunt.[83]

- Deep Throat disclosed to Woodward that Mitchell and Colson were behind Watergate.[84] In Chapter 10 and subsequent chapters, I discuss the unlikelihood of Mitchell and Colson sanctioning Watergate.

- Deep Throat disclosed to Woodward that Haldeman "pushed" Mitchell into authorizing a wiretapping operation for the 1972 campaign, which included relocating Hunt and Liddy from the White House "vigilante operation" to the C.R.P.[85] In Chapters 9 and 10, I demonstrate that Magruder was responsible for Liddy merging with the C.R.P., and he was likely chosen at Dean's behest.

In, Chapter 13 "Revenge of the Key," I discussed Alfred Baldwin, McCord's lackey and the "gauchest character" Martha Mitchell had ever encountered, crooning to the F.B.I. and D.C.'s U.S. attorney approximately three weeks after the Watergate bust in exchange for immunity.[86] At the time Baldwin was crooning to the F.B.I. in July of 1972, Mark Felt, ostensibly, in the guise of Deep Throat, was the F.B.I.'s associate director and overseer of the F.B.I.'s Watergate investigation.[87] But Felt didn't cough up Baldwin's name to Woodward: Baldwin's name surfaced publicly in a September *Los Angeles Times* article.[88] If Woodward and Felt were actually in cahoots with each other starting in June of 1972, I find it nearly inconceivable that Felt wouldn't have edified him about Baldwin's status as a government canary in July.

Many Watergate researchers and authors have concluded that Deep Throat was a composite, and Jim Hougan, in *Secret Agenda,* identified a likely Deep Throat source – Hunt's boss at the Robert Mullen Company.[89] Woodward allegedly chatted with him over the phone when he wrote his early scoop on Hunt, connecting Hunt to both the White House and the Watergate burglars.[90]

The Robert Mullin Company was a C.I.A. front, and its C.E.O. was a C.I.A. agent or a C.I.A. asset.[91, 92] Mullin's C.E.O. met with his C.I.A. case officer less than a month after the Watergate bust, and his case officer deemed his information so sensitive that he wrote a handwritten memorandum on the meeting and personally handed it to C.I.A. Director Richard Helms.[93] At that meeting, Mullin's C.E.O. boasted to his C.I.A. case officer that he had deterred reporters at the *Washington Post* and *The Washington Star* from implicating the C.I.A. in Watergate.[94] A second C.I.A. memorandum on Mullin's C.E.O. stated that he was "feeding stories to Bob Woodward" under the caveat of anonymity, and a "suitably grateful" Woodward "protects" him as a source and also protects the Mullen Company.[95]

Woodward may also have had a cozier relationship to the C.I.A. than merely his relationship with Mullin's C.E.O. The Watergate Committee's senior Republican had a hunch that Woodward was affiliated with the C.I.A., and he directed one of the Watergate Committee's counsels to inquire about the association.[96] But the C.I.A. rebuffed the counsel's inquiries.[97] So, the senator dispatched the counsel's request and a letter to C.I.A. Director William Colby, Helms' succesor, inquiring about Woodward's relationship to the C.I.A.[98] A "few hours" after the senator dispatched the letter, he received a phone call from an "incensed" Woodward.[99] His relatively prompt phone call to the senator suggests that he may have had a very snug rapport with the C.I.A. director.

CHAPTER 25

BALDERDASH BOB AND HOT CARL FOREVER

B ob Woodward and Carl Bernstein have become as inseparable as Huck Finn and Tom Sawyer in American lore, even though the tandem had antithetical backgrounds and personalities. The 29-year-old Woodward was a conservative W.A.S.P. and a byproduct of Midwestern prosperity who attended Yale. Conversely, 28-year-old Bernstein was born into working class Washington, D.C., and his parents were members of the American Communist Party.[1]

An early sense of alienation would've been difficult for Bernstein to avoid, because of his parents' political affiliation and the likes of Joe Mc-Carthy, J. Edgar Hoover, Richard Nixon, and their ilk assailing American Communists. As a teenager, Bernstein was short, and his face was pitted by acne, which would've served to exacerbate the estrangement of an already alienated teen.[2] As an adolescent, Bernstein attempted to assuage his alienation by embracing Judaism.[3] Though his parents were atheists, he insisted on a bar mitzvah.[4] He then became a member of an international fraternal organization for Jewish teenagers, which was affiliated with B'nai B'rith.[5]

Bernstein also developed chops as a dancer, and he flourished on Washington's homespun version of *American Bandstand – Milt Grant's Record Hop*.[6] In fact, Bernstein and his partner, who was a mere five feet tall, won several jitterbug contests.[7] As a teenager, he also developed an affinity for smoking, drinking, and playing pool.[8] His nascent forays into dissipation didn't enhance his academic performance, and he barely graduated from high school.[9]

After Bernstein's high school graduation, his father's connections enabled him to land a job at the *Washington Star* as a copy boy, which entailed hustling typed stories to different sections of the newspaper and also running errands.[10] The teeming excitement and buzz of a daily newspaper gave him an exhilarating sense of belonging.[11] Bernstein's evolution at the newspaper was expeditious: copy boy, dictationist, obituary writer, and then part-time reporter.[12]

The University of Maryland allowed Bernstein to enroll, based on his exceptional writing, but his enrollment was probationary, because of his lackluster high school grades.[13] Bernstein's efforts at school were quickly eclipsed by his five-day employment at the newspaper, and his collegiate aspirations atrophied.[14] Though he yearned to become a full-time reporter, the *Star* implemented a policy that only reporters with college degrees could be elevated to an exalted, full-time status.[15]

An editor at the *Star* received an offer to become the managing editor of a modest New Jersey daily, the *Daily Journal,* near Manhattan, and Bernstein implored the editor to liberate him from his glass ceiling at the *Star.*[16] The editor employed him as his personal assistant.[17] He also told Bernstein that he could pursue and write stories in his spare time.[18]

In 1965, Bernstein was in Manhattan when the great blackout of 1965 occurred.[19] The spirit of carpe diem inspired him to compose a staccato, Kerouacian flow of consciousness article that was accentuated by streaming gerunds, colorful medleys of adjectives, and exclamation marks.[20] The article was replete with fanciful tales: hitchhikers wearing Brook Brothers suits, fifteen people squeezed into a cab, and a thousand people splayed on the floor of the Americana Hotel's "multi-level lobby."[21]

The article garnered Bernstein the New Jersey Press Association award for Best News Writing Under a Deadline.[22] He received additional accolades for an exposé on underage drinking in Manhattan.[23] As Bernstein was collecting kudos for his reporting at the New Jersey daily, he estranged his coworkers: A former coworker disclosed that Bernstein was perpetually behind on his rent, and he was in arrears to many of the people who worked at the paper due to his incessant mooching.[24] His rather unflattering nickname at the paper was "the rotten kid."[25]

After about a year, Bernstein accrued a portfolio of clips that enabled him to matriculate to the *Washington Post.*[26] Though Bernstein had the talent to conjure up resplendent prose, he continued to estrange colleagues.[27] At the *Post,* he was frequently A.W.O.L., tardy on stories, submitting absurdly high expense accounts, and he, once more, displayed a flair for mooching.[28]

Bernstein befriended a notorious D.C. pimp who owned an adult bookstore, and he made repeated visits to the pimp's porn parlor.[29] The pimp even lavished Bernstein with pornographic materials.[30] Bernstein was also a participant in a swingers' club that was primarily composed of C.I.A. officers and their girlfriends or wives.[31] Interestingly, the C.I.A.'s liaison to the Plumbers was a participant in that swingers' club, too.[32]

After Bernstein's Watergate celebrity, his voracious libidinal cravings did not seem to wane, because, after all, fame and power are the ultimate aphrodisiacs. In fact, *New York* magazine recounts an anecdote of Bernstein hitting on a 16-year-old at a dinner party.[33] Though Bernstein brought a date to the dinner party, he, nevertheless, encountered the 16-year-old in the kitchen and rubbed his body against hers as he attempted to solicit a date.[34]

In 1976, Bernstein married a woman who became a renowned writer and director.[35] Bernstein, however, couldn't put a brake on his philandering and the marriage disintegrated by 1980.[36] The ex-wife exacted revenge by writing a thinly veiled novel about their marriage.[37] In the novel, Bernstein's former wife wrote that her satyr of a husband would have sex with a venetian blind.[30]

All the President's Men wielded inexplicable lies that were apparently incorporated to heighten dramatic tension. In *All the President's Men*, Bernstein reportedly drove to McLean, Virginia on September 18, 1972 to interview the C.R.P.'s treasurer.[39] According to *All the President's Men*, the jaunt would've usually taken one-half hour, but an afternoon downpour prolonged his drive to "an hour and a quarter."[40] Bernstein, of course, became "soaked" when he exited the car and, on foot, searched for the C.R.P.'s treasurer's house.[41] But the National Oceanic and Atmospheric Administration begs to differ with Bernstein's account, recording that the day in question had a miniscule two-hundreds of an inch of rain between 4:00 P.M. and 5:00 P.M. and four-hundreds of an inch between 5:00 P.M. and 6:00 P.M.[42]

All the President's Men wielded an additional lie about Bernstein's interview with the C.R.P. treasurer: Bernstein reportedly discovered that the C.R.P. treasurer wouldn't be home until 7:30 P.M., and he again braved the rain when he returned to his house later that night.[43] But, yet again, the National Oceanic and Atmospheric Administration begs to differ with Bernstein's account, recording that there was no rain after 6:00 P.M. that day.[44]

All the President's Men espoused a whopper about Bernstein ducking a subpoena on February 26, 1973: Woodward and Bernstein wrote that the C.R.P. attempted to serve Bernstein with a subpoena, but, when he was in the *Washington Post's* lobby, Bernstein was alerted that the server was in the newsroom.[45] He then sprinted to the stairwell and swiftly ascended seven flights to the accounting department.[46] Bernstein then ducked into an office and phoned the *Post's* executive editor who told him to go see a movie.[47] In *All the President's Men*, Bernstein spent the afternoon watching the porno flick *Deep Throat*.[48]

Although *Deep Throat* would seem to meld naturally with Bernstein's sense of esthetics, his anecdote about watching the porno flick on that day was an unabashed lie. The film *Deep Throat* had played in D.C. during the summer and fall of 1972.[49] However, four months prior to Bernstein's reported evasion of the subpoena, D.C. police raided D.C.'s adult theaters and confiscated hard-core pornographic films.[50] At the time, the fate of hard-core pornography was in the midst of being adjudicated in the courts: The film *Deep Throat* wasn't even listed in Washington's newspapers in February of 1973, and the theaters that had previously shown *Deep Throat* were forced to run either soft porn or action adventure movies.[51]

In *All the President's Men*, Bernstein cultivates an exceptional source – "Z" – who imparts information about the malfeasance of the president's men in truncated sentences that read like Zen koans.[52] Woodward later said that Z was as important a source as Deep Throat.[53] In the passage where Bernstein made his first contact with Z, Woodward and Bernstein carefully crafted and manipulated their semantics, implying that Z was an employee of the Nixon White House or C.R.P.[54] But Z was a Watergate grand juror![55] And to compound the lie, Woodward and Bernstein maintained in *All the President's Men* that Watergate grand jurors never granted them an interview.[56]

Bernstein had punctured the sanctity of the grand jury probing Watergate, and he gave his notes on the contact to Ben Bradlee, the *Post's* salty, Boston Brahmin executive editor, to apparently safeguard from subpoenas emanating from the D.C. U.S. attorney's office.[57] The latter action demonstrated that the *Post's* executive editor was, likely, in on the charade. In fact, Bradlee plays an integral role in the demise of the Nixon administration, and he also oozes a morass of lies about his relationship to the C.I.A.

In the previous chapter, I demonstrated that Woodward's cover story about Deep Throat was extremely defective, and in this chapter I've discussed Bernstein's turpitude. Woodward and Bernstein are not the honorable knights for truth and justice depicted by Robert Redford and Dustin Hoffman in the film *All the President's Men*. Indeed, their lives and their Watergate reporting are, unfortunately, a sprawling net of lies that are moored to the monolithic lie of Deep Throat. An extremely charitable interpretation of their deceit would relegate them to a pair of ethical eunuchs who repeatedly lied to heighten *All the President's Men's* dramatic friction. But Woodward and Bernstein were guilty of absurd lies that eclipsed accentuating the dramatic.

CHAPTER 26

CRYPTO FASCISM SAVES DEMOCRACY

D
espite the fabricated tales of Woodward and Bernstein, Nixon and his presidency survived the slings and arrows of outrageous fortune and hobbled into the spring of 1973. The televised hearings of the Watergate Committee commenced in May of 1973. Nine million Americans sat spellbound before their televisions, hoping that the hearings would finally expose the truth about Watergate.[1] The first supernova of the hearings was John Dean. The Senate granted Dean "use immunity," which is a form of immunity that prevented the Senate from using Dean's testimony or evidence derived from Dean's testimony to be held against him, but it, nonetheless, left Dean susceptible to prosecution by evidence that was not derived by his testimony.[2]

Throughout his protracted testimony, Dean lost his contacts in favor of round, tortoise shell glasses, and he dressed like an extremely conservative young man. His beautiful and dutiful blonde wife sat behind him, her face taut with concern. Dean should have received an Oscar nod as he unfurled his cautionary tale of woe.

Despite Dean's masterful performance, the Watergate Committee didn't have incontrovertible proof of Nixon's collusion in the Watergate cover-up, because it was Dean's word against Nixon's word – a zero sum stalemate. But Nixon had a secret that was privy to a select cabal within his administration: He had the Oval Office, Cabinet Room, his office in the Executive Office Building, the Aspen Lodge at Camp David, and the Lincoln Sitting Room wired to record his conversations.[3] Nixon also tapped the phones in the Oval Office and in his Executive Office Building office.[4] Nixon wrote that he would "consult the tapes in preparing whatever books or memoirs I might write" after his presidency.[5]

Haig learned of Nixon's secret taping system shortly after becoming Nixon's chief-of-staff in May of 1973.[6] After he became privy to the taping system, he attempted to expose it: Haig had inherited a former Haldeman apparatchik, who was privy to the taping system, and Haig instructed him to "tell the truth" about the taping system when interviewed by Watergate Committee staffers in July.[7] Conversely, Haldeman had told the apparatchik that if the Watergate Committee staffers ever questioned him about a taping system, he should immediately default to executive privilege.[8] When the Watergate Committee staffers interviewed the Haldeman-Haig apparatchik, he deftly danced around the issue and didn't surrender the taping system.[9]

Alexander Butterfield, a former Haldeman aide, ultimately coughed up the secret taping system to the Watergate Committee. In the preceding chapters, I've discussed the Nixon administration as a porous sieve for C.I.A. personnel, and Butterfield seemed to be a variation on that theme. Testifying before the House Judiciary Committee, Butterfield maintained that he and H.R. Haldeman had been friends when they attended U.C.L.A.[10] Butterfield also testified that Haldeman unexpectedly phoned him in January of 1969 and offered him a position on Haldeman's staff, even though they hadn't seen each other in more than 20 years.[11]

An implausible story indeed – and also a lie!

In actuality, Butterfield was an Air Force colonel stationed in Australia when he wrote Haldeman a letter, seeking employment at the White House.[12] In his letter to Haldeman, Butterfield neglected to mention that he had been the principal liaison between the military and the C.I.A. in Australia.[13] Nixon's personal secretary suspected that Butterfield was a C.I.A. plant, and Haldeman, in retrospect, also harbored suspicions that Butterfield was a plant due to Butterfield's lies before the House Judiciary Committee.[14]

According to *All the President's Men*, Deep Throat ostensibly disclosed Butterfield's name to Woodward in October of 1972.[15] Moreover, a former treasurer for the C.R.P.'s finance committee allegedly dropped Butterfield's name to Woodward and Bernstein, describing his position as supervising "internal security"[16] Woodward and Bernstein wrote that Woodward drove to Butterfield's suburban Virginia home in January of 1973, but no one answered the door.[17]

Abruptly in May, after Haig became Nixon's chief-of-staff, Woodward imbued Butterfield's name with a newfound gravitas: In *All the President's Men*, Woodward reportedly approached a Watergate Committee staff member and inquired if Butterfield had been interviewed.[18] In the middle of May, the televised Watergate Committee hearings had commenced, and Woodward's entreaty to interview Butterfield was purportedly rebuffed by the Committee, because the staff was "too busy."[19] But Woodward wouldn't be discouraged: "Some weeks later," he ostensibly told "another staffer" that Butterfield's duties in Haldeman's office related to "internal security."[20] Woodward and Bernstein wrote that the Watergate Committee's chief counsel, whose name appears in Rikan's little black book, finally slated Watergate Committee investigators to interview Butterfield on Friday, July 13.[21]

I find it telling that Butterfield's name ostensibly lay dormant in the notes of Woodward and Bernstein for months before it suddenly and inexplicably achieved a gravitas that compelled Woodward to presumably contact Watergate Committee staffers *twice* about Butterfield. Woodward's perplexing behavior aligns with Haig learning about Nixon's taping system in May.[22]

After Woodward's lobbying, Butterfield initially unveiled the existence of Nixon's taping system to Watergate Committee staffers on Friday July 13, 1973.[23] In *All the President's Men*, Woodward and Bernstein wrote that Butterfield was a "reluctant witness."[24] But Butterfield's perjury before the House Judiciary Committee, and his connections to the military and C.I.A. seemingly belie his apparent reluctance. Butterfield's perjury before the House Judiciary Committee, which potentially translated into years in prison, indicated that he either had skeletons in the closet or bats in the belfry. After Butterfield divulged the existence of Nixon's taping system to Watergate Committee staffers on Friday, the Committee promptly scheduled him to testify the following Monday.[25]

According to *All the President's Men*, the day after Butterfield's initial disclosure about the taping system, a "senior" member of the Watergate Committee's investigative staff allegedly relayed Butterfield's revelations to Woodward.[26] But Woodward claimed that the Saturday phone call marked his first encounter with information about Nixon's taping system, even though he had ostensibly proffered Butterfield's name to the Watergate Committee on two prior occasions.[27]

When Woodward claimed to have discovered the existence of Nixon's taping system, he and Bernstein were allegedly plunged into the throes of ambivalence: They reportedly thought that the taping system could be a diabolical plot, whereby the Nixon administration would surrender falsified tapes that exonerated Nixon.[28]

In *All the President's Men*, Woodward phoned *Washington Post* executive editor Bradlee on Saturday night and told him of the volatile, revelatory scoop.[29] Bradlee, however, ostensibly said that the revelatory scoop was a "B-plus" story that required additional excavation.[30] Bradlee's relegation of Woodward's information on Butterfield to a "B-plus" story is rather perplexing, because Butterfield's disclosure of Nixon's secret taping system was pyrotechnic and would irrevocably alter history.

At the time Bradlee was making an apparently irrational decision by vetoing a scoop that would alter the trajectory of history, Haig was making an apparently irrational decision about Butterfield's upcoming testimony, too. On Saturday, Haig also purportedly learned that Nixon's taping system was in jeopardy of being exposed.[31] On Sunday, a Watergate Committee counsel phoned Buzhardt and told him that he should be prepared to surrender the tapes.[32] The unfurling of Nixon's taping system to the Watergate Committee and the American public should've been a strident DEFCON 1 alarm for Haig and Buzhardt, but they didn't tell Nixon about the impending testimony over the weekend![33]

The reason Haig offered for not disclosing Butterfield's upcoming testimony to Nixon was that he was ill with viral pneumonia.[34] Though Nixon was indeed hospitalized for pneumonia that weekend, he was quite cogent as evinced by the series of protracted phone conversations he had from his hospital bed.[35] In *RN*, Nixon wrote about his hospitalization: "I was determined to show that even in the hospital I was able to carry out my duties.... I ended up staying on the phone until late at night, checking on the day's events."[36] Haig finally informed Nixon of Butterfield's upcoming testimony on Monday morning.[37] Nixon was shocked that his aides hadn't invoked executive privilege.[38]

Haig's actions and inactions make it apparent that he was determined to ensure that Nixon's secret taping system was made public: First, he instructed the Haldeman-Haig apparatchik to "tell the truth" about the taping system; second, he kept Nixon in the dark over the weekend about Butterfield's impending testimony.

Nixon discussed whether or not the tapes should be destroyed with Haig and Buzhardt.[39] Haig advised against destruction of the tapes, because that would be an indelible mark of guilt in the collective mind of the public.[40] Interestingly, Buzhardt argued for the destruction of the tapes.[41] Nixon decided not to destroy the tapes: He felt that the tapes would exonerate him from Dean's accusations that he and Nixon had conspired to obstruct justice for eight months prior to Dean's exodus from the administration.[42]

The Butterfield testimony before the Watergate Committee merges a quartet of military and/or intelligence personnel in the emergent demise of Nixon's presidency: Woodward, Butterfield, Haig, and the *Post's* executive editor Bradlee. Woodward ostensibly pressed Butterfield on the Watergate Committee and, over the weekend, Haig didn't disclose Butterfield's impending testimony to Nixon, which paralyzed his recourse to block it with the imprimatur of executive privilege or national security. Bradlee ensured that Nixon wouldn't be edified about Butterfield's impending testimony via the *Washington Post* by a rather disingenuous pretext: Butterfield outing Nixon's secret taping system, an article that would've been a supernova, was a mere "B-plus" story.

I've previously elucidated the military and/or intelligence connections of Haig, Woodward, and Butterfield, but Bradlee, too, had a history that was enmeshed in intelligence, even though he's shielded his connections to the C.I.A. with brazen mendacity. A book written by journalist Deborah Davis, *Katherine the Great: Katherine Graham and The Washington Post,* is a biography of *Washington Post* publisher Katharine Graham. Davis' book also addresses the clandestine connections between the C.I.A. and *Washington Post,* and Bradlee's former connections to the C.I.A. In 1979, a large, mainstream publisher, Harcourt Brace Jovanovich, published the book.[43]

In *Katharine the Great,* Davis reported that Bradlee was the wellspring of C.I.A. material in response to a popular French newspaper that featured an article asserting that the United States had framed Ethel and Julius Rosenberg, an American couple sentenced to death for smuggling A-bomb secrets to the Soviet Union.[44] Davis wrote that the C.I.A. chief in Paris directed Bradlee to write a propaganda analysis of the Rosenberg case, depicting the Rosenbergs as guilty and deserving of the death penalty.[45]

Bradlee didn't appreciate Davis' *Katharine the Great,* and he penned an extremely caustic letter to the president of Harcourt Brace Jovanovich, accusing Davis of lying.[46] Bradlee even threatened to banish Harcourt Brace to "that special little group of publishers who don't give a shit for the truth."[47] The president of Harcourt Brace ultimately capitulated to Bradlee's threats: Six weeks after *Katherine the Great*'s release, he withdrew the book from bookstores and 20,000 copies of the book were shredded, even though Harcourt Brace had previously nominated the book for an American Book Award.[48] Davis was also subjected to a smear campaign: Two respected publications portrayed her as unprofessional and mentally unstable.[49]

In 1987, a small publisher was willing to republish Davis' radioactive book.[50] In the interim, Davis filed a Freedom of Information Act request and acquired government documentation that unequivocally demonstrated that Bradlee was the progenitor of C.I.A. propaganda.[51] The C.I.A. chief in Paris had indeed sent Bradlee to New York to harvest documentation about the Rosenberg case from their prosecutors.[52] Bradlee then wrote a protracted opus of propaganda on the Rosenbergs with the C.I.A.'s topspin.[53]

The government documentation apodictically linked Bradlee to the C.I.A., so his brazen mendacity about zero affiliation with the C.I.A. is perplexing, unless, of course, Bradlee continued to disseminate C.I.A. propaganda. In that case, he would deploy every fabrication and resource at his disposal to ensure that his C.I.A. affiliation wasn't breached, because, if he were exposed as an Agency shill, his executive editorship of the *Washington Post* had the potential to be severely tainted. Moreover, the stories that he sanctioned as the executive editor of the *Washington Post*, including Watergate, had the potential to be tainted and subjected to renewed scrutiny. Bradlee, like his two ace reporters, Woodward and Bernstein, was an unabashed liar.

CHAPTER 27

SATURDAY NIGHT FEVER

In Chapter 22, "The Berlin Wall Crumbles," I discuss the "resignations" of Ehrlichman, Haldeman and Attorney General Richard Kleindienst in the wake of the revelations emanating from Daniel Ellsberg's trial. Nixon ultimately tapped Secretary of Defense Elliot Richardson to be his new and improved attorney general.[1] Nixon, however, had to make a pact with the Democrat-controlled Senate to secure Richardson's nomination: Richardson would have to appoint an independent special prosecutor to investigate Watergate.[2] Nixon reluctantly consented, and Richardson was confirmed as attorney general by an 82 to 3 margin in the Senate.[3]

The 52-year-old Richardson was married with three children.[4] He was a tall, svelte, and soft-spoken Boston blueblood. Richardson looked like a Clark Kent doppelgänger: He had a thatch of dark brown hair, fastidiously parted to the side, and patrician facial features that were accentuated by boxy black glasses. Richardson was the son of a distinguished physician, who was a professor of medicine at Harvard Medical School.[5] Shortly after Richardson enrolled in Harvard as an undergraduate, he took a leave of absence to fight in World War II.[6] He enlisted in the Army and stormed the beaches of Normandy as a first lieutenant, earning a Bronze Star and two Purple Hearts.[7]

After World War II, Richardson returned to Harvard.[8] He joked that he expended the majority of his time as an undergraduate drawing cartoons for *The Harvard Lampoon*.[9] But he, nonetheless, graduated near the top of his class and enrolled in Harvard Law School, where he became president and editor of the prestigious *Harvard Law Review*.[10] When Richardson clerked for a Supreme Court justice, he negotiated a pact with the justice that allowed him to read Shakespeare every morning for an hour.[11]

After Richardson served as the U.S. Attorney for the District of Massachusetts, the newly elected Richard Nixon appointed him to be undersecretary of state.[12] In 1970, he became Secretary of the Department of Health, Education, and Welfare, a cabinet level post.[13] Nixon then selected him to be the Secretary of Defense at the beginning of 1973 – he became the U.S. Attorney General four months later.[14]

Nixon had been good to Richardson, and he thought Richardson would reciprocate. But Richardson promptly appointed an antagonistic Archibald Cox as the special prosecutor of the Watergate Special Prosecution Force (W.S.P.F.)[15] Cox and the W.S.P.F. would displace the federal prosecutors who had previously prosecuted Watergate and launch various task forces focusing on different facets of the Nixon administration's malfeasance and criminality.[16] The 61-year-old Cox, tall and gaunt, was an esteemed Harvard Law School professor and a bit of an eccentric: He had a bristling flattop of white hair, he sported three-piece suits, button-down shirts, and svelte bow ties.[17] He also had an affinity for driving his pickup truck to Harvard.[18] Richardson had been a protégé of Cox's at Harvard Law School.[19]

Cox was a dedicated Democrat who had served as a speechwriter and adviser to President John Kennedy, and Kennedy had appointed him solicitor general, the third highest rank in the Department of Justice.[20] Cox quickly stocked the W.S.P.F. with Democrats and Ivy Leaguers – Nixon's favorite cross-section of society.[21] The eccentric, unassuming Harvard professor would spare Nixon no quarter.

Cox had been the special prosecutor of the W.S.P.F. for a month and half when Butterfield's revelations about the Nixon tapes echoed around the world.[22] Cox immediately pounced. He had the daily logs of Nixon's activities, including meetings and phone calls, and he wrote a letter to Buzhardt requesting that Nixon provide him with eight taped conversations that he thought would incriminate Nixon in the Watergate cover up.[23] Cox then amended his original request to include nine taped conversations.[24] Nixon wasn't amenable to Cox's request, so Cox announced that he would subpoena the tapes.[25] The Watergate Committee also sought the tapes.[26]

Naturally, Cox had to obtain a subpoena from a judge to acquire the tapes, and, lo and behold, that judge was none other than Maximum John Sirica. The last time we encountered Sirica was Chapter 20, "The Pugilist at Wrest," but now he's back with a vengeance and as draconian as ever. Sirica oversaw Cox and the W.S.P.F.'s grand jury investigations, so he presided over a hearing where the legality of subpoenaing Nixon's tapes was debated.[27]

In a crowded courtroom, the August hearing pitted the grand jury's special prosecutor, Archibald Cox, against one of Nixon's recently recruited attorneys.[28] Nixon's attorney contended that the president should be the sole authority on whether or not the tapes should be made public due to the risk of compromising national security.[29] Cox argued that the

W.S.P.F. needed the tapes to properly adjudicate the crimes committed by the Nixon administration, because there was "strong reason to believe that the integrity of the executive office has been corrupted, although the rot is not yet clear."[30]

After listening to arguments from both sides, Sirica made a ruling a week later that disappointed both Cox and Nixon: Sirica ordered that Nixon surrender the tapes to him.[31] He had decided that he would personally listen to the tapes and determine the tapes that should be parsed out to the W.S.P.F. grand jury and the tapes that would compromise national security.[32]

Nixon's cadre of attorneys and Cox appealed Sirica's ruling to the U.S. Circuit Court of Appeals, and, in October of 1973, the appellate court sided with Sirica, ordering that Nixon surrender the tapes to Sirica.[33] Nixon felt the jungle encroaching on him, but drinking and sedatives had negated his ability to repel his new mortal foes: One night, Britain's prime minister phoned Nixon about a war erupting in the Middle East, but Kissinger found Nixon in a debilitated state of intoxication and opted not to interrupt his stupor.[34]

In addition to Nixon's desire to sack Cox, Haig had become disenchanted with him too. The W.S.P.F. special prosecutor was investigating crimes that fell outside the purview of the Watergate break-ins: He had also declared open season on the Plumbers.[35] Cox encountered sheer recalcitrance when he sought documentation about the Plumbers.[36] An investigation into the Plumbers could potentially intersect with Haig's treasonous role in the Moorer-Radford affair.

When Cox was about to indict former Nixon administration personnel for their roles in the Plumbers' dirty and illicit deeds, Buzhardt adamantly maintained that a trial of former Plumbers would breach national security issues.[37] Buzhardt's appeal temporarily postponed Cox's prosecution of the Plumbers.[38] But the pesky Cox also started investigating the Nixon administration's illegal wiretaps, which had the potential to entangle Haig in additional illegalities.[39] An outraged Haig phoned Richardson about Cox's probe into the administration's illegal wiretaps and brandished a threat to fire Cox.[40] For Haig's sake, Cox had to be jettisoned, and the foxtrot that Haig and Buzhardt choreographed to purge Cox proved to be very effective.

One Monday, October 15, Haig summoned Richardson to the White House under the auspices of Richardson, Haig, and Nixon discussing a crisis in the Mideast.[41] When Richardson arrived at the White House, he discovered that Haig had summoned him under a false pretense.[42] Haig instructed Richardson to sack Cox and thus negate the subpoenaing of the tapes.[43] Nixon would then submit summaries of the nine subpoenaed tapes to Sirica.[44]

But Richardson replied that Cox's requests hadn't usurped his mandate, and he would resign as attorney general before firing Cox.[45] After Richardson returned to the Justice Department, Haig phoned him with a compromise of sorts.[46] Haig proposed that a particular senator independently summarize the tapes for Sirica.[47] The 72-year-old senator in question was hard of hearing, and he had the epithet of the "Undertaker" due to his deft abilities to bury problems.[48] Haig phoned Richardson an hour later and relayed to him that Nixon accepted the Undertaker Compromise.[49] Haig also tossed in a wee bit of coercion: He told Richardson that Cox had to refrain from subpoenaing additional tapes or documents beyond the Undertaker Compromise or Richardson should summarily banish him.[50]

Richardson desperately sought to avert the Constitutional crisis that was looming on the horizon, and he rendezvoused with Haig and Buzhardt later in the day to forge a consensus.[51] He disclosed to Haig that he would urge Cox to cosign the Undertaker Compromise.[52] Richardson, however, warned Haig that he would resign if he were ordered to sack Cox – if Cox were merely seeking additional taped conversations.[53] Haig was now perfectly positioned to ice Cox and severely damage Nixon: Haig assured Nixon that Cox would, indeed, accept the Undertaker Compromise, and he also told Nixon that Richardson would support him if Cox didn't accept the Undertaker Compromise.[54]

After Richardson's meeting with Haig and Buzhardt, he relayed the Undertaker Compromise to Cox.[55] The following morning, Tuesday, October 16, Cox discussed the Undertaker Compromise with his aides.[56] Though Cox was dubious of the Undertaker's Cliff Notes, he requested that Richardson put the proposal in writing.[57] Richardson's proposal incorporated the Undertaker Compromise, and it also specified that the arrangement only applied to the tapes that had been previously subpoenaed.[58] Haig and Buzhardt insisted that Cox adopt the proposal by Friday night at midnight, which was Nixon's deadline to appeal the U.S. Circuit Court of Appeals decision on the subpoenaed conversations to the Supreme Court.[59] So, now, Richardson was attempting to avert a Constitutional crisis in a pressure cooker.

Richardson and Cox discussed the Undertaker Compromise twice on Wednesday, October 17.[60] On Thursday, Cox wrote a response that Richardson delivered to the White House on Thursday night: Cox wasn't compatible with the Undertaker Compromise, but he was amenable to negotiation.[61] On Thursday night, Richardson met with Haig, Buzhardt, and an attorney Haig and Buzhardt had recently conscripted to presumably aid Nixon with his litigation over the tapes.[62] The recently conscripted attorney lauded the Undertaker Compromise as a magnanimous concession.[63] Richardson was starting to suffer from Undertaker Compromise Fatigue Syndrome, and he suggested that the attorney phone Cox.[64]

The conversation between Nixon's newly acquired attorney and Cox was bellicose and devoid of latitude for negotiation, but Cox, nevertheless, requested that the attorney commit his response to paper.[65] The subsequent letter, delivered on Friday morning, unequivocally stated that Cox would refrain from subpoenaing additional evidence beyond the Undertaker Compromise.[66] Cox's response to the missive was a categorical rejection: He would never accept such restrictions, because they would prevent him from discharging his duties as the W.S.P.F. special prosecutor.[67] Throughout the crisis with Cox, Haig continued to hoodwink Nixon: Haig told Nixon that Richardson wouldn't tender his resignation if Cox resigned.[68]

After Cox received the letter on Friday morning, Richardson phoned Haig and inquired about the status of the negotiations with Cox: Haig replied that the negotiations were hunky-dory.[69] Shortly after Haig talked to Richardson, a letter from Cox, rejecting the Undertaker Compromise, arrived at the White House.[70] Richardson had informed Haig that he wanted to see the president if the negotiations with Cox collapsed.[71] Richardson's request was a clear-cut warning to Haig that he would resign if Cox were fired.[72] In fact, the previous night Richardson wrote a list of reasons "Why I Must Resign."[73]

Richardson was fortified with his resignation letter when Haig summoned him to the White House on that fateful Friday morning.[74] Richardson met with Haig, Buzhardt, and the attorney who had the acrimonious phone call with the Cox the night before.[75] Richardson's implied threat to resign had, apparently, resuscitated the negotiations: Haig conveyed to Richardson that the administration would commit to the Undertaker Compromise without canning Cox.[76]

In an effort to frame an accord, Richardson recommended that Nixon's new attorney write a second letter to Cox containing a caveat that merely shelved the idea of Cox subpoenaing additional evidence beyond the Undertaker Compromise.[77] The new attorney did, indeed, write Cox a second letter with a declaration that was as accommodating as a nihilist answering the front door to proselytizing Jehovah Witnesses: "The differences between us remain so great that no purpose would be served by further discussion."[78] Conversely, on Friday afternoon, Haig said to Nixon about the impasse with Richardson: "It's no big problem."[79]

Haig then phoned Richardson and told him that he was about to receive a letter from Nixon.[80] The letter mandated that Richardson give Cox an ultimatum: The Undertaker Compromise or bust.[81] Richardson was enraged that he was not consulted about the decisions yielding the ultimatum.[82] Haig responded that he had informed Nixon twice about Richardson's misgivings, but Nixon wasn't willing to concede a nanometer beyond the Undertaker Compromise.[83] The high-speed collision between Nixon and Cox, as engineered by Haig, was now inevitable.

On Friday night, without informing Richardson or Cox, Nixon released a statement about his impasse with Cox: He would consent to the Undertaker Compromise, but the subpoenaing of additional evidence would be unequivocally rejected.[84] On Saturday afternoon, October 20, Cox held a news conference: He protested Nixon's obdurate evasion of the subpoenaed materials.[85] Cox also stated that he would not resign as the W.S.P.F. special prosecutor, and Nixon would have to endure the radioactive fallout if he were fired.[86]

After Cox's press conference, Haig summoned Richardson to the White House.[87] Richardson told Nixon that he had come to resign, because he would not fire Cox.[88] Nixon pleaded with Richardson not to resign until a crisis in the Middle East had been resolved, but Richardson was inflexible.[89] Haig then phoned the deputy attorney general and ordered him to sack Cox, but he rebuffed Haig's directive and resigned.[90] Finally, the solicitor general agreed to sack Cox, and he was promptly elevated to acting attorney general.[91] At about 8:30 that night, Nixon's press secretary announced the resignations of Richardson, the deputy attorney general, Cox's dismissal, and also the abolishment of the W.S.P.F.[92] In the annals of American history, this ignominious interlude is coined the "Saturday Night Massacre."

Americans were stunned by the Saturday Night Massacre's wanton perversion of justice: Letters, telegrams, and telephone calls deluged D.C.[93] The drumbeat of impeachment also started reverberating from the House of Representatives.[94] The Saturday Night Massacre put Nixon's presidency on life support – he had to backpedal at Mach 3 speed. Nixon was forced to ameliorate the congressional unrest, and he promised that the acting attorney general would appoint a new W.S.P.F. special prosecutor.[95] Nixon also decided to relinquish the subpoenaed conversations to Sirica.[96] When Nixon decided to surrender the taped conversations, he wrote that he could take a modicum of solace because the tapes would prove Dean had lied to the Watergate Committee.[97]

Nixon also hemorrhaged credibility and popularity from lacerations that weren't even inflicted by Watergate. Prior to the Saturday Night Massacre, Nixon had to contend with Vice President Spiro Agnew coming under investigation for graft – bribery, extortion, and tax violations – when he served as Maryland's governor.[98] Of course, the vice president adamantly disavowed the charges and relegated them to "damned lies."[99] Indeed, he made an impassioned speech in Los Angeles that reached its crescendo when he declared: "I will not resign if indicted!"[100] Eleven days later he resigned as vice president and ultimately pled "no contest" to one count of tax evasion.[101] Agnew resigned ten days before the Saturday Night Massacre.[102] He later claimed that he resigned because Haig brandished a death threat – he would be assassinated if he didn't resign.[103]

As Nixon was tenaciously fighting for survival in the jungle, he found himself in the crosshairs of the Internal Revenue Service in the summer of 1974. The I.R.S. concluded that Nixon owed $432,000 in back taxes for his first four years as president.[104] Tricky Dick became too tricky with the I.R.S. when he claimed a deduction of $567,000 when submitting his vice-presidential papers to the national archives: He belatedly discovered that a 1969 law prohibited such deductions.[105] The I.R.S. had considered charging Nixon with fraud, but he received a consolation prize – a $14,000 fine.[106]

CHAPTER 28

THE TALE OF THE TAPE

As the Nixon administration was surging towards its demise, Nixon was descending into entropy. His conversations increasingly approached incoherence: One aide encountered a mumbling Nixon in a White House hallway, and he thought he heard: "The bastards! The bastards!"[1] Nixon was also opting for seclusion and developed an affinity for nocturnal piano playing.[2] He started to sweat profusely, stutter, and tremble at news conferences.[3] He even forcefully shoved his press secretary on national television.[4] Tricky Dick was running out of tricks.

Within two weeks of Richardson's resignation, Nixon nominated a Republican senator from Ohio to be the acting attorney general.[5] Four days later, Leon Jaworski was sworn in as the new and improved W.S.P.F. special prosecutor.[6] The 68 year-old Jaworski was born in Waco, Texas, and he was the senior partner of a large Houston law firm.[7] Jaworski was medium height and stocky. He had receding silver-hair and a suntan that had been cultivated in the Lone Star sun. His impeccably tailored suits had compliant creases in all the right places, and black square glasses enlarged his reflective eyes. He also had a relaxed southern hospitality and charm that belied the persona of a high-powered lawyer. Jaworski had been married for more than forty years, and he and his wife had three children.[8] His specialty was corporate law, and he appeared to be the antithesis of the eccentric Archibald Cox.

Jaworski was a prodigy of sorts: He had graduated from high school at 15, and then was awarded a scholarship to Baylor University.[9] At the ripe age of 20, he received a law degree, becoming the youngest person to ever be admitted to the Texas bar.[10] Jaworski's distinguished legal career included serving as a prosecutor at the Nuremberg trials of Nazi war criminals and as the president of the American Bar Association.[11] Jaworski was close to Nixon's predecessor – Lyndon Johnson. He represented Johnson against voter fraud charges – L.B.J. was exonerated.[12]

Like many of the individuals enmeshed in Watergate, Jaworski had covert connections to the C.I.A.[13] He was the attorney and also a "director" of the Texas-based M.D. Anderson Foundation, which funded medical research and covertly acted as a C.I.A. conduit to disburse funds in the 1960s.[14] Jaworski initially denied his involvement in the foundation's clandestine disbursement of C.I.A. funds.[15] However, he confessed to his complicity after a former law partner said that he, Jaworski and a third director of the foundation unanimously consented to act as a C.I.A. funding conduit.[16] A portion of the funds were earmarked for the National Student Association, which confronted Communist leaning student organizations on U.S. campuses. Like the *Washington Post's* Ben Bradlee, Jaworski lied about his former affiliation with the C.I.A. Although he may have had a number of reasons for lying about his former Agency affiliation, it's within the realm of reason that he continued his relationship with the C.I.A., and he didn't want his role as the W.S.P.F. special prosecutor to be tainted by an ongoing association with Langley.

The W.S.P.F. staff, stocked with Ivy Leaguers, initially thought they had been "sold down the Rio Grande" when Jaworski's appointment was announced.[17] Cox and Jaworski had antithetical styles: Cox managed the W.S.P.F. like a law professor conducting a seminar, and Jaworski ran the W.S.P.F. as if it were the litigation team of a major law firm.[18] A primary factor that differentiated Cox from Jaworski was that Richardson had chosen Cox – Haig had chosen Jaworski.[19] Interestingly, Jaworski wouldn't disclose how he met Haig.[20] Haig assured Nixon that Jaworski was a swell guy, and he would be an easier foe than Cox. Nixon was utterly blind to the fact that Haig would use Jaworski to raze his administration.

As mentioned in the last chapter, Nixon decided to relinquish the subpoenaed conversations for political self-preservation after the Saturday Night Massacre:[21]

> 1. A meeting on June 20, 1972, of Nixon, Ehrlichman, and Haldeman from 10:30 A.M. until approximately 12:45 P.M.
>
> 2. A telephone call on June 20, 1972, between Nixon and John Mitchell from 6:08 P.M. to 6:12 P.M.
>
> 3. A meeting on June 30, 1972, of Nixon, Mitchell, and Haldeman for an hour and 15 minutes.
>
> 4. A meeting on September 15, 1972, among Nixon, Haldeman, and Dean from 5:27 P.M. to 6:17 P.M., which was the day the grand jury returned the indictments against the Watergate burglars.
>
> 5. A meeting on March 13, 1973, between Nixon and Haldeman from 12:42 P.M. to 2:00 P.M.

6. A meeting on March 21, 1973, of Nixon, Haldeman and Dean from 10:12 A.M. to 11:55 A.M.

7. A meeting on March 21, 1973, of Haldeman, Ehrlichman, Dean, and Nixon's press secretary from 5:20 P.M. to 6:01 P.M.

8. A meeting on March 22, 1973, among Nixon, Ehrlichman, Haldeman, Mitchell and Dean from 2:00 P.M. to 3:43 P.M.

9. A meeting on April 15, 1973, between Nixon and Dean from 9:17 P.M. to 10:12 P.M.

Nixon had decided to scrutinize the subpoenaed tapes' content, and he instructed his secretary to transcribe the subpoenaed conversations.[22] On an early October afternoon, Nixon's secretary of 22 years, who was usually the quintessence of prim and proper, was in the midst of transcribing the tapes when she anxiously burst into Nixon's office in the Executive Office Building.[23]

She told Nixon that she had inadvertently erased approximately five minutes of a taped conversation between Nixon and Haldeman three days after the Watergate break-in.[24] Buzhardt had previously conveyed to Nixon that the Haldeman conversation hadn't been subpoenaed, so Nixon assuaged his secretary's anxiety.[25] Haig then allegedly phoned Buzhardt about the accidental erasure by Nixon's secretary to confirm that Nixon's conversation with Haldeman hadn't been subpoenaed, and Buzhardt allegedly replied that the Haldeman conversation hadn't been subpoenaed.[26]

In the original subpoena, Cox mistakenly thought that Nixon had met with Ehrlichman and Haldeman simultaneously.[27] Cox, however, had realized his error, and he sent a memo to Buzhardt stating that he sought the two respective conversations Nixon had with Ehrlichman and then Haldeman three days after the Watergate bust on June 20th.[28] The Haldeman conversation had, indeed, been subpoenaed.[29] Haig and Buzhardt were either extremely duplicitous or extremely incompetent, but, given their behavior thus far and their subsequent behavior, the smart money would ride on extremely duplicitous.

In late October, Buzhardt met with Sirica in the judge's chamber and informed him that two of the subpoenaed conversations had not been recorded.[30] As figurative smoke surged from his ears, Sirica ordered a hearing on the matter the following day.[31] At the public hearing the next day, Buzhardt announced to the world that two of the subpoenaed conversations were non-existent: The conversation between John Mitchell and Nixon on June 20, 1972, and the conversation between Dean and Nixon on April 15, 1973.[32] After Buzhardt's admission, the *New York Times* and *Time Magazine* published editorials calling for Nixon's resignation.[33] The two missing conversations were the beginning of the next phase of the Nixon tapes' imbroglio.

The next month, early November, Sirica held hearings about the tapes' missing conversations, and the presidential aide who had become the curator of the tapes imparted to the courtroom that Nixon's secretary had told him of a "gap" in one of the tapes.[34] The aide in question was a retired general who Haig had conscripted to act as his deputy chief-of-staff.[35] Nixon's secretary testified the following day, and she denied that she had erased portions of the tape, despite erasing five minutes of the conversation between Nixon and Haldeman.[36]

The day Nixon's personal secretary testified in Sirica's courtroom that the tapes didn't have a gap, November 8, the *Washington Post* published a Woodward and Bernstein article on page one – "Parts Inaudible."[37] In their article, Woodward and Bernstein had gleaned information from five "White House sources" who said the tapes were blemished by "background noise," "periods of silence," and "gaps in the conversations."[38] One source, however, divulged that the problems with the tapes were of "a suspicious nature" and "could lead someone to conclude that the tapes have been tampered with."[39]

In *All the President's Men*, Woodward and Bernstein revealed that the source for the article's incriminating tidings was none other than Deep Throat.[40] Woodward had ostensibly moved his balcony flowerpot in the first week of November of 1973, signaling Deep Throat that he sought a meeting that night.[41] At that meeting, Deep Throat supposedly edified Woodward that "one or more of the tapes contained deliberate erasures."[42]

As I mentioned in Chapter 24, Woodward went a bridge too far when he named former G-man, Mark Felt, as his sole source for Deep Throat. Felt had resigned from the F.B.I. in June – five months earlier.[43] For Woodward's account to be truthful, Felt would've had to drive into D.C. every day from Fairfax County, Virginia and scrutinize Woodward's balcony.[44] Even if the reader is willing to swallow the absurd tale of Felt's treks into D.C. every day after leaving the F.B.I., it would be extremely unlikely that he would've been aware of *deliberate erasures*.

Time magazine narrowed the field of Deep Throat contenders to those who were privy to gaps in the tapes and, excluding Nixon and his secretary, the list included Haig, Buzhardt, a Nixon aide, an attorney who replaced Dean as counsel to the president, and an attorney the administration recruited to assist with Nixon's burgeoning legal travails – Mark Felt isn't on the list.[45] Woodward's account of clandestine, nocturnal sojourns to an underground parking garage in Virginia is utterly absurd when compared to Haig simply relaying to his former briefer, Bob Woodward, that the tapes contained suspicious and deliberate erasures. .

After Woodward and Bernstein's page-one article about erasures on the Nixon tapes, which, odds-on, Sirica would've read, Buzhardt and a lawyer that Nixon had enlisted to assist with his mounting legal quandaries inexplicably decided to listen to the June 20 conversation between Nixon and Haldeman – with a stopwatch.[46] Buzhardt had assured Nixon *twice* that the June 20, 1972 conversation between Nixon and Haldeman hadn't been subpoenaed.[47] But the recently enlisted attorney read Cox's August memo and told Buzhardt that the June 20 conversation between Nixon and Haldeman had definitely been subpoenaed.[48] The attorney who listened to the tape with Buzhardt told the authors of *Silent Coup* that it would've been next to impossible for Buzhardt to gaffe on that conversation not being subpoenaed, especially after Cox's August clarification memo.[49]

When listening to the subpoenaed conversation, they encountered an 18-and-a-half minute gap instead of the five-minute gap created by Nixon's secretary.[50] Haig told Nixon about the gap the next day, and Nixon wrote: "It was a nightmare."[51] The following week, Buzhardt revealed the protracted gap to Sirica.[52] Haig informed Sirica that the protracted erasure had been the work of a "sinister force."[53] Sirica was rightfully apoplectic about Buzhardt's disclosure – probably to the point of displaying Tourette's Syndrome-like symptoms. Sirica demanded that Nixon surrender the tapes or he would be subject to legal ramifications that would force him to surrender the tapes.[54]

The Nixon administration complied near the end of November.[55] Sirica ruled that the majority of two tapes and part of a third tape were covered by executive privilege and wouldn't be surrendered to the W.S.P.F.[56] He also found that a subpoenaed conversation among Nixon, Haldeman and Dean didn't mention Watergate.[57] In fact, the subpoenaed conversations didn't incriminate Nixon one iota in the Watergate burglaries or the cover-up.[58]

Tricky Dick had dodged a bullet, but he wasn't unscathed. Sirica announced the formation of a six-man panel composed of White House and W.S.P.F. personnel to investigate the integrity of the tapes.[59] In the middle of January, the panel rendered its report: The 18-and-a-half minute gap had "almost surely" been deliberately doctored.[60]

Over the years, Watergate lore has universally accepted that Nixon was culpable for the additional minutes being erased from the tape. But the *Silent Coup* authors have suggested that the protracted erasure might have been courtesy of Haig and/or Buzhardt, because they sought to accelerate the necrosis of Nixon's presidency: Haig and/or Buzhardt certainly had the means to erase the tape and, thus far, they've been proficient at mutilating Nixon's integrity.[61]

The tape that contained the 18-and-a-half minute gap was a conversation between Nixon and Haldeman that wended from 11:26 A.M. to 12:45 P.M. June 20, 1972 – three days after the break-in.[62] Nixon wrote that he was able to reconstruct slices of the conversation from Haldeman's notes, and he and Haldeman revisited the topic of Watergate later in the day.[63] On that morning, Nixon and Haldeman were utterly in the dark about who spearheaded the botched Watergate burglary.[64] Consequently, the likelihood of Nixon and Haldeman acting upon a definitive criminal conspiracy to obstruct justice was improbable.

In addition to Nixon dealing with a fuming Sirica, the media reported that the honeymoon between the Nixon administration and Jaworski had been short-lived and hostilities quickly began to flare.[65] Despite the professed antipathy between the White House and Jaworski, Haig and Jaworski were in "constant communication" and having quasi-secret meetings.[66] To ensure the secrecy of their meetings, Jaworski entered the White House through the Diplomatic Entrance, which was established to protect the anonymity of diplomats.[67] After Jaworski slipped into the White House, he and Haig would meet in the Map Room, a parlor where Franklin Roosevelt frequently retired to study battle maps during World War II.[68]

As 1973 wended into 1974, Haig seemingly started to expedite Nixon's presidential expiration date. In December of 1973, Haig approached Nixon and proffered an agreement ostensibly on behalf of the W.S.P.F. special prosecutor: Jaworski wouldn't seek additional tapes if Nixon surrendered a collection of specified tapes that hadn't been subpoenaed.[69] Jaworski, however, claimed that he never made such a pact.[70] Nixon consented to the pact as explained by Haig, but Jaworski didn't find the collection of tapes provided by Haig to be relevant to the W.S.P.F. grand jury's investigation.[71]

In January, Jaworski requested to listen to a tape recorded on June 4, 1973.[72] The June 4, 1973 tape – or "tape of tapes'" – was a recording of Nixon listening to previous conversations he'd had about Watergate and riffing on their contents.[73] The tape was essentially a treasure map for Jaworski to find the administration's criminal activity.[74] At this point, two very different narratives emerge about the "tape of tapes": The Woodward and Bernstein version and the Nixon version.

The Woodward and Bernstein version recounted Haig surrendering the innocuous collection of tapes in December.[75] Their version also included Haig talking Nixon into relinquishing the "tape of tapes," because it would, most likely, be the "last request from Jaworski."[76] In the Woodward and Bernstein version, Nixon instructed Buzhardt to listen to the tape.[77] After Buzhardt listened to the tape, he lobbied for Nixon not to relinquish the recording.[78] But Haig urged Nixon to yield the tape – and he prevailed.[79] Haig then allowed Jaworski to take a copy of the tape of tapes back to his office![80]

In the Nixon version, Haig said that if Nixon surrendered the benign collection of tapes in December, Jaworski would cease and desist from requesting additional tapes.[81] According to Nixon, Haig only came to him once – in December – and requested that Nixon allow Jaworski to listen to the benign collection of tapes.[82] Ergo, if Nixon is telling the truth, Haig relinquished the "tape of tapes" without consulting Nixon.

Woodward, Bernstein, and Nixon are three consummate practitioners of mendacity. In fact, if black belts were awarded for mendacity, Woodward, Bernstein, and Nixon would effortlessly qualify for 10th degree black belts. But rudimentary reasoning indicates that Nixon is telling the truth: Nixon fought tooth and nail to preserve his presidency, so it defies logic that he would surrender the June 4 tape, especially without a subpoena. Haig was delivering a deathblow to the Nixon administration.

After Jaworski listened to the "tape of tapes," he wrote a letter to the White House, requesting 25 additional tape recordings.[83] But Nixon refused to knuckle under.[84] In April, Nixon's recalcitrance compelled Jaworski to request that Sirica issue a subpoena for 64 additional taped conversations.[85] Sirica acquiesced.[86] After Sirica issued the subpoena, Jaworski developed a Vito Corleone streak and made Nixon an offer he couldn't refuse: Jaworski would publicly name Nixon as an unindicted co-conspirator if Nixon didn't surrender 18 of the 64 taped conversations.[87]

Nixon wrote that Jaworski's deal was tantamount to "blackmail," but he nonetheless started listening to the 18 taped conversations that Jaworski had specified."[88] He eventually encountered the June 23, 1972, conversation in which he told Haldeman to deploy the C.I.A. to block the F.B.I.'s investigation into the C.R.P.'s money laundering that I discussed in Chapter 17 – "The Whole Bay of Pigs Thing." The conversation would be the smoking gun for Nixon's obstruction of justice.[89]

Instead of surrendering the tapes, Nixon decided to take his chances in the courts.[90] Jaworski opted to circumvent the appellate court and shepherded the case before the U.S. Supreme Court.[91] On July 24, the Supremes voted 8 to 0 that Nixon had to surrender the tapes.[92] The smoking gun conversation of June 23, 1972, was quickly scattered to the four winds.

Though Buzhardt appeared to be contoured from the same crypto-fascist mold as Haig, he occasionally embraced views that were seemingly antithetical to Haig's and intended to safeguard Nixon. But when the Supreme Court ruled in favor of Jaworski, Buzhardt demonstrated his true colors: Before the White House even released the transcripts of the June 23, 1972 conversation between Nixon and Haldeman, Buzhardt became a Paul Revere of sorts as he showed the smoking gun transcripts to various congressmen.[93] The House minority leader was determined to vote against the House's articles of impeachment against Nixon until Buzhardt presented the smoking gun transcripts to him. [94] He then opted for impeachment.[95]

Nixon announced his resignation on August 9.[96]

Tricky Dick had run out of tricks . . . and the jungle devoured him.

CHAPTER 29

GUILTY!

As Haig ushered Nixon's presidency to its doom, the ghosts of the Moorer-Radford affair made a visit to him. The *Chicago Tribune* reported that the Joint Chiefs' Chairman Admiral Moorer had received pilfered documentation from Kissinger's office.[1] But the following day, the *Washington Post* and Woodward came to the rescue of Haig: A Woodward and Bernstein article exonerated Admiral Moorer and, for that matter, Alexander Haig from the pilfering of top secret documents.[2] The article pinned the Moorer-Radford affair pilfering exclusively on Radford and stated that he delivered insignificant material to unnamed individuals at the Pentagon.[3] Woodward conveniently neglected to mention his former affiliation with Haig, Moorer, and Welander.[4]

Two days after Woodward and Bernstein published their article on the Moorer-Radford affair, the *New York Times* reported that a White House investigation had discovered that the Chairman of the Joints Chief of Staff, Thomas Moorer, had received "secret National Security Council documents."[5] The article penned by Woodward and Bernstein in the *Washington Post* merely implicated Radford in innocuous shenanigans, but the *Chicago Tribune* and *New York Times'* articles framed the Moorer-Radford affair as potentially treasonous.

In early February of 1974, the Senate Armed Services Committee held a hearing on the Moorer-Radford affair.[6] The chairman of the Senate Armed Services Committee just happened to be the Senate's 72-year-old Undertaker.[7] The Undertaker oversaw the closed-door hearing on the Moorer-Radford affair.[8] The fix was in. Before the Senate Armed Services Committee, Admiral Moorer testified that Radford had handed him documents on two occasions, even though he hadn't directed Radford to purloin the documents and the purloined documents contained meaningless information.[9] The Senate Armed Services Committee called Kissinger as a witness, and he cleverly evaded stating whether or not he had been spied upon.[10] Moreover, he told the hearing that he and Moorer were swell pals, and Moorer concurred with Kissinger's various diplomatic endeavors.[11] The Undertaker gave both Moorer and Kissinger a clean bill of health.[12]

The following day, Radford testified that Admiral Robinson and Admiral Welander recruited him to pinch National Security Council secrets, and he implicated Haig in the spy ring, too.[13] The day after Radford testified, Admiral Welander demolished Radford's credibility and testified that Radford was solely responsible for the pilfering of National Security Council's documents.[14] Welander's statement to Ehrlichman that implicated Haig in the Moorer-Radford affair was not offered to the senators.[15]

The final witness to be called by the Senate Armed Services Committee hearing was a beacon of truth: Fred Buzhardt.[16] Buzhardt brought a copy of his reinterview of Welander to the hearing.[17] He testified that there was not a substantial difference between the interview he conducted of Welander and the interview Ehrlichman conducted of Welander.[18] Buzhardt didn't mention that Ehrlichman's interview pointed to Haig's culpability in the spy ring, and his reinterview absolved Haig of such a transgression.

The hearing then became slightly surreal. The Undertaker announced that he was in the midst of sensitive negotiations for both the Ehrlichman and Buzhardt interviews of Welander: He said the Senate Armed Services Committee had a 50-50 chance of landing both interviews.[19] As senators were leaving the hearing, one senator was dumfounded by the obvious cover-up: The disconcerted senator demanded that additional witnesses should be called, especially Ehrlichman.[20] The Undertaker detonated, demanding that Buzhardt not share his reinterview of Welander with the Senate Armed Services Committee.[21] The hearing may have ended with a bang, but additional witnesses were not called and neither interview was proffered to the Senate Armed Services Committee. Haig, Moorer, and Welander had walked scot-free from their treasonous scheme.[22] The Undertaker had delivered!

As the Undertaker was burying the Moorer-Radford affair, the next phase of Watergate was for the W.S.P.F. grand jury to return indictments against all the president's men. In early March of 1974, the W.S.P.F. charged Mitchell, Haldeman, Ehrlichman and four others with multiple indictments, including conspiracy, obstruction of justice, and perjury.[23] For the sake of simplification, I'll focus on the charges levied against Mitchell, Haldeman, and Ehrlichman:

- John Mitchell was charged with conspiracy, obstruction of justice, and perjury.[24] He was also charged with making false statements to the F.B.I. and grand jury.[25] He faced a maximum of 30 years in prison and $42,000 in fines.[26]

- H. R. Haldeman was charged with conspiracy, obstruction of justice, and perjury.[27] He faced a maximum of 25 years in prison and $16,000 in fines.[28]

- John Ehrlichman was charged with conspiracy, obstruction of justice, and making false statements to the F.B.I. and grand jury.[29] He faced a maximum of 25 years in prison and $40,000 in fines.[30]

The indictments were handed up to Sirica, and it was undoubtedly a joyous day for him: He was convinced that the Watergate burglars had acted on a higher authority than Liddy, and his convictions were en route to being a Holy Writ. But for Sirica's beliefs to be wholly sanctified, he and the W.S.P.F. prosecutors had to engage in a little skullduggery to ensure the indictments translated into guilty verdicts.

A February memo written by Jaworski, discussing a meeting with Sirica, detailed Sirica's desire to have the W.S.P.F. grand jury return indictments against all the president's men "as soon as possible."[31] Sirica was turning 70 years old in the middle of March, which meant that he would have to relinquish the position of D.C.'s chief judge and be precluded from assigning the "cover-up trial" to himself.[32] Jaworski and the W.S.P.F. grand jury acquiesced and delivered the indictments about two and half weeks before Sirica's 70th birthday, giving Sirica the authority to appoint himself as the judge in the cover-up trial.[33]

The W.S.P.F. prosecutors' two star witnesses against Mitchell et al. were Dean and Magruder. Magruder didn't particularly impress the W.S.P.F. prosecutors with his veracity.[34] As I mentioned in Chapter 14, Magruder was so terrified of a stint in prison that he recited multiple variations of his story in an effort to please the prosecutors. The W.S.P.F. prosecutors identified about four-dozen potential discrepancies in Magruder's numerous tales to various entities, including the grand jury and Watergate Committee.[35] In fact, Magruder's variations on his story were so contradictory that federal prosecutors reportedly debated whether or not they could, in good faith, call him as a witness.[36]

Dean also had a fluid story.[37] But Dean had proved to be a superlative witness before the Watergate Committee and, apparently, before the W.S.P.F. grand jury, so now he would be called on to be a superlative witness against Mitchell, Haldeman, and Ehrlichman. Although the W.S.P.F. and Sirica would grant Dean a sweetheart deal, Jaworski's predecessor, Archibald Cox, wasn't so gracious concerning Dean, because Cox reportedly said: "If everything else goes down the drain, the one thing I can cling to is Dean's venality."[38]

The W.S.P.F. grand jury concluded that the seven Watergate perps had participated in a criminal conspiracy.[39] In a criminal conspiracy case, at least one of the perps has made an "overt act" in furtherance of the conspiracy. An overt act, in the context of a criminal conspiracy, is an action that might be innocent by itself unless it is made in the furtherance of a crime. For example, phone calls are an innocent act, but if a phone call links two conspirators to a crime then that phone call is an overt act. When criminal conspiracies are prosecuted, overt acts are the web that connects the conspirators. The W.S.P.F. grand jury listed 45 overt acts that connected Nixon administration officials to the Watergate cover-up.[40] Some of the overt acts were firmly based in reality, but some of the overt acts were only part and parcel of the government's conspiracy theory.

The first overt act listed by the grand jury occurred on the day of the Watergate bust, when John Mitchell and Magruder were in Los Angeles on a C.R.P. fund-raising junket.[41] It stated that Mitchell told an aide to phone Liddy, and instruct him to approach the attorney general.[42] As per Mitchell's ostensible instructions, Liddy approached the attorney general and requested that he spring "one or more" of the Watergate burglars from the pokey.[43]

In Chapter 15, "The Burning Man," I discussed the reality of that chain of events. That overt act, like the official Watergate narrative, contravened the laws of physics: Liddy and a White House aide had their golf course rendezvous with Attorney General Kleindienst at 12:30 P.M. E.S.T.[44] But Mitchell's security log showed that Magruder and the Mitchell aide initially talked at 9:55 P.M. W.S.T. or 12:55 P.M. E.S.T.[45] Only time travel can account for that overt act.

Cunning is an apt description of "overt act nine," dated June 28, 1972, eleven days after the Watergate bust, when Dean conscripted Ehrlichman to use the president's personal attorney to raise hush money.[46] Dean testified before the Watergate Committee that Mitchell proposed Nixon's personal attorney raise hush money when they met in Mitchell's office on June 28, and Dean should discuss that contingency with Ehrlichman.[47]

Testifying before the Watergate Committee, Mitchell vigorously denied Dean's contention that he had endorsed using the president's personal attorney to raise funds for the burglars.[48] As I mentioned in Chapter 18, "Pay the Piper," Mitchell had an irrefutable alibi for contesting Dean's account of their meeting: Mitchell was in New York on that day, June 28, when Dean testified that they met in Mitchell's D.C. office. Even the *Washington Post* reported that Mitchell had been in New York that day.

The W.S.P.F. undoubtedly realized the flaw in its conspiracy theory, so "overt act nine" didn't name Mitchell, even though he was ostensibly the prime mover of hush money.[49]

A July 1974 memorandum written by a W.S.P.F. attorney addressed the quandary with Dean's story, and it also demonstrated that the ends justified the means for the W.S.P.F. "Our case will probably have to be based on the theory that Mitchell asked Dean on Saturday, June 24, to explore both the C.I.A. and Kalmbach [Nixon's personal attorney] possibilities; or that Mitchell's logs are incomplete."[50] The memorandum also conceded that Dean had "exercised somewhat more discretion himself to forge ahead with getting Kalmbach into the picture than he has admitted…"[51] At the cover-up trial, Dean testified that he spoke to Mitchell, via the telephone, from Mitchell's office![52]

Many of the overt acts and indictments were predicated on lies and outright absurdities: I've only discussed the claptrap involved in two overt acts: If I deconstructed every overt act and indictment, *The Truth About Watergate* would weigh in at an additional 200 pages. However, those two examples demonstrate that the W.S.P.F. was willing to contravene the Earth's space-time continuum and suborn perjury, too.

The W.S.P.F. prosecutors also had an ace up their collective sleeves: Sirica had inveigled himself to be the trial judge. The synergy between Sirica and the zeal of W.S.P.F. prosecutors generated a theater of the absurd. James Rosen, in *The Strong Man,* summed up Sirica's various absurdities and ineptitude at the cover-up trial: "At various points, he forgot to excuse a witness; forgot key dates in the case's chronology; permitted forms of cross-examination he later barred, without ever admitting error; proposed, unfathomably, that a witness be cross-examined outside the presence of the jury, then withdrew the idea; admitted he 'maybe' allowed the prosecution to pose leading questions to a witness on redirect examination, a flagrant violation of courtroom procedure; admitted he 'may' have improperly allowed the prosecution to make a closing argument to the jury during the questioning of a witness; admitted he 'probably' gave the prosecution 'too much latitude' in the questioning of a witness; admitted he couldn't always discern the speakers on the Nixon tapes, the trial's most important evidence; mocked Nixon from the bench; and he shrugged 'when you have a situation like we have, that has been highly publicized, you just can't have a perfect trial.'"[53]

Though Sirica was guilty of malfeasance, he was accurate on the latter point: Mitchell, Haldeman, and Ehrlichman could never have received a fair trial, regardless if the W.S.P.F. prosecutors had not suborned perjury and Sirica had ceased and desisted from his antics, because they had been so thoroughly enmeshed in the real and imagined crimes of Richard Nixon. They probably couldn't have received a fair trial in Timbuktu. On January 1, 1975, the jury pronounced Mitchell, Haldeman, and Ehrlichman guilty on all counts.[54]

When Dean pled guilty to one count of conspiring to obstruct justice, Sirica initially hammered him with a one- to four-year sentence.[55] Magruder also pled guilty to one count of conspiring to obstruct justice, and Sirica hammered him with a ten-month to four-year sentence.[56] Sirica's ploy with the harsh sentences levied against Dean and Magruder was designed to enhance their credibility, because the attorneys for Mitchell, Haldeman, and Ehrlichman couldn't argue that Dean and Magruder were testifying on behalf of the W.S.P.F. prosecutors due to their sweetheart deals.[57]

But after Dean and Magruder performed consummately for the W.S.P.F. prosecutors, Sirica reduced Dean's sentence to four months and Magruder's sentence to six months. The New York Times, apparently, didn't comprehend Sirica's ploy, because it lauded Sirica's "mercy."[58] The paper also published an article about how Dean and Magruder had "cleansed" themselves with the ablutions of truth.[59]

Though Mitchell, Haldeman, and Ehrlichman should have been indicted for the actual crimes they committed, the W.S.P.F. and Sirica perpetrated a great disservice to America. The W.S.P.F. and Sirica looked upon Nixon as the anti-Christ and weren't concerned with the truth: Their objective was to exact a pound of flesh, and their malfeasance deprived us of the truth about Watergate. When the ends justify the means, truth is invariably the first casualty.

EPILOGUE

Our present-day understanding of Watergate is embroidered with grand deceptions and fictions that are difficult to renounce, because we yearn to believe that Watergate was the byproduct of an incorruptible Fourth Estate and an unassailable democracy that expunged Nixon and his malignant ilk from government. Unfortunately, the incorruptible Fourth Estate was quite corrupt and the unassailable democracy was the fountainhead of numerous fabrications. The government conspiracy theory of Watergate repeatedly usurps the laws of physics, suborns perjury, and it is buttressed by the profuse lies of Woodward and Bernstein.

In "Revenge of the Key," I elucidated the extensive corroboration validating that the D.N.C. served as a conduit to Rikan's Columbia Plaza brothel. Indeed, a former assistant U.S. attorney was among those who corroborated the "call girl theory." As I stated earlier, the overwhelming evidence should force the "call girl theory" of Watergate as a "conspiracy theory" into mandatory retirement. Despite profuse proof of the "call girl theory," I acknowledge that divergent agendas were in play that obfuscate the actual motives for the break-ins. The motive of Liddy by means of Magruder was to collect D.N.C. intelligence and tap the D.N.C.'s chairman's phone. The motives of McCord, and probably Hunt, were to protect the Columbia Plaza brothel and damage the Nixon administration.

McCord tapping the phone in the usually vacant office used by Spencer Oliver and the D.N.C. secretaries, and burglar Martinez having a key to Maxie Wells' desk during the second break-in would seem to shine a light on the Columbia Plaza honey trap. But McCord's lies to Liddy about the incompatibility of the receiver and recorder, his strict control over the logs given to Liddy, and his lies to the Department of Justice helped to ensure that the Columbia Plaza brothel was unscathed throughout the Watergate investigation. And, unquestionably, federal prosecutors being ordered to "shut down" an investigation into the Columbia Plaza also significantly aided and abetted McCord's task of protecting Rikan et al.

Nixon attempted to quash the F.B.I.'s investigation into the C.R.P.'s Watergate-related money laundering by having the C.I.A. play its national security trump card. Though the C.I.A. Director Richard Helms initially acquiesced to Nixon, he ultimately double-crossed him, which unleashed the F.B.I. to conduct an unabated investigation. But the C.I.A.'s national security trump card seems to have been played in other facets of the Watergate saga. The Department of Justice was cognizant of the Columbia Plaza operation and an assistant U.S. attorney felt that blackmail was involved, but federal prosecutors were ordered to cease and desist their investigation. In addition to the Columbia Plaza, a second example of a honey trap, blackmail operation has emerged in the Watergate narrative: Russell tipped off a federal prosecutor to a honey trap/blackmail operation near Dupont Circle, replete with video cameras, targeting judges and other elite Washingtonians. Though an assistant U.S. attorney concluded that Russell was attempting to divert his attention from the Columbia Plaza, he, nevertheless found Russell's information about the Dupont Circle honey trap to be correct. However, the Justice Department again shut down the assistant U.S. attorney from pursuing that case. So, yet again, individuals affiliated with a honey trap had the capability to shut down a federal investigation.

I discussed the basement apartment in Chevy Chase, Maryland that was rented by McCord as a possible honey trap. In *Secret Agenda*, Jim Hougan speculated that the basement apartment was a blackmail operation, because it was furbished with extensive bugging equipment and "young girls" recurrently visited the apartment. And McCord's former landlady also identified E. Howard Hunt as a visitor.

I also examined McCord's employment by murky milieus within the C.I.A.'s Office of Security. In *Secret Agenda*, Jim Hougan reported on the dirty deeds perpetrated by the shadowy enclaves of the Office of Security, which included domestic blackmail. A Washington, D.C. police captain who helmed the D.C. police's "sex squad" was a profuse fountainhead of prurient dirt on all and sundry in the capital for both the C.I.A. and F.B.I. The captain, via confiscated "trick books," had the names and sexual preferences of the prostitutes' clients, who included congressmen, diplomats, judges, and spooks.

J. Edgar Hoover's propensity for blackmail over decades emerged only after his death. Politicians who had become blackmail fodder for Hoover had zero motivation to speak out about their compromised status, especially if Hoover had pictures of their incriminating or extramarital sexual conduct. Blackmail pictures disseminated publicly would mark the demise of their careers, devastate their families, and reduce their lives to public ignominy. Thus, the F.B.I. and C.I.A. have the ability to blackmail politicians and powerbrokers with impunity. The C.I.A. began with a mandate to collect and collate information, but it also seems to be in the business of collecting and collating people.

The Nixon administration was also willing to deploy blackmail in order to nullify a Watergate investigation. The conversation among Nixon, Haldeman, and Dean involved Dean mentioning that the Speaker of the House was marshaling forces to have the House's Banking and Currency Committee commence a Watergate investigation. Haldeman then said that the Speaker of House would be vulnerable to being leveraged due to his excessive drinking and scrapes with law enforcement.

After Haldeman said the Speaker of the House was ripe for blackmail, Dean chimed in and told Nixon and Haldeman that he was scrutinizing campaign finance reports to discover the congressmen on the House's Banking and Currency Committee who were guilty of violating campaign finance laws. This last example of prospective political blackmail demonstrates that our politicians are prone to blackmail from various angles that are divorced from a runaway libido and sexcapades.

The hawks in the military and in the C.I.A. infiltrated the Nixon administration, and it was ultimately the C.I.A.'s James McCord who acted as the catalyst to trigger the avalanche that engulfed and then overwhelmed Nixon. The grand irony of the silent coup of 1974 is that the history books praise it as a shining example of American democracy, even though the C.I.A. has been extremely inimical towards democracy at home and abroad.

Domestically, the C.I.A. has infiltrated African-American and antiwar groups, illegally opened Americans' mail, committed domestic spying operations, and perpetrated sadistic mind control programs, shredding the Constitutional rights of untold Americans.[1] The Agency has also toppled numerous *democracies* abroad or clandestinely manipulated their elections: Iran,[2] Italy,[3] Guatemala,[4] Ecuador,[5] Chile,[6] Brazil,[7] El Salvador,[8] etc. are countries that have been subjected to C.I.A.-sponsored coups or C.I.A.-manipulated elections. The C.I.A. has also supported and/or colluded with homicidal and even genocidal dictators in the Congo,[9,10] Chile,[11,12] Peru,[13,14] Panama,[15,16] Haiti,[17,18] Iraq,[19] Indonesia,[20] etc.

The countries and dictators I've listed are not exhaustive of the C.I.A.'s interventions or its cronyism with murderers. Indonesia, for example, epitomizes the C.I.A.'s nadir of malevolence and the bloodlust of its dictators of choice. In Indonesia, the C.I.A.-supported General Suharto murdered more than 500,000 Indonesians and tortured at least 750,000 before or after imprisoning them in concentration camps.[21] In fact, U.S. diplomats and C.I.A. officials supplied the bloodthirsty Suharto with the names of 5,000 alleged Communists who became slated for extermination.[22] Democracy isn't an overriding priority of genocidal dictators – or the hawks in the C.I.A.

Journalism's two superstars – Woodward and Bernstein – are superstar charlatans. In the prior chapter, I discussed a Woodward and Bernstein article exonerating Haig from the top-secret document pilfering that was integral to the Moorer-Radford affair. After absolving Haig and the Joint Chiefs, they pinned the larceny exclusively on lowly yeoman Radford and wrote that Radford delivered insignificant documentation to unnamed individuals at the Pentagon. As I have mentioned, Woodward conveniently neglected to mention his former affiliation with Moorer, Haig, and Welander.

After Woodward and Bernstein exonerated Haig from the Moorer-Radford affair, their three respective fates would continue to be inextricably intertwined, even though Haig and Woodward deployed deception and grand theatrics to perpetuate the extravagant farce of disavowing their prior connection. When Gerald Ford replaced Nixon as president, Haig was eventually bumped up to Supreme Commander of the North Atlantic Treaty Organization (N.A.T.O.) and headquartered in Brussels, Belgium.[23] When Haig was in Brussels, Woodward flew to Belgium and attempted to interview Haig, but he was unceremoniously spurned.[24] Haig's rebuff ostensibly served as absolute proof that Haig and Woodward were never in cahoots.

But before Woodward and Haig's faux impasse, Woodward, Bernstein, and Haig had a clandestine conclave at Haig's D.C. home on the night of September 10, 1974 – about a month after Nixon's resignation.[25] Haig was on the homestretch of serving as President Gerald Ford's chief-of-staff, and he greeted Woodward and Bernstein in a tuxedo, because he had attended a formal dinner at the British Embassy that night.[26] The conclave of those three beacons of veracity lasted 80 minutes and ended shortly before 1:00 A.M.[27]

Woodward and Bernstein had jockeyed *All the President's Men* to fame and fortune, but now they needed an encore to perpetuate their newfound status as journalism's rock stars. As Haig held court, in his tuxedo, chain-smoking Marlboro Lights, he generously presented Woodward and Bernstein with their encore to *All the President's Men*.[28] Haig nourished his lapdogs with the premise for *The Final Days:* A commander-in-chief freefalling in an abyss of madness who had the potential to trigger nuclear Armageddon – until super-hero Alexander Haig intervened and saved humanity.[29]

Haig also imparted a structural scaffolding for *The Final Days:* He told Woodward and Bernstein that their encore shouldn't focus a magnifying glass on the "last days" of the Nixon administration, but, rather, on the "last 15 months" of the Nixon presidency, which just happened to be in sync with Haig's tenure as Nixon's chief-of-staff.[30] Haig conveyed to his lapdogs that he had "extensive notes" that would help them to "reconstruct everything."[31]

If the reader harbors reservations about Haig ushering Nixon's presidency down the primrose path to ruin, Woodward's notes from that night should erase such doubts: Haig knew "from the beginning … the inevitability of Nixon's leaving office prematurely."[32] After publication of *The Final Days,* the thoughtful Haig sent Nixon a telegram from Brussels: "I do not have a copy of the book but I want to reassure you that I have not contributed in any way to the book … [33]

The Final Days was a runaway best seller for Woodward and Bernstein, but both experienced existential misfires in the Land of Milk and Honey. Bernstein resigned from the *Washington Post* in January of 1977.[34] In September of 1977, *Rolling Stone* published a twelve-thousand-word article penned by Bernstein – "The C.I.A. and the Media" – elucidating the C.I.A.'s extensive infiltration of the American media.[35] Bernstein's choice of subject matter for his first offering after leaving the *Washington Post* was noteworthy.

The *Rolling Stone* article was a searing indictment of the media's collusion with the C.I.A., but, alas, it was written by Bernstein, so its unconditional authenticity is, of course, suspect. However, *Washington Post* executive editor Ben Bradlee, who brazenly lied about his C.I.A. affiliation, wasn't fond of Bernstein's *Rolling Stone* article.[36] So, perhaps, Bernstein's article about the C.I.A.'s infiltration of the media had swaths of veracity? After the *Rolling Stone* article, Bernstein's prolificacy floundered, and he was hemorrhaging his newfound wealth.[37] But his post-Watergate fame and momentum allowed a 1979 segue to become ABC television's Washington, D.C. news bureau chief.[38]

Bernstein's tenure at ABC was troubled. In addition to his excessive libidinal appetites, his substance abuse also came to the fore.[39] Bernstein found himself demoted at ABC from a bureau chief to a plebian reporter.[40] A network correspondent described Bernstein's abysmal ABC performance: "I gotta tell you, at ABC, he was just a terrible screw-up. It's awful to say it. It was awful to watch it."[41] Indeed, the long-time reigning president of ABC news confessed that hiring Bernstein was the "biggest mistake of my television career."[42] Life in the fast lane had taken its toll on Bernstein, and in 1983 he skidded into hospitalization for depression, exhaustion, and severe migraine headaches.[43]

Woodward, too, wasn't immune from post-Watergate scandal. After his Watergate celebrity, he was bumped up to assistant managing editor of the Post's Metro section and thought to be the heir apparent to executive editor Ben Bradlee.[44] But Woodward developed an autocratic reputation as an assistant managing editor of the Metro section.[45] A Yale history professor described Woodward's conservative bent as "crypto-fascist" and autocrats are highly susceptible to major gaffes, because they're reluctant or unwilling to solicit advice or suggestions.

Woodward made a spectacular gaffe in 1980. A reporter for the Post's District Weekly wrote an article about the plight of an eight-year-old heroin addict – "Jimmy's World."[46] The illustrious Washington Post didn't vet the reporter's résumé, which was riddled with fabrications, and "Jimmy's World" just happened to be a fantastic fabrication, too.[47] But Woodward loved the story, and he promoted the prevaricating reporter from the District Weekly section of the Post to the Metro section, and she became one of his acolytes.[48]

Though "Jimmy's World" received a strong gale of incredulity from various editors at the Post, Woodward ascribed their incredulity to "professional jealousy."[49] D.C. Mayor Marion Barry mobilized the police force, and sunk thousands of man-hours into searching for the eight-year-old heroin addict, and he, too, became incredulous of the story when Jimmy was nowhere to be found.[50]

Despite rampant incredulity, Woodward backed "Jimmy's World" for a Pulitzer Prize for local reporting, and, lo and behold, the prevaricating reporter joined the rarified ranks of Pulitzer Prize recipients.[51] But "Jimmy's World" proved to be a work of fiction, and its progenitor was exposed as a fraud.[52] The Pulitzer Prize was relinquished.[53]

In addition to "Jimmy's World," Woodward has produced various gaffes over the years that might have impeded the careers of run-of-the-mill journalists. He wrote a book about the life and death of John Belushi – Wired – but he was less than forthcoming about his motives as he preyed on Judy Belushi, John Belushi's widow. Judy Belushi was appalled by a *Chicago Tribune* magazine article that reported on her late husband's affinity for heroin and cocaine and the macabre condition of his cadaver, and she made the grave mistake of trusting that Woodward would revive her late husband's legacy.[54] Both John Belushi and Woodward were from Wheaton, Illinois, and Woodward professed his admiration for Belushi.[55]

Woodward initially said that he intended to write a book about Belushi's life but Belushi's widow nixed that idea, because she had planned to write a book about her deceased husband.[56] With the belief that Woodward was embarking on a series of articles about John Belushi, his wife arranged for him to access Belushi's cloistered and apprehensive celebrity friends, and she also granted him 21 interviews.[57] Woodward stressed to Judy Belushi that she could trust him, but, unbeknownst to her, he had signed a book deal with Simon and Schuster, which gave him the considerable advance of $600,000 for a book on Belushi that was to include photographs.[58]

In January of 1984, *People* magazine announced *Wired* to the world.[59] Shocked, Judy Belushi phoned Woodward, and he confessed that the newspaper series had morphed into a book.[60] She had intense disdain for the title, too, because it implied that Belushi's life was being distilled into a rather unflattering state.[61] At a meeting in New York City, Woodward told Judy Belushi that *Wired* was merely a working title. But Belushi's widow had arrived at a tipping point with Woodward's duplicity: she requested that Woodward return the photographs she had given to him.[62]

Belushi's widow received a letter from Woodward on the *Post's* letterhead, and the letter contained the requested photographs.[63] The letter, however, stated that the photos were being included in the book.[64] Belushi's widow sued Woodward and Simon and Schuster for $100,000 and also sought an injunction against distribution of the book.[65] But the injunction wasn't granted.[66] Judy Belushi settled with Simon and Schuster for $35,000, and the publisher excised the photographs from subsequent editions of the book.[67] Unfortunately, Judy Belushi's lawsuit became a fantastic promotional vehicle for *Wired*.[68]

I could comment further on Woodward's shameful exploits, but they would be merely redundant variations on the meme. Though Woodward has been largely unscathed for being an ethical eunuch, the publisher of the *Washington Post* ultimately realized that Ben Bradlee's heir apparent wasn't Ben Bradlee's heir apparent.[69] He took Woodward to dinner and told him he wouldn't inherit the executive editorship of the *Post*.[70] Woodward is now an associate editor of the *Post*.

The silent coup of 1974, abetted by Haig and Woodward, delivered the U.S. presidency to Vice President Gerald Ford. Haig served briefly as President Ford's chief-of-staff before Ford appointed Donald Rumsfeld to replace him.[71] Rumsfeld then chose Dick Cheney to be his principal aide.[72] Rumsfeld ultimately soared to Secretary of Defense under Ford, and Cheney became Ford's deputy chief-of-staff.[73] Bob Woodward and the *Washington Post* had enabled the neocons to have their first considerable taste of power: The hawks had triumphed over Nixon's détente with the Soviets and China.

Woodward also came to the rescue of Haig after Haig had been nominated to be President Ronald Reagan's secretary of state: The Senate's Foreign Relations Committee subpoenaed the logs of Nixon's meetings with Haig in an effort to determine if the Nixon tapes implicated Haig in malfeasance when he was Nixon's chief-of-staff.[74] With the imprimatur of the *Washington Post,* Woodward wrote a screed strongly criticizing the Foreign Relations Committee for attempting to subpoena the logs of Nixon's tapes.[75] Woodward, in part, argued that Haig shouldn't be held accountable for his remarks on the tapes, because they were made in an effort to placate Nixon.[76] Astonishingly, Nixon continued to think that Haig was a swell guy, and he refused to surrender the logs.[77] The Senate ultimately confirmed Haig as Secretary of State by a resounding margin – 93 to 6.[78]

Watergate propelled Woodward to superstar status, and his name is synonymous with the "left" toppling Nixon. Since Watergate, however, his reporting has promoted the beliefs of the government's militaristic hawks. Woodward acted as an apologist for the lies of the Bush II administration about Iraq's weapons of mass destruction, which resulted in the tragic Iraq invasion: He wrote that C.I.A. Director George Tenet told Bush II that finding weapons of mass destruction was a "slam dunk."[79] Woodward's superlative vantage point to push the Iraq War to liberals served the neocons extremely well as they were revving up their war machine.

Like Woodward, Dean has had an interesting run since Watergate. Earlier, I cited a *New York Times* article reporting that Dean had been "cleansed" by the ablutions of truth. But Dean has had a tenuous relationship with Mr. Clean, because *Silent Coup* tarnished him: *Silent Coup* depicted Dean as the prime mover in the Watergate break-ins and subsequent cover-up, and it also discussed Maureen Dean's connection to Heidi Rikan. Dean and Mo unleashed a $150 million libel lawsuit against the publisher of *Silent Coup,* St. Martin's Press, the authors of *Silent Coup,* and G. Gordon Liddy.[80] The lawsuit claimed that St. Martin's Press et al.

sought to "impute Maureen with improper, immoral and criminal conduct" by conveying that she was "an associate, member or intimate of a call girl ring" serving the Democratic National Committee.[81]

The discovery in the case would prove to be problematic for Dean, whose autobiographical *Blind Ambition* contradicted his Senate testimony and his W.S.P.F. cover-up trial testimony.[82] Dean, however, had a plausible excuse for the contradictions: His ghostwriter fabricated passages of the book![83] Dean testified in a deposition that his ghostwriter, a Pulitzer Prize-winning historian, fabricated sections of the book "out of whole cloth."[84]

But Dean's ghostwriter begged to differ: He said that Dean approved everything in *Blind Ambition*, which was written when he lived in Dean's home.[85] "Every morning we would do tapings and discussions and I would draft all day and he would read what I would write," said the ghostwriter. "The collaboration was intense. Very intense."[86] Perhaps Dean was having memory difficulties again and forgot about the "intense" collaboration?

The libel lawsuit against St. Martin's wended for years before the Deans and St. Martin's came to an out-of-court settlement in 1997.[87] The terms of the lawsuit were confidential, but both litigants asserted a triumph.[88] Dean said, "We're satisfied."[89] When questioned about the financial facets of the settlement, St. Martin's attorney responded: "I didn't say any dollars were paid."[90] St. Martin's did not retract a single word of *Silent Coup*, but the publisher relinquished the rights of *Silent Coup* to its authors.[91,92]

Unlike St. Martin's Press, the Deans would find that *Silent Coup* author Len Colodny wasn't compatible with a settlement. Colodny and his attorney filed a motion for a summary judgment against the Deans' lawsuit.[93] If granted, a motion for a summary judgment confirms that the opposing party's claim or claims are without merit. Colodny and his attorney were quite serious about seeking a summary judgment: Their motion included "4,000 pages of transcripts, interviews, and other evidence backing up" *Silent Coup*.[94] After the Deans' attorneys promised a point-by-point rebuttal to the motion but never delivered on it, the lawsuit became slightly surreal.[95] State Farm, Colodny's personal liability insurance carrier, ultimately elected to remunerate Colodny with $410,000 if he dismissed his motion for a summary judgment against Dean.[96] State Farm also remunerated the Deans with an undisclosed amount.[97] According to Colodny, the U.S. District Court judge overseeing the case ruled that Dean could not sue Colodny for libel if Colodny republished *Silent Coup*.[98]

Dean may have been once more plagued by memory problems prior to inking the settlement with Colodny: Less than a week before the settlement, he boldly told a Fox News' reporter that he "can't wait to go to court" and "unpeel the story publicly for the first time."[99] Following the settlement, the Deans' attorney declared with bravado that if Colodny republished *Silent Coup,* "we'd sue him" again for defamatory statements.[100] Colodny has since republished *Silent Coup,* and Dean hasn't sued him.[101] Despite Dean's sound and fury, he sidestepped the courtroom to adjudicate the lawsuits he initiated.

And, alas, Dean would eventually withdraw his lawsuit against G. Gordon Liddy, but the backstory of his retraction is quite interesting.[102] Liddy salivated at the thought of a courtroom showdown with Dean. In fact, the opportunity of finally cornering Dean in a courtroom may have stimulated his salivary glands far more than a rotisserie Wister rat basted with butter. Liddy goaded Dean by publicly and repeatedly declaring that Mo had been a prostitute.[103] Though Dean evaded facing Liddy in a courtroom, his legal team encouraged former D.N.C. secretary Maxie Wells to sue Liddy for libel: Liddy had publicly stated that the Watergate burglars were searching Wells' desk for a package of call-girl photos that were used to arrange dalliances, and the package contained a photo of Mo.[104,105]

Wells had become a community college teacher in Louisiana, and her libel lawsuit sought to bleed Liddy for $5.1 million.[106,107] In 2001, Liddy and Maxie Wells faced off in a U.S. district courtroom in Baltimore. Wells projected the persona of a naïve girl who played the organ in a Baton Rouge, Louisiana church before relocating to Washington, D.C.: She asserted that Liddy's comments about her desk being the repository for the pictures of prostitutes were slanderous and impeded her pursuit of a doctorate in English literature.[108] In Wells' courtroom showdown against Liddy, she testified that her desk merely contained "office supplies, hand lotion, and reports in progress."[109] If Wells' kept those items under lock and key, she must have considered them to be of great value!

Dean was scheduled to testify at the trial, but Wells' attorney withdrew his name as a witness.[110] Dean finally had a chance to defend his wife's honor in a court of law, but he offered the following explanation for not testifying at the trial: 'I'd like to testify and I'd love to have the jury see all the evidence that shows the falsity of Gordon Liddy's claim. But this case isn't Liddy vs. John Dean."[111]

In closing arguments, Liddy's lawyer said that Dean was behind the defamation lawsuit, because he sought to squelch the idea that he masterminded the Watergate break-in.[112] Liddy's attorney also asserted that Dean was "using the judicial process to enforce his own official story of

Watergate, a story he created in 1973."[113] After a three-week trial, the jury deadlocked in Liddy's favor at 7 to 2.[114] When the jury announced to the judge that it was hopelessly deadlocked, he declared a mistrial and dismissed the case.[115] Liddy proclaimed: "John Dean has just had a stake pounded through his heart, and I pounded it in there."[116]

After the trial, the *Washington Post* published an editorial diatribe that was aimed at the fallibility of judicial proceedings and also freethinking.[117] The editorial stated that the jury sided with Liddy "in spite of the fact that Mr. Liddy relies, for his theory, on a disbarred attorney with a history of mental illness."[118] In the last paragraph of the editorial, the *Post* diatribe stated the hazards of such a verdict: "The danger of such outcomes as this one is that this sort of thinking spreads."[119] We certainly don't want freethinking to spread! The *Washington Post's* motto is "Democracy Dies in Darkness." Democracy also dies when a newspaper's executive editor and its two star reporters are serial liars.

Wells appealed the judge's decision, and an appellate court granted a *Wells v. Liddy* sequel.[120] So, in 2002, Wells and Liddy locked horns once more. In the second trial, the jurors deliberated a mere four hours before returning a unanimous verdict for Liddy.[121] Liddy had scored a resounding knockout over Dean's surrogate.

Since 2008, various books have been published that implicate Dean as integral to the Watergate burglary.[122,123,124,125] Dean threatens lawsuits, but the levy of lies is finally crumbling. Dean threatened to sue author James Rosen whose *The Strong Man,* published by Doubleday, implicated Dean as the prime mover of the Watergate break-ins, but Rosen didn't seem too concerned about the bite of a paper tiger: "Dean himself is well aware that his historical reputation has suffered enormously in the last two decades, and so he resorts to frivolous litigation and bullying tactics to rehabilitate himself," said Rosen. "Not since Albert Speer [a Nazi minister convicted at the Nuremberg Trials] has a historical figure so assiduously used his post-prison writings to muddy and distort the historical record of the events in which he was culpable."[126]

Contrary to Liddy, I believe that Mo wasn't a prostitute in Heidi Rikan's stable if the chronologies in her book, *Mo: A Woman's View of Watergate* and *Blind Ambition* are correct. According to Mo and Dean, she moved in with Dean in January of 1971, when she relocated from Los Angeles to D.C.[127] And after six weeks in D.C., she landed a job at the Bureau of Narcotics and Dangerous Drugs, and then the National Commission on Marijuana and Drug Abuse employed her.[128]

If Mo's chronology is accurate, she was living with Dean after she relocated to D.C., and shortly thereafter the federal government employed her, so it doesn't square that she would need to be a prostitute to support herself. However, a *Washington Post* article reported that Mo met Dean when she was working for the "National Committee [sic] on Marijuana and Drug Abuse."[129] If the *Washington Post* is correct about Mo meeting Dean when she was working for the government, then her chronology collapses.

And, finally, I feel compelled to have a pithy discussion about Nixon: The *Washington Post* published a 1996 article on Nixon, "Our Last Liberal President," written by celebrated journalist Mark Shields.[130] Shields noted that Nixon championed a guaranteed minimal family income of $5,500 for every family with children.[131] Nixon's comprehensive welfare reform also mandated free job training for parents and free childcare for their children. Nixon sought to underwrite his welfare reform by spending 131 percent more on the poor.

Congress ultimately discarded Nixon's plan, because it allocated less capital to affluent states.[132] "We reject that argument because we are one country," said Nixon. "Consider the name of this nation: the United States of America. We establish minimum national standards because we are united. We encourage local supplements because we are a federation of states. And we care for the unfortunate because this is America."[133]

Nixon also made a national healthcare plan his number one domestic priority.[134] Under the plan, Americans' employers would be required to offer healthcare insurance to employees that included dental care, mental health, and freedom of choice regarding doctors and hospitals.[135] The plan also called for Medicare to be expanded, so the poor would be the recipients of the same benefits, but Congress discarded the Nixon healthcare plan.[136]

The Nixon administration increased spending on education by more than 50 percent.[137] Nixon also created the Occupational Safety and Health Administration to ensure safer workplaces for Americans.[138] And the Environmental Protection Agency was established during the Nixon administration.[139] Nixon's attempted alterations to the welfare system and his sweeping changes in education allocations, workplace safety, and environmental protection are the reasons Mark Shields deemed him the "last liberal American president."[140]

When it came to foreign policy, Nixon had a split personality. He ardently attempted to forge peace with the Red Menace, and he sought to reduce the nuclear arsenals of both the U.S. and the U.S.SR. He also extracted America from the bloody quagmire in Vietnam that killed more than 58,000 Americans and between two and three million Vietnamese.[141] Nixon, however, sowed untold carnage in Vietnam, because of his recurrent bombing of North Vietnam.[142] During his watch, 20,000 Americans also perished in Vietnam.[143] Nixon's carpet-bombing of neutral Cambodia to eradicate North Vietnamese sanctuaries yielded Cambodian food shortages and a tsunami of Cambodian refugees, which enabled the genocidal Khmer Rouge to flourish.[144] In addition to having the bloodlust of the Khmer Rouge dripping from his hands, Nixon buttressed genocidal dictators like General Suharto and Augusto Pinochet.[145,146]

Nixon's split personality on foreign policy included making significant yearly cuts to defense spending: In 1968, defense spending accounted for 46 percent of U.S. government outlays and by 1974 defense spending had diminished to 29.5 percent of government outlays.[147] So, in addition to cutting out the hawks from his principal geopolitical moves, Nixon incrementally cut defense spending by a hefty 64 percent.

In 2022, national defense outlays for the U.S. are estimated to be about $877 billion.[148] The United States accounted for about 39 percent of the world's military expenditures in 2018, and China was a distant second at about 13 percent.[149] Russia, India, Saudi Arabia, and the United Kingdom respectively ranked third, fourth, fifth, and sixth vis-à-vis the percentages of the world's military expenditures at 3.9 percent, 3.6 percent, 3.3 percent, and 3.1 percent.[150]

"The War on Terror" has the ring of a Madison Avenue jingle, and it's plunged America into a nearly two-decade conflict. The hawks have gorged themselves since the onset of the War on Terror and the U.S. has been the Earth's preeminent Merchant of Death: Between 2018 to 2022, the U.S. accounted for 40 percent of the world's market share of armaments.[151] Though I believe that Nixon should've been arrested for treason when he tampered with the Paris Peace Accords prior to the 1968 election, negating his presidency, I have also come to believe that a U.S. president who sought peace at the expense of the military-industrial complex would be a welcome novelty.

≠≠≠

Endnotes

Prologue

1. Mark Silk, "Before the Scandal Broke," *Smithsonian,* November 2016, p. 32.

2. Ibid.

3. Ibid.

4. Ibid.

5. Ian Urbina, "Arrest Near in 2001 Killing of Intern, Authorities Say," *New York Times,* Feb 22, 2009, Late Edition, p. 16.

6. Michael D. Shear, "Race in Va.'s 2nd District Turns Fierce," *Washington Post,* October 29, 2004, B7.

7. Emily Langer, "Steven LaTourette, Ohio Republican with an Independent Streak, Dies; He Served Nine Terms in Congress Before Stepping Down in 2012, Citing Rancorous Partisanship," *Washington Post,* August 4, 2016, https://www.washingtonpost.com/politics/steven-latourette-ohio-republican-with-an-independent-streak-dies/2016/08/04/864e20ca-5a35-11e6-831d-0324760ca856_story.html?utm_term=.9d18712b5650. Accessed September 4, 2019.

8. "Arnie Ally Ducks Film Awards," *New York Post,* October 1, 2004, p. 12.

9. Kimberly Hefling, "Congressman Sherwood Settles Suit Filed by Mistress, Lawyer Says," Associated Press State and Local Wire, BC Cycle, November 8, 2005.

10. Abby Goodnough and Kate Zernike, "A Complex and Hidden Life Behind Ex-Representative's Public Persona," *New York Times,* Late Edition, October 5, 2006, p. A27.

11. Campbell Robertson, "In Louisiana, Tainted Senator Rides Anti-Obama Sentiment," *New York Times,* September 11, 2009, Late Edition, p. A1.

12. Adam Cohen, "Editorial Observer: Larry Craig's Great Adventure: Suddenly, He's a Civil Libertarian," *New York Times,* September 24, 2007, Late Edition, p. A22.

13. Ian Urbina, "Sex Scandal Shakes Race for Congress in Florida," *New York Times,* October 14, 2008, Late Edition, p. A12.

14. Alan Feuer, "From a Bright Past to a Cloudy Future: D.W.I. Arrest, a Secret Child. So What's Next for Fossella?" *New York Times,* May 10, 2008, Late Edition, p. B1.

15. Kim Severson, "Candidate, Philanderer and Juggler, Too: Edwards Trial Shows Deception's Strains," *New York Times,* May 21, 2012, Late Edition, p. A12.

16. "The Ensign Investigation, to be Continued," *New York Times,* May 14, 2011, Late Edition, p. A18.

17. Maureen Dowd, "Pharisees on the Potomac," *New York Times,* July 19, 2009, Late Edition, p. WK11.

18. Gail Collins, "Sex Scandals to Learn By," *New York Times,* March 18, 2010, Late Edition, p. A31.

19. Carl Hulse, "Citing Affair, Republican Gives Up House Seat," *New York Times,* May 19, 2010, Late Edition, p. A14.

20. Susan Milligan, "Shirtless Christopher Lee Shows More Class than Other Scandal Pols," *US News and World Report,* February 10, 2011, https://www.usnews.com/opinion/blogs/susan-milligan/2011/02/10/shirtless-christopher-lee-shows-more-class-than-other-scandal-pols. Accessed September 4, 2019.

21. Benjamin Weiser, "Anthony Weiner Gets 21 Months in Prison for Sexting with Teenager," *New York Times,* September 25, 2017, https://www.nytimes.com/2017/09/25/nyregion/anthony-weiner-sentencing-prison-sexting-teenager.html. Accessed September 4, 2019.

22. Campbell Robertson, "Politicians are Slowed by Scandal, but Many Still Win the Race," *New York Times,* July 18, 2013, Late Edition, p. A11.

23. Katherine Seelye, "Oregon Congressman Named in Sex Case, Says He'll Resign," *New York Times,* July 27, 2011, Late Edition, p. A11.

24. Jonathan Weisman, "Despite Ethics Pledge, Response by G.O.P. Varies," *New York Times,* April 29, 2014, Late Edition, p. A18.

25. Emily Cochrane, "Texas Congressman Who Settled Harassment Case with Taxpayer Funds Resigns," *New York Times,* April 6, 2018, https://www.nytimes.com/2018/04/06/us/politics/farenthold-harassment-case-resigns.html. Accessed September 4, 2019.

26. Michael D. Shear and Michael S. Schmidt, "Hastert Payouts Said to be Linked to Sexual Abuse," *New York Times,* May 30, 2015, Final Edition, p. A1.

27. Emily Cochrane, "G.O.P. Congressman to Retire After Reports He Asked Woman to Have Abortion," *New York Times,*

October 4, 2017. https://www.nytimes.com/2017/10/04/us/politics/representative-tim-murphy-retire-abortion.html. Accessed September 4, 2019.

28. Sheryl Gay Stolberg, Yamiche Alcindor and Nicholas Fandos, "Al Franken to Resign From Senate Amid Harassment Allegations," *New York Times,* December 7, 2017, https://www.nytimes.com/2017/12/07/us/politics/al-franken-senate-sexual-harassment.html. Accessed September 4, 2019.

29. Nicholas Fandos and Jonathan Martin, "Congressman Caught in Storm Over Explicit Photo," *New York Times,* November 23, 2017, Late Edition, p. A20.

30. Nicholas Fandos, "House Republican Trent Franks Resigns Amid Harassment Investigation," *New York Times,* Dec. 7, 2017, https://www.nytimes.com/2017/12/07/us/politics/trent-franks-house-member-resigns.html. Accessed September 4, 2019.

31. Michael S. Schmidt, et al., "Gaetz Said to Face U.S. Inquiry Over Sex with an Underage Girl." *New York Times,* March 31, 2021, Late Edition, p. A1.

32. Sheryl Gay Stolberg, "First-Term Democrat, Rising Star in House, Denies Relationship with an Aide." *New York Times,* October 23, 2019, Late Edition, p. A19.

33. Gabriel Trip and Isabella Grullon Paz, "North Carolina Survey Gives Democrats Edge," *New York Times,* Oct. 30, 2020, Late Edition, p. A22.

34. Yamiche Alcindor, "John Conyers to Leave Congress Amid Harassment Claims," *New York Times,* December 5, 2017, https://www.nytimes.com/2017/12/05/us/politics/john-conyers-election.html. Accessed September 4, 2019.

35. Thomas Kaplan, "Pennsylvania Congressman Who Settled Harassment Case Resigns Amid Ethics Inquiry," *New York Times,* April 27, 2018, https://www.nytimes.com/2018/04/27/us/politics/pennsylvania-congressman-meehan-resigns.html. Accessed September 4, 2019.

36. John Miller, "Idaho Senator Quits Amid Sex Scandal," *Sunday Gazette-Mail,* September 2, 2007, p. 1A.

37. Henry Vinson with Nick Bryant, *Confessions of a D.C. Madam: The Politics of Sex, Lies, and Blackmail,* (Walterville: Trineday, 2014), p. 79.

38. "Senator, Arrested in an Airport Bathroom, Pleads Guilty," *New York Times,* August 28, 2007, Late Edition, p. A19.

39. Carl Hulse, "Once-Calming Leader and a Stunning Turn," *New York Times,* May 30, 2015, Late Edition, p. A11.

40. Ibid.

41. Julie Phillips, Dave Bosman, "Woman Says Her Brother was Victim of Hastert: Sex Abuse Hidden For Years, She Adds," *New York Times,* June 6, 2015, Late Edition, p. A10.

42. Phillip Giraldi, "Did Foreign Governments Blackmail Denny Hastert?" *The American Conservative,* October 20, 2015, https://www.theamericanconservative.com/articles/how-a-plea-deal-for-hastert-may-hide-the-truth. Accessed September 4, 2019.

43. Jeff Zeleny, "Report Finds Negligence in Foley Case: Ethics Inquiry Faults Republicans," but Cites No Rule Violations" *New York Times,* December 9, 2006, Late Edition, p. A14.

44. Giraldi, "Did Foreign Governments Blackmail Denny Hastert?" (Sibel Edwards was the name of the F.B.I. whistleblower.)

45. Walter Goodman, "Revelations about J. Edgar Hoover," *New York Times,* February 9, 1993, Late Edition, p. C16.

Chapter One

1. Roger Morris, *Richard Milhous Nixon: The Rise of an American Politician,* (New York: Henry Holt and Company, 1990), pp. 40-41.

2. Ibid., p. 65.

3. Ibid., pp. 65-66.

4. Ibid., p. 66.

5. Ibid., p. 67.

6. Ibid., p. 98.

7. Ibid., pp. 98-99.

8. Ibid., p. 65.

9. Ibid., pp. 83-84.

10. Ibid., pp. 146-147.

11. Ibid., p. 140.

12. Ibid., p. 110.

13. Ibid.

14. Ibid., pp. 110-111.

15. Ibid., p. 111.

16. Ibid., p. 118.

17. Ibid., p. 125.

18. Ibid., p. 131.

19. Ibid., p. 156.

20. Ibid., p. 160.

21. Ibid., p. 140.

22. Ibid., p. 141.

23. Ibid., p. 163.

24. Ibid., p.178.

25. Ibid., p. 181.

26. Ibid., pp. 179-181.

27. Ibid., p. 187.

28. Ibid., p. 194.

29. Ibid., p. 200.

30. Ibid., p. 218.

31. Ibid., pp. 209-211.

32. Ibid., pp. 220-221.

33. Ibid., p. 220.

34 Ibid., p. 227.

35 Ibid., p. 242.

36 Ibid., p. 247.

37 Ibid., p. 271.

38 Ibid., p. 259. (Horace Voorhis was the ten-term incumbent).

39. Ibid., p. 284.

40 Ibid., p. 340.

41. Robert Bruskin, "New Congress Members Hit Housing Lack," *Washington Post,* December 29, 1946, p. M4.

42. Morris, *Richard Milhous Nixon: The Rise of an American Politician*, p. 341.

43. Ibid., p. 396.

44. Ibid., p. 386.

45. Ibid., p. 396. (Whitaker Chambers was the name of Hiss' accuser.)

46. Ibid., p. 397.

47. Ibid., p. 403.

48. C. P. Trussell, "Alger Hiss Admits Knowing Chambers; Meet Face to Face," *New York Times,* August 18, 1948, Late City Edition, p. 1.

49. Ibid.

50. William Fitzgibbon, "The Hiss-Chambers Case: A Chronology Since 1934," *New York Times,* June 12, 1949, Late City Edition, p. E8.

51. Ibid.

52. William R. Conklin, "Hiss Is Sentenced to Five-Year Term; Acheson Backs Him," *New York Times,* January 26, 1950, Late City Edition, p. 1.

53. Ibid.

54. Morris, *Richard Milhous Nixon: The Rise of an American Politician*, pp. 539-541.

55. Rudy Abramson, "From Beginning to End, Nixon Was a Fighter," *Los Angeles Times,* April 24, 1994, Sunday Final, p, A1.

56. Morris, *Richard Milhous Nixon: The Rise of an American Politician*, p. 611.

57. "Nixon motto: 'The worst thing a politician can be is dull,'" *Chicago Tribune,* April 24, 1994, Chicagoland Final, Section 1, p. 6.

58. James Reston, "Nominee Asks Unity at Home and Just, Sure Peace Abroad," *New York Times,* July 12, 1952, Late City Edition, p. 1.

59. Ibid.

60. Morris, *Richard Milhous Nixon: The Rise of an American Politician*, p. 734.

61. Ibid., p. 734.

62. Ibid., p. 733.

63. Ibid., p. 762.

64. Ibid., p. 781.

65. Ibid., p. 798.

66. Ibid., p. 802.

67. John W. Finney, "Defense Recalls 'Checkers' Speech By Nixon," *New York Times,* July 31, 1972, Late City Edition, p. 12.

68. Lee Huebner, "The Checkers Speech After 60 Years," *The Atlantic,* September 22, 2012, https://www.theatlantic.com/politics/archive/2012/09/the-checkers-speech-after-60-years/262172. Accessed September 4, 2019.

69. "Text of Senator Nixon's Broadcast Explaining Supplementary Expense Fund," *New York Times,* September 24, 1952, Late City Edition, p. 22.

70. Ibid.

71. Ibid.

72. Ibid.

73. Ibid.

74. Ibid.

75. Morris, *Richard Milhous Nixon: The Rise of an American Politician*, p. 844.

76. Huebner, "The Checkers Speech After 60 Years."

77. Gladwin Hill, "Nixon Denounces Press as Biased," *New York Times,* November 8, 1962, Late City Edition, p. 1.

78. Ibid.

79. Ibid.

80. Evan Thomas, *Being Nixon: A Man Di-*

vided, (New York: Random House, 2015), p. 137.

81. Ray Locker, *Nixon's Gamble: How a President's Own Secret Government Destroyed His Administration,* (Guilford: Lyons Press, 2016), p. 7.

82. Ibid.

83. James Rosen, *The Strong Man: John Mitchell and the Secrets of Watergate,* (New York: Doubleday, 2008), p. 38.

84. Ibid., p. 5.

85. Ibid., p. 6

86. Ibid.

87. Ibid.

88. Ibid., p. 7.

89. Ibid.

90. Ibid.

91. Ibid.

92. "John N. Mitchell Dies at 75; Major Figure in Watergate," *New York Times,* November 10, 1988, Late Edition, p. A1.

93. Rosen, *The Strong Man,* p. 11.

94. Ibid,. p. 11.

95. Ibid., p. 13.

96. Ibid., p. 16.

97. Ibid., p. 17.

98. Ibid.

99. Ibid., p. 18.

100. Ibid., p. 19.

101. Ibid., p. 20.

102. Ibid.

103. Ibid., p. 21.

104. Ibid., p. 23.

105. Ibid., p. 27.

106. Ibid., p. 33.

107. Ibid., p. 34.

108. Ibid., p. 41.

Chapter Two

1. Max Frankel, "It All Adds Up For Richard Nixon," *New York Times,"* August 11, 1968, Late City Edition, p. E1.

2. Harrison E. Salisbury, "Nixon: Then and Now," *New York Times,* September 16, 1968, Late City Edition, p. 1.

3. Ibid.

4. Arthur Schlesinger Jr., "A Skeptical Democrat Looks at President Nixon," *New York Times, Sunday Magazine,* November 17, 1968.

5. Donald Janson, "The Violence That Hurt the Ticket," *New York Times,* September 1, 1968, Late City Edition, p. E2.

6. Len Colodny and Tom Shachtman, *The Forty Years War,* (New York: HarperCollins, 2009), p. 17.

7. Ibid.

8. Robert B. Semple Jr., "Presidential Race: Nixon's View: It's Not in the Bag – Not Yet," *New York Times,* September 22, 1968, Late City Edition, p. E1.

9. Colodny and Shachtman, *The Forty Years War,* p. 17. (Nguyen Thieu was the president of Vietnam.)

10. Ibid. (The intermediary was Anna Chennault and the president of South Vietnam was Nguyen Van Thieu.)

11. Locker, *Nixon's Gamble,* p. 12.

12. Colodny and Shachtman, *The Forty Years War,* p. 17.

13. Richard Severo, "H.R. Haldeman, Nixon Aide Who Had Central Role in Watergate, Is Dead," *New York Times,* November 13, 1993, Late Edition, p. 31.

14. J. Anthony Lukas, *Nightmare: The Underside of the Nixon Years,* (Athens: Ohio University Press, 1999), p. 224.

15. Ibid., p. 225.

16. Ibid., p. 224.

17. Ibid.

18. Ibid.

19. Ibid.

20. Ibid.

21. Ibid., p. 225.

22. Ibid.

23. Ibid.

24. Ibid.

25. Ibid.

26. Ibid.

27. Ibid.

28. Rupert Cornwell, "Obituary: John Ehrlichman," *Independent,* February 17, 1999, https://www.independent.co.uk/arts-entertainment/obituary-john-ehrlichman-1071331.html. Accessed September 4, 2019. Accessed September 4, 2019.

29. Lukas, *Nightmare,* p. 62.

30. Ibid.

31. Ibid.

32. Colodny and Shachtman, *The Forty Years War,* p. 124.

33. David Stout, "John D. Ehrlichman, Nixon Aide Jailed for Watergate, Dies at 73," *New York Times,* February 16, 1999, Late Edition, p. A1.

34. Ibid.

35. Lukas, *Nightmare,* p. 62.

36. Ibid.

37. Ibid.

38. Ibid.

39. John Ehrlichman, *Witness to Power: The Nixon Years,* (New York: Simon and Schuster, 1982), pp. 22-23.

40. Ibid., p. 35.

41. Lukas, *Nightmare,* p. 62.

42. Ibid.

43. Ibid.

44. Ibid.

45. Colodny and Shachtman, *The Forty Years War,* p. 13.

46. Lukas, *Nightmare,* p. 62.

47. Richard Nixon, *RN: The Memoirs of Richard Nixon,* (New York: Grosset & Dunlap, 1978), p. 6.

48. Colodny and Shachtman, *The Forty Years War,* p. 33.

49. Locker, *Nixon's Gamble,* p. 14.

50. Colodny and Shachtman, *The Forty Years War,* p. 37.

51. Locker, *Nixon's Gamble,* p. 14.

52. Ibid., p. 18.

53. Jefferson Morley, *Scorpions' Dance: The President, the Spymaster, and the CIA,* (New York: St. Martin's Press,2022), pp. 24-25.

54. Ibid.

55. Ibid.

56. Ibid.

57. Chris Whipple, *The Spymasters: How the CIA Directors Shape History and the Future,* (New York: Scribner, 2020), p. 42.

58. Ibid.

59. Colodny and Shachtman, *The Forty Years War,* pp. 36-38.

60. Ibid., p. 31.

61. Ibid., pp. 17-18.

62. Schlesinger Jr., "A Skeptical Democrat Looks at President Nixon."

63. Locker, *Nixon's Gamble,* p. 14.

64. Ibid., p. 14. (The candidate was Nelson Rockefeller.)

Chapter Three

1. Colodny and Shachtman, *The Forty Years War,* p. 37.

2. Ibid., p. 36-37.

3. Ibid., p. 81.

4. Sabrina Tavernse, "Thomas H. Moorer, 91, Dies; Head of Joint Chiefs in 70's," *New York Times,* February 7, 2004, Late Edition, p. A13.

5. Ibid.

6. Ibid.

7. Ibid.

8. Ibid.

9. Ibid.

10. Ibid.

11. Len Colodny and Robert Gettlin, *Silent Coup: The Removal of a President,* New York: St. Matin's Press, 1991), (Paperback), p. 4.

12. Colodny and Shachtman, *The Forty Years War,* p. 70.

13. Ibid., p. 54.

14. Ibid., p 81.

15. Ibid.

16. Ibid.

17. Colodny and Gettlin, *Silent Coup,* p. 5.

18. Ibid.

19. Colodny and Shachtman, *The Forty Years War,* p. 81.

20. Colodny and Gettlin, *Silent Coup,* p. 5.

21. Ibid., pp. 25-30.

22. Ibid.

23. Ibid., p. 29.

24. Ibid., p. 28.

25. Ibid., p. 13.

26. Ibid., p. 29.

27. Ibid., p.14.

28. Ibid. (Yahya Khan was the name of Pakistan's bloodthirsty president.)

29. Ibid., p. 29.

30. Ibid., p. 30.

31. Ibid., p. 14.

32. Ibid., p. 58.

33. Ibid., p. 21.

34. Ibid., p. 50.

35. Ibid., p. 51.

36. Ibid., p. 21.

37. Ibid., p. 22.

38. Ibid.

39. Ibid.
40. Ibid.
41. Ibid.
42. Ibid., p. 24.
43. Colodny and Shachtman, *The Forty Years War,* p. 125.
44. Ibid.
45. Colodny and Gettlin, *Silent Coup,* p. 49. (Melvin Laird was the secretary of defense.)
46. Ibid.
47. Ibid.
48. Ibid., p. 50.
49. Ibid.
50. Ibid., p. 58.
51. Ibid., p. 51.
52. Ehrlichman, *Witness to Power,* p. 304. (David Young was the name of the Kissinger subordinate.)
53. Colodny and Gettlin, *Silent Coup,* p. 35-39.
54. Ehrlichman, *Witness to Power,* p. 304.
55. Ibid.
56. Ibid., p. 307.
57. Colodny and Gettlin, *Silent Coup,* p. 48.
58. Ibid., p. 45.
59. Ibid.
60. Ibid.
61. Ibid., p. 53.

Chapter Four

1. William Beecher, "Raids in Cambodia by U.S. Unprotested," *New York Times,* May 9, 1969, Late City Edition, p. 1.
2. Colodny and Gettlin, *Silent Coup,* p. 55.
3. Ibid., pp. 56-57. (Morton Halperin was the name of the NSC staffer whose phone was tapped.)
4. Ibid.
5. Neil Sheehan, "Vietnam Archive: Pentagon Study Traces 3 Decades of Growing U. S. Involvement," *New York Times,* June 13, 1971, Late City Edition, p. 1.
6. James M. Naughton, "Arguments to be Heard Today: Federal Warrant is Issued for the Arrest of Ellsberg," *New York Times,* June 26, 1971, Late City Edition, p. 1.
7. Colodny and Gettlin, *Silent Coup,* p. 15.
8. Lukas, *Nightmare,* p. 73-74.
9. Ibid., p. 74.
10. Ibid., p. 75.
11. Hougan, *Secret Agenda,* p. 33.
12. Ibid., p. 3.
13. Ibid.
14. Ibid.
15. Ibid., p. 33.
16. Morley, *Scorpions' Dance,* p.145.
17. Hougan, *Secret Agenda,* p. 33.
18. Ibid., p. 8.
19. Ibid.
20. Tim Weiner, "E. Howard Hunt, Agent Who Organized Botched Watergate Break-In, Dies at 88," *New York Times,* January 24, 2007, Late Edition, p. C13.
21. Ibid.
22. Ibid.
23. Ibid.
24. Jim Hougan, *Secret Agenda,* p. 109.
25. Ibid., p. 6.
26. Ibid.
27. Ibid.
28. Ibid.
29. Ibid. (Hunt's non de plume was David St. John.)
30. Ibid.
31. Ibid.
32. Ibid., p. 265.
33. Ibid., p. 78.
34. Ibid., p. 6.
35. Ibid., p. 27.
36. Ibid., p. 29.
37. Ibid.
38. Ibid.
39. Ibid., p. 28.
40. Ibid., p. 29.
41. Ibid., p. 109.
42. Ibid., pp. 109-110. (Miami's C.I.A. station chief was Jake Esterline, and the C.I.A. superior who quashed his concerns was Cord Meyer.)
43. Ibid., pp. 109-110.
44. Lukas, *Nightmare,* p. 86.
45. G. Gordon Liddy, *Will: The Autobiography of G. Gordon Liddy,* (New York: St. Martin's Press, 1980), p. 24.
46. Ibid.
47. Ibid.

48. Ibid.

49. Ibid., p. 156-157.

50. Ibid., p. 58.

51. Ibid., p. 59.

52. Ibid., p. 102.

53. James Feron, "Poughkeepsie Recalls Liddy: Gung-Ho Deputy Prosecutor," New York Times, July 13, 1973, Late City Edition, p. 37.

54. Gordon Liddy, Will, p. 104.

55. Ibid., p. 107.

56. Ibid., p. 118.

57. Laura Mansnerus, "Timothy Leary, Pied Piper of Psychedelic 60's, Dies at 75," New York Times, June 1, 1996, Late Edition, p. 1.

58. Liddy, Will, p. 122-124.

59. Ibid., p. 124.

60. Feron, "Poughkeepsie Recalls Liddy: Gung-Ho Deputy Prosecutor."

61. Ibid.

62. Ibid.

63. Ibid.

64. Ibid.

65. Hougan, Secret Agenda, p. 41.

66. Ibid.

67. Ibid.

68. Liddy, Will, p. 158.

69. Ehrlichman, Witness to Power, p. 399.

70. Liddy, Will, pp. 162-163.

71. Ibid.

72. Ibid. p. 162.

73. Ibid.

74. Ibid., p. 163.

75. Ibid.

76. Ibid., p. 164.

77. Ibid.

78. Jim Hougan, Secret Agenda, p. 43.

79. Ibid.

80. Ibid. (Steve Greenwood was the name of the CIA employee.)

81. Ibid.

82. Ibid., p. 44 (General Robert Cushman was the name of the C.I.A.'s deputy director.)

83. Ibid.

84. Ibid., p. 45.

85. Liddy, Will, p. 162.

Chapter Five

1. Hougan, Secret Agenda, p. 44. (Egil Krogh was the name of the Ehrlichman subordinate.)

2. Ibid.

3. Lukas, Nightmare, p. 99.

4. U.S., Congress, Senate. The Final Report of the Select Committee on Presidential Campaign Activities United States Senate, 93d Congress, 2nd Session, Report No. 93-981 (Washington: U.S. Government Printing Office,1974), p. 696.

5. Hougan, Secret Agenda, p. 46.

6. Ibid.

7. Ibid.

8. Ibid.

9. Ibid.

10. Ibid.

11. Ibid., pp. 46-47.

12. U.S., Congress, Senate, Hearings before the Select Committee on Presidential Campaign Activities: Watergate and Related Activities, Book 1, 93rd Congress, 1st Session, (Washington: U.S. Government Printing Office, 1973), p. 378.

13. New York Times Staff, The Watergate Hearings: Break-in and Cover-up, (New York: Bantam Books, 1973), p. 69.

14. Hougan, Secret Agenda, p. 47.

15. Ibid.

16. Ibid., p. 48.

17. Ibid., p. 141.

18. Ibid., p. 48.

19. Ibid., p. 57.

20. Ibid., p. 9.

21. Ibid, p. 57.

22. Ibid. (Jack Caulfield was the name of the White House operative.)

23. Ibid. (Alfred Wong was the name of Secret Service supervisor at the White House.)

24. Ibid.

25. Rosen, The Strong Man, p. 281.

26. Hougan, Secret Agenda, p. 57.

27. Ibid., p. 58. (William McMahon was the name of the former C.I.A. employee.)

28. Lukas, Nightmare, p. 170.

29. Ibid.

30. Hougan, Secret Agenda, p. 9.31. Ibid.

32. Ibid., pp. 10-11.

33. Ibid., p. 11.

34. Ibid., p. 9.
35. Rockefeller Commission. *Report to the President by the Commission on C.I.A. Activities Within the United States,* (Washington: U.S. Government Printing Office, 1975), p. 249.
36. Hougan, *Secret Agenda,* p. 13-14. (Captain Roy Blick was the name of MPD officer who oversaw the "sex squad.")
37. Ibid.
38. Ibid., p. 14.
39. Ibid., p 12. (Security Research Staff was the name of the C.I.A. branch.)
40. Ibid., p. 11.
41. Rosen, *The Strong Man,* p. 281.
42. Hougan, *Secret Agenda,* p. 9.
43. Ibid., p. 234. (Lee Pennington Jr., was the name of the C.I.A. contract agent.)
44. Ibid.
45. Ibid., p. 9.
46. Ibid.
47. Ibid., p. 19. (Miriam Furbershaw was the name of McCord's landlady.)
48. Ibid.
49. Ibid., pp. 19-20.
50. Ibid., p. 19.
51. Ibid., p. 20.
52. Ibid.
53. Ibid.
54. Ibid.
55. Ibid.
56. Ibid.
57. Ibid., pp.17-18.
58. E. Howard Hunt, *Undercover: Memoirs of an American Secret Agent,* (New York: Berkley Publishing Corporation, 1974) p. 274.
59. Ibid.
60. Liddy, *Will,* p. 191.
61. Ibid.
62. Ibid., p. 217.
63. Ibid.
64. Hougan, *Secret Agenda,* p. 123.
65. Ibid.
66. Rosen, *The Strong Man,* 2008, p. 281. (Allen Dulles was the name of the C.I.A. director.)

Chapter Six

1. John Dean, *Worse than Watergate: The Secret Presidency of George W. Bush,* (New York: Little, Brown & Company, 2004).
2. Patrick Anderson, "Rushing Toward a Footnote in History," *New York Times Magazine,* July 8, 1973.
3. Ibid.
4. Ibid.
5. Ibid.
6. Ibid.
7. Ibid.
8. Ibid.
9. Ibid.
10. Colodny and Gettlin, *Silent Coup,* p. 98.
11. Ibid.
12. Ibid.
13. Ibid., p. 99.
14. Ibid.
15. Anderson, "Rushing Toward a Footnote in History."
16. Ibid.
17. Colodny and Gettlin, *Silent Coup,* p. 98.
18. Ibid.
19. Ibid.
20. Ibid., p. 99.
21. Ibid.
22. Ibid.
23. Ibid.
24. Ibid.
25. Ibid., p. 100.
26. Ibid.
27. Ibid.
28. Ibid., p. 101.
29. Ibid.
30. Ibid.
31. Ibid.
32. Ibid.
33. Ibid.
34. Ibid.
35. Ibid.
36. Ibid., pp. 101-102.
37. U.S. Congress, Senate, Hearings, *Book 3,* (Exhibit 41) pp. 1334-1337.
38. Colodny and Gettlin, *Silent Coup,* p. 102.
39. U.S. Congress, Senate, *Hearings, Book 4,* (Exhibit 48) pp. 1689-1690.
40. Ibid., p. 1411.
41. Ibid.

42. U.S. Congress, Senate, *Hearings, Book 7*, p. 2684.
43. Colodny and Gettlin, *Silent Coup*, p. 102.
44. Ibid., p. 98.
45. Matt Schudel, "Nixon Operative Devised Some 'Dirty Tricks'" *Washington Post*, June 24, 2012, p. C6.
46. Ibid.
47. Ibid.
48. Douglas Martin, "Jack Caulfield, 83, Bearer of a Watergate Message," *New York Times*, June 22, 2012, Late Edition, p A23.
49. Ibid.
50. Ibid.
51. Colodny and Gettlin, *Silent Coup*, p. 102. (Tony Ulasewicz was the name of the second N.Y.P.D. detective.)
52. Ibid., pp. 97-98.
53. Ibid., p. 108.
54. Ibid.
55. Ibid. (The New York madam was Xaviera Hollander, author of *The Happy Hooker*.)
56. Ibid.
57. Ibid.
58. Ibid.
59. Ibid., p. 109.
60. Ibid.
61. Ibid., p. 108.
62. Ibid., p. 109.
63. Ibid., p. 110.
64. Ibid.
65. Ibid., p. 109.
66. Ibid., p. 110.

Chapter Seven

1. Phil Stanford, *White House Call Girl*, (Port Townsend: Feral House, 2013), p. 18.
2. Ibid.
3. Ibid., p. 21-22.
4. Ibid., p. 21.
5. Ibid.
6. Ibid.
7. Ibid.
8. Ibid.
9. Ibid.
10. Ibid.
11. Ibid., p. 22.
12. Ibid.

13. Ibid., pp. 22-24. (Loren "Buzzy" Patterson was the name of Rikan's husband.)
14. Ibid.
15. Ibid.
16. Ibid.
17. Ibid.
18. Ibid.
19. Ibid.
20. Ibid., p.28.
21. Ibid.
22. Ibid., p.38. (Josephine Alvarez was the name of Joe Nesline's mistress.)
23. Ibid., p. 37.
24. Ibid., p. 39.
25. Ibid.
26. Ibid., p. 45. (George Owen was name of the Dallas Cowboys' scout.)
27. Ibid., p. 163.
28. Maureen Dean with Hays Gorey, *Mo: A Woman's View of Watergate*, (New York: Simon and Schuster, 1977) p. 38.
29. Stephanie Mansfield, "Sex! Power! Mo Dean! And Sex!: The Stockbroker Turns Novelist with Her Racy 'Washington Wives,'" *Washington Post*, October 24, 1977, Final p. B1.
30. Dean with Gorey, *Mo: A Woman's View of Watergate*, p. 35. (G. Stedman Huard was the name of the affluent suitor.)
31. Ibid.
32. Ibid., p. 36.
33. Ibid., p. 37.
34. Stanford, *White House Call Girl*, p. 53. (Jack Garfield was the name of the dentist.)
35. Ibid. (The two actors were Jacques Bergerac and Hugh O'Brian.)
36. Dean with Gorey, *A Woman's View of Watergate*, p. 37.
37. Ibid., 38.
38. Stanford, *White House Call Girl*, p. 49.
39. Dean with Gorey, *A Woman's View of Watergate*, p. 38.
40. Ibid., p. 39. (Michael Biner was the name of Mo's second husband.)
41. Ibid.
42. Ibid., p. 40.
43. Ibid.
44. Ibid.
45. Ibid.
46. Ibid.

47. Ibid., p. 41.

48. Ibid., pp. 16-17. (Mo's roommate, Patricia Hornung, was separated from Paul Hornung.)

49. Stanford, *White House Call Girl*, p. 53.

50. Dean with Gorey, *A Woman's View of Watergate*, p. 21.

51. Ibid. (Bill McClain was the mutual friend.)

52. Ibid., p. 22.

53. Ibid., pp. 26-27.

54. Ibid., p. 46.

55. Ibid., p. 47.

56. Ibid., p. 48.

57. Stanford, *White House Call Girl*, p. 59.

58. Dean with Gorey, Mo: *A Woman's View of Watergate*, p. 79. (Beverly Sills was the famous opera singer.)

59. Ibid.

60. Stanford, *White House Call Girl*, p. 60.

60. Stephanie Mansfield, "Sex! Power! Mo Dean! And Sex!: The Stockbroker Turns Novelist with Her Racy 'Washington Wives.'"

Chapter Eight

1. Stanford, *White House Call Girl*, p. 65.

2. Hougan, *Secret Agenda*, p. 112.

3. Colodny and Gettlin, *Silent Coup*, pp. 156-157.

4. Ibid., p. 128.

5. Ibid.

6. Ibid., p. 129.

7. Stanford, *White House Call Girl*, p. 69.

8. Ibid.

9. Ibid.

10. Ibid., p. 65.

11. Ibid.

12. Ibid.

13. Ibid., p. 66.

14. Ibid.

15. Ibid.

16. Ibid.

17. Colodny and Gettlin, *Silent Coup*, p. 129.

18. Stanford, *White House Call Girl*, p. 66.

19. Ibid.

20. Ibid.

21. Ibid., p.67.

22. Ibid.

23. Ibid.

24. Ibid.

25. Ibid.

26. Ibid.

27. Ibid.

28. Ibid.

29. Ibid., p.70.

30. Ibid.

31. Ibid.

32. Ibid.

33. Ibid.

34. Ibid.

35. Ibid.

36. Ibid., p. 73.

37. Ibid.

38. Ibid.

39. Ibid.

40. Ibid.

41. Hougan, *Secret Agenda*, p. 116.

42. Ibid.

43. Ibid.

44. Stanford, *White House Call Girl*, p. 74.

45. Ibid.

46. Ibid.

47. Ibid.

48. Ibid.

49. Ibid.

50. Ibid.

51. Ibid.

52. Ibid.

53. Ibid.

54. Ibid.

55. Ibid.

56. Ibid.

57. Ibid.

58. Ibid., p. 77.

59. Colodny and Gettlin, *Silent Coup*, p. 129.

60. Stanford, *White House Call Girl*, p. 77.

61. Ibid.

62. Ibid.

63. Ibid.

64. Ibid.

65. Colodny and Gettlin, *Silent Coup*, p. 130.

66. Ibid.

67. Stanford, *White House Call Girl*, p. 77.

68. Ibid.

69. Ibid., p. 78.

70. Ibid.

71. Ibid.

72. Ibid., p. 81.
73. Ibid.
74. Ibid., p. 83.
75. Hougan, *Secret Agenda,* p. 116.
76. Ibid.
77. Stanford, *White House Call Girl,* p. 83.
78. Ibid.
79. Ibid.
80. Hougan, *Secret Agenda*, p. 9.
81. Stanford, *White House Call Girl.,* p. 81.
82. Ibid.
83. Ibid.
84. Ibid.
85. Ibid.
86. Ibid.
87. Ibid.
88. Ibid., p. 82.
89. Ibid.
90. Ibid.
91. Ibid.
92. Ibid.
93. Ibid.
94. Ibid.
95. Ibid.
96. Ibid.
97. Ibid.
98. Ibid.
99. Ibid.
100 Ibid.

Chapter Nine

1. Colodny and Gettlin, *Silent Coup*, p. 117.
2. Roger Stone with Mike Colapietro, *Nixon's Secrets: The Rise, Fall, and Untold Truth about the President, Watergate, and the Pardon.* (New York: Skyhorse, 2014), p. 279.
3. Douglas Martin, "Jeb Magruder, 79, Nixon Aide Jailed for Watergate, Dies," *New York Times,* May 17, 2014, Late Edition, p. D8.
4. Ibid.
5. Ibid.
6. Ibid.
7. Ibid.
8. Ibid.
9. Ibid.
10. Ibid.
11. Ibid.

12. Ibid.
13. Ibid.
14. Ibid.
15. John Dean, III, *The White House Years: Blind Ambition,* (New York: Simon and Schuster, 1976), p. 76.
16. Ibid. (Egil Krogh was the name of the Ehrlichman aide.)
17. Liddy, *Will*, p. 133.
18. Ibid.
19. Ibid., p. 181. (Egil Krogh was the name of the Ehrlichman aide.)
20. Ibid.
21. Ibid., p. 182.
22. Ibid.
23. Ibid.
24. Ibid.
25. U.S. Congress, Senate, *Hearings, Book 3,* p. 927.
26. Hunt, *Undercover,* p. 186.
27. Liddy, *Will*, p. 212.
28. U.S. Congress, Senate, *Hearings, Book 3,* p. 928.
29. Ibid., p. 1150.
30. Liddy, *Will*, p. 185.
31. U.S. Congress, Senate, *Hearings, Book 3,* p. 928.
32. Liddy, *Will*, p. 186.
33. Ibid., p. 189.
34. Ibid., p. 196.
35. Ibid., p. 193.
36. U.S. Congress, Senate, *The Final Report of the Select Committee on Presidential Campaign Activities United States Senate*, p. 21.
37. Liddy, *Will*, p. 198.
38. Ibid.
39. Ibid.
40. Ibid., p. 199.
41. Ibid.
42. Ibid.
43. Ibid., pp. 196-197.
44. Ibid., p. 197.
45. Ibid.
46. Ibid.
47. Ibid., p. 191.
48. U.S. Congress, Senate, *Hearings, Book 4,* p. 1610.
49. Liddy, *Will*, p. 200.

50. Ibid.

51. Ibid., p. 198.

52. Ibid.

53. U.S. Congress, Senate, *Hearings, Book 4,* p. 1610.

54. Ibid.

55. Ibid.

56. Liddy, *Will,* pp. 202-203.

57. Ibid., p. 203.

58. Ibid.

59. Ibid.

60. Ibid., p. 207.

61. Ibid.

62. Ibid.

63. Ibid.

64. Ibid.

65. Stanford, *White House Call Girl,* p. 94.

66. Ibid., p. 78.

67. Ibid., 92.

68. Ibid.

69. Ibid.

70. Ibid.

71. Ibid.

72. Ibid.

73. Ibid., p. 94.

74. Ibid.

75. Ibid.

76. Ibid., pp. 103-104.

Chapter Ten

1. Colodny and Gettlin, *Silent Coup,* p. 122.

2. Ibid.

3. Liddy, *Will,* p. 212.

4. Ibid.

5. Ibid.

6. Jeb Stuart Magruder, *This American Life: One Man's Road to Watergate,* (New York: Atheneum, 1974), p. 192. (Gordon Strachan was the name of the Haldeman aide.)

7. Ibid., p. 193.

8. Colodny and Gettlin, *Silent Coup,* pp. 126-127.

9. Ibid., p. 125.

10. Ibid. (Frederick LaRue and Harry Flemming were the names of Mitchell's aides.)

11. Ibid.

12. Ibid. (Harry Flemming was the name of the Mitchell aide who left the room.)

13. U.S. Congress, Senate, *The Final Report of the Select Committee on Presidential Campaign Activities United States Senate,* p. 25.

14. Ibid.

15. Ibid.

16. Ibid. (Frederick LaRue was the name of the Mitchell aide who testified before the Watergate Committee.)

17. Rosen, *The Strong Man,* 2008, p. 273.

18. Colodny and Gettlin, *Silent Coup,* p. 126.

19. Ibid., p. 127.

20. Liddy, *Will,* p. 215. (Robert Reisner was the name of the Magruder subordinate.)

21. Ibid., p. 219.

22. Ibid., p. 215.

23. Hougan, *Secret Agenda,* p. 111.

24. Hougan, *Secret Agenda,* pp. 124-125. (Michael Stevens was the name of McCord's Chicago-based wireman.)

25. Ibid., p. 125.

26. Ibid.

27. Ibid.

28. Stanford, *White House Call Girl,* p. 106.

29. Ibid.

30. Ibid.

31. Hougan, *Secret Agenda,* p. 111.

32. Ibid.

33. Ibid.

34. Stanford, *White House Call Girl,* p. 106.

35. Ibid.

36. Hougan, *Secret Agenda,* p. 112.

37. Stanford, *White House Call Girl,* p. 106.

38. Hougan, *Secret Agenda,* p. 118. (John Rudy was the name of the assistant U.S. attorney for Washington, D.C.)

39. Ibid., pp. 118-119.

40. Ibid., p. 119.

41. Liddy, *Will,* p. 219. (Lawrence O'Brien was the name of the D.N.C. chairman.)

42. Ibid.

43. Hougan, *Secret Agenda,* pp. 123-124.

44. Liddy, *Will,* p. 219.

45. Colodny and Gettlin, *Silent Coup,* p. 108.

46. Ibid., p. 135.

47. Tom Condon, "From Hartford 25 Years Later, A Watergate Player Reflects," *Hartford Courant,* June 15, 1997, A.1.

48. Ibid.

49. Ibid.

50. Ibid.

51. Ibid.
52. Ibid.
53. Ibid.
54. Hougan, *Secret Agenda*, p. 135.
55. Ibid., pp. 135-136.
56. Ibid., p. 135.
57. Ibid.
58. Ibid., p. 136.
59. Ibid.
60. Ibid., p. 135.
61. Condon, "From Hartford 25 Years Later, A Watergate Player Reflects."
62. Hougan, *Secret Agenda*, p. 136.
63. Ibid.
64. Ibid.
65. Ibid.
66. Ibid.

Chapter Eleven

1. Hougan, *Secret Agenda*, p. 137.
2. U.S. Congress, Senate, *Hearings, Book 1*, p. 398.
3. Ibid.
4. Ibid., p. 399.
5. Hougan, *Secret Agenda*, p. 153.
6. Ibid., p. 155.
7. Ibid., p. 137.
8. Ibid., p. 139.
9. Ibid., p. 141.
10. United Press International, "Paper Says Girl was Sent to Kill Castro," *Los Angeles Times, June* 13, 1976, Final, p. 5.
11. Hougan, *Secret Agenda*, p. 82.
12. Ibid., p. 140.
13. Ibid., p. 143.
14. Ibid., p. 141.
15. Ibid., p. 142.
16. Ibid., p. 141.
17. Ibid.
18. Ibid.
19. Hunt, *Undercover*, p. 223.
20. Ibid., p. 220.
21. Ibid., p. 223.
22. Hougan, *Secret Agenda*, p. 144.
23. Ibid., p. 145.
24. Ibid., p. 144.
25. Ibid., pp. 148-149.
26. Ibid., p. 149.
27. Ibid.
28. Ibid.
29. Ibid., p. 149.
30. Ibid., p. 207.
31. Ibid., p. 149.
32. Ibid.
33. Ibid., p. 151.
34. Ibid., p. 150.
35. Ibid.
36. Ibid.
37. Liddy, *Will*, p. 231.
38. Ibid.
39. Ibid., p. 232.
40. Ibid.
41. Hougan, *Secret Agenda*, p. 151.
42. Ibid.
43. Liddy, *Will*, p. 232.
44. Ibid.
45. Ibid.
46. Hougan, *Secret Agenda*, p. 152.
47. Ibid.
48. Ibid.
49. Ibid.
50. Colodny and Gettlin, *Silent Coup*, p. 144.
51. Hougan, *Secret Agenda*, p. 152
52. Ibid., p. 156.
53. Ibid.
54. Ibid.
55. Ibid.
56. Ibid., p. 157.
57. Ibid.
58. Ibid.
59. Colodny and Gettlin, *Silent Coup*, p. 140.
60. Hougan, *Secret Agenda*, p. 161.
61. Liddy, *Will*, p. 234.
62. Ibid.
63. Ibid.
64. Ibid.
65. Ibid., p. 235.
66. Ibid.
67. Ibid.
68. Ibid.
69. Ibid.
70. Ibid.
71. Ibid.
72. Ibid.
73. Ibid.

74. Ibid.

75. Hougan, *Secret Agenda,* p. 161.

76. Ibid., pp. 161-162.

77. Ibid., p. 162.

78. Lukas, *Nightmare,* p. 201.

79. Ibid.

80. Ibid.

81. Colodny and Gettlin, *Silent Coup,* p. 143. (Earl J. Silbert was the name of the assistant U.S. attorney.)

Chapter Twelve

1. Colodny and Gettlin, *Silent Coup,* p. 146.

2. Ibid., pp. 146-147

3. Hougan, Secret Agenda, p. 172. (John Rudy was the name of the assistant U.S. attorney.)

4. Colodny and Gettlin, *Silent Coup*, p. 148.

5. Ibid. (Dean Smith was the name of John Rudy's boss.)

6. Ibid.

7. Stanford, *White House Call Girl*, p. 116.

8. Colodny and Gettlin, *Silent Coup*, p. 149.

9. Hougan, Secret Agenda, p. 173.

10. Colodny and Gettlin, *Silent Coup*, p. 149.

11. Stanford, *White House Call Girl,* pp. 116-117.

12. Colodny and Gettlin, *Silent Coup*, p. 149.

13. Ibid.

14. Ibid.

15. Ibid.

16. Ibid., p. 130.

17. Ibid.

18. Stanford, *White House Call Girl,* p. 117. (Roemer McPhee was the name of the attorney and council to the Republican National Committee)

19. Colodny and Gettlin, *Silent Coup,* pp. 153-154. (Charles Richey was the name of the federal judge.)

20. Ibid., p. 153. (Edwin C. Brown was the name of Bailley's attorney.)

21. Ibid., p. 154.

22. Ibid.

23. Ibid.

24. Ibid., p. 155.

25. Ibid.

26. Wallace Turner, "California Curbs Mental State as Trial Defense: Odd Twist to Defense," *New York Times,* September 13, 1981, Late City Edition, p. 35.

27. Colodny and Gettlin, *Silent Coup*, p. 156.

28. Ibid., p. 155.

29. Ibid.

30. Ibid., p. 234.

31. Ibid.

32. Ibid., p. 236.

33. Ibid., pp. 156-157. (As previously mentioned, John Rudy was the name of Bailley's federal prosecutor.)

34. Liddy, *Will,* p. 237.

35. Ibid.

36. bid., p. 239.

37. Ibid. p. 237.

38. Ibid.

39. Ibid.

40. Ibid.

41. Ibid., p. 238

42. Colodny and Gettlin, *Silent Coup*, p. 152.

43. Ibid.

44. Lukas, *Nightmare*, p. 203.

45. Hougan, *Secret Agenda*, p. 183.

46. Ibid., p. 186.

47. Ibid., p 191.

48. Ibid., p. 187.

49. Ibid.

50. Ibid., p. 207.

51. Ibid., p. 189.

52. Ibid.

53. Ibid., pp. 189-190. (Frank Wills was the name of the security guard.)

54. Ibid., p. 190.

55. Ibid.

56. Ibid., pp. 190-191. (Bobby Jackson was the name of Wills' supervisor.)

57. Ibid., p. 191. (Ira O'Neal was the name of Bobby Jackson's supervisor.)

58. Ibid. (Bruce Givens was the name of the D.N.C. volunteer.)

59. Ibid., p. 192.

60. Ibid., p. 194.

61. Ibid., p. 192.

62. Ibid., p. 193.

63. Ibid.

64. Ibid., p. 193.

65. Ibid., pp. 193-194.

66. Ibid., p. 195.

67. Ibid.

68. Ibid., p. 196.
69. Ibid.
70. Ibid.
71. Ibid.
72. Ibid.
73. Ibid., p 197.
74. Ibid.
75. Ibid.
76. Ibid., p. 197.
77. Ibid., p. 198.
78. Ibid.
79. Ibid., p. 199.
80. Hunt, *Undercover*, p. 240.
81. Liddy, *Will*, p. 243.
82. Ibid.
83. Hougan, *Secret Agenda*, p. 199.
84. Ibid.
85. Ibid.
86. Ibid.
87. Ibid., p. 200.
88. Ibid., 199.
89. Ibid. (Walter Hollams was the name of the Federal Reserve Board's roving guard.)
90. Ibid., pp. 199-200.
91. Ibid., p. 200.

Chapter Thirteen

1. Hougan, *Secret Agenda,* p. 200.
2. Ibid., pp. 200-201.
3. Ibid., p. 200.
4. Ibid.
5. Lukas, *Nightmare,* p. 206. (Paul Leeper and John Barrett were the names of Shoffler's colleagues.)
6. Hougan, *Secret Agenda,* p. 201.
7. Ibid.
8. Ibid.
9. Ibid.
10. Lukas, *Nightmare,* p. 207.
11. Ibid.
12. Hougan, *Secret Agenda,* p. 201.
13. Ibid.
14. Ibid., p. 195.
15. U.S. Congress, Senate, *Hearings, Book 1,* p. 404.
16. Ibid.
17. Liddy, *Will*, p. 245.
18. Ibid.
19. Hougan, *Secret Agenda,* p. 202.
20. Ibid.
21. Stanford, *White House Call Girl,* p. 130.
22. Hougan, *Secret Agenda,* p. 202.
23. Ibid.
24. Ibid.
25. Ibid.
26. Stanford, *White House Call Girl,* p. 130.
27. Hougan, *Secret Agenda,* p. 203.
28. Ibid.
29. Ibid.
30. Ibid.
31. Ibid.
32. Ibid.
33. Ibid.
34. Ibid.
35. Colodny and Gettlin, *Silent Coup,* p. 164.
36. Ibid.
37. Hougan, *Secret Agenda,* pp. 203-204.
38. Ibid., p. 204.
39. Ibid.
40. Ibid.
41. Ibid., p. 235.
42. Ibid.
43. Ibid., p. 241.
44. Ibid.
45. Liddy, *Will*, p. 246.
46. Ibid.
47. Ibid.
48. Hougan, *Secret Agenda,* p. 118. (In addition to telling prominent attorney Bud Fensterwald about the Columbia Plaza honey trap, Russell also told the Committee to Investigate Assassination's employee Bob Smith, and former Treasury agent Ken Smith.)
49. Rosen, *The Strong Man,* p. 291. (John Rudy was the name of the former federal prosecutor.)
50. Colodny and Gettlin, *Silent Coup,* p. 161.
51. Ibid., p. 138.
52. Ibid.
53. Stanford, *White House Call Girl,* p. 130.
54. Colodny and Gettlin, *Silent Coup,* p. 142.
55. Chris Kahn, "Appeals Court Orders New Trial in Defamation Suit Against Watergate Burglar G. Gordon Liddy," Associated Press, March 1, 2002.
56. Ibid.

57. Manuel Roig-Franzia, "Arguments in Liddy Trial Focus on Dean: Jury Begins Deliberations in Defamation Suit," *Washington Post*, February 1, 2001, Final, p. A6.

58. Gail Gibson, "Jury Rejects Claim that Liddy Hurt Reputation; Repeating Watergate Call-Girl Ring Theory didn't Defame ex-D.N.C. Secretary," *Baltimore Sun*, July 4, 2002, Final Edition, p. A1.

59. Brian Witte, "Jury Rejects Defamation Lawsuit Against Watergate Conspirator G. Gordon Liddy," Associated Press, BC Cycle, July 3, 2002.

60. Gail Gibson, "Dean won't Take Stand in Liddy Defamation Lawsuit," *Baltimore Sun*, January 29, 2001, p. 6B. (James Rosen was the name of the Fox reporter, and Robert Strauss was the name of the former D.N.C. treasurer.)

61. Hougan, *Secret Agenda*, p. 236. (Carmine Bellino was the name of the former F.B.I. agent and chief investigator for the Watergate Committee.)

62. Ibid.

63. Elizabeth MacDonald, "The Kennedys and the I.R.S.," *Wall Street Journal*, January 28, 1997, p. A16.

64. Bart Barnes, "Carmine Bellino Dies at 84; was Congressional Investigator," *Washington Post*, February 28, 1990, Final, p. B4.

65. Hougan, *Secret Agenda*, p. 236. (William Birely was the name of Carmine Bellino's friend.)

66. Andrew Barnes, "GOP's Birely Named to County Council; Power Shift Seen," *Washington Post*, December 29, 1965, p. B1.

67. Hougan, *Secret Agenda*, pp. 236-237.

68. Ibid., p. 236.

69. Ibid., p. 239.

70. Ibid., p. 183.

71. Ibid.

72. Ibid.

73. Ibid.

74. Ibid.

75. Ibid.

76. Ibid.

77. Ibid.

78. Ibid., p. 239.

Chapter Fourteen

1. U.S. Congress, Senate, *The Final Report of the Select Committee on Presidential Campaign Activities United States Senate*, p. 25.

2. Colodny and Gettlin, *Silent Coup*, p. 152.

3. Rosen, *The Strong Man*, 2008, p. 294.

4. U.S. Congress, Senate, *The Final Report of the Select Committee on Presidential Campaign Activities United States Senate*, p. 25.

5. Colodny and Gettlin, *Silent Coup*, pp. 126-127. (As I've previously mentioned, Fred LaRue was the Key Biscayne witness.)

6. Ibid., p. 151.

7. Ibid.

8. Ibid.

9. "Judge Sirica's Mercy," *New York Times*, January 10, 1975, Late City Edition, p. 36.

10. Martin, "Jeb Magruder, 79, Nixon Aide Jailed for Watergate, Dies."

11. Ibid.

12. Ray Locker, "Watergate Figure Jeb Magruder Dies at 79," *USA Today*, May 16, 2014, https://www.usatoday.com/story/news/nation/2014/05/16/jeb-magruder-watergate-figure-dies-at-79/9174989. Accessed September 10, 2019.

13. Stanford, *White House Call Girl*, p. 94.

14. Martin, "Jeb Magruder, 79, Nixon Aide Jailed for Watergate, Dies."

15. Ibid.

16. Ibid.

17. Ibid.

18. Geoff Shepard, *The Real Watergate Scandal*, (Washington, D.C.: Regency History, 2015), p. 175.

19. Ibid.

20. Hougan, *Secret Agenda*, p. 213.

21. Ibid., p. 320.

22. Ibid., p. 321.

23. Ibid., p. 320.

24. Ibid.

25. Ibid.

26. Ibid.

27. Ibid., p. 321. (Edmund Chung was the name of Shoffler's former superior.)

28. Ibid.

29. Ibid.

30. Stanford, *White House Call Girl*, p. 174. (Karl

Milligan and Robert Puglisi were the names of Shoffler's fellow vice squad officers.)

31. Ibid. (Ledra Brady was the name of the clerk.)

32. Hougan, *Secret Agenda,* p. 217.

33. Ibid.

34. Rosen, *The Strong Man,* p. 281.

35. Hougan, *Secret Agenda,* p. 63. (James Jesus Angleton was chief of C.I.A. counterintelligence.)

36. Lukas, *Nightmare,* p. 304.

37. Ibid., p. 236.

Chapter Fifteen

1. Liddy, *Will,* p. 248.

2. Ibid. pp. 249-250.

3. Colodny and Gettlin, *Silent Coup,* p. 165.

4. Liddy, *Will,* p. 250.

5. Colodny and Gettlin, *Silent Coup,* p. 166.

6. Liddy, *Will,* p. 250.

7. Ibid.

8. Ibid. p. 251.

9. Magruder, *This American Life,* p. 214. (Fred LaRue was the name of the Mitchell aide.)

10. Ibid.

11. Ibid.

12. U.S. Congress, Senate, *Hearings, Book 2,* p. 798. (The four individuals ostensibly huddling were John Mitchell, Fred LaRue, Robert Mardian, and Jeb Magruder.)

13. U.S. Congress, Senate, *The Final Report of the Select Committee on Presidential Campaign Activities United States Senate,* p. 32. (Robert Mardian was the name of the Mitchell aide.)

14. Liddy, *Will,* p. 251.

15. Ibid.

16. Ibid.

17. Ibid. (The White House aide was Powell Moore.)

18. Ibid., p. 252-253.

19. U.S. Congress, Senate, *Hearings, Book 9,* p. 3562.

20. Ibid.

21. U.S. Congress, Senate, *The Final Report of the Select Committee on Presidential Campaign Activities United States Senate,* p. 32.

22. U.S. Congress, Senate, *Hearings, Book 4,* p. 1662.

23. U.S. Congress, Senate, *Hearings, Book 6,* p. 2353. (The Mitchell aide was Robert Mardian.)

24. Ibid.

25. Liddy, *Will,* p. 251.

26. Colodny and Gettlin, *Silent Coup,* p. 170.

27. Ibid., p. 168.

28. Ibid., p. 172.

29. H.R. Haldeman with Joseph DiMona, *The Ends of Power,* (New York: Times Books, 1978), p. 10.

30. Ibid.

31. Ibid.

32. Ibid., p. 11.

33. Ehrlichman, *Witness to Power,* p. 347.

34. Ibid.

35. Ibid.

36. Rosen, *The Strong Man,* p. 308.

37. Haldeman with DiMona, *The Ends of Power,* p. 12.

38. Magruder, *An American Life,* p. 226.

39. Ibid.

40. Hougan, *Secret Agenda,* p. 225.

41. Ibid., p. 228. (Lucille Sweany and Donald Sweany were the respective names of McCord's secretary and her husband.)

42. Ibid., pp. 227-228. (Lee Pennington Jr., was the name of the C.I.A. asset.)

43. Ibid., p. 228.

44. Ibid.

45. Ibid.

46. Ibid., p. 229.

47. Colodny and Gettlin, *Silent Coup,* p. 188.

48. Ibid.

49. Magruder, *An American Life,* p. 223.

50. Ibid., pp. 223-224.

51. Ibid., p. 224.

52. Liddy, *Will,* p. 255.

53. Ibid.

54. Dean, *Blind Ambition,* p. 96.

55. Liddy, *Will,* p. 254.

56. Ibid., p. 255.

57. Ibid., p. 256.

58. Dean, *Blind Ambition,* p. 98.

59. Liddy, *Will,* p. 256. (Gordon Strachan was the Haldeman aide named by Liddy.)

60. Dean, *Blind Ambition,* p. 98.

61. Liddy, *Will,* p. 257.

62. Ibid.

63. Dean, *Blind Ambition,* p. 98.

64. Liddy, *Will,* p. 258.

65. Ibid.

66. Ibid.

67. Ibid., pp. 258-259.

68. Ibid., p. 259.

Chapter Sixteen

1. Colodny and Gettlin, *Silent Coup,* p. 185.

2. U.S. Congress, Senate, *Hearings, Book 3,* p. 934.

3. U.S. Congress, Senate, *Hearings, Book 7,* p. 2822.

4. Ibid. (Bruce Kehrli was the name of the Haldeman aide, and Ken Clawson was the name of the deputy press secretary.)

5. U.S. Congress, Senate, *Hearings, Book 3,* p. 934.

6. Ibid.

7. U.S. Congress, Senate, *Hearings, Book 7,* p. 2718.

8. Colodny and Gettlin, *Silent Coup,* p. 186.

9. Hunt, *Undercover,* pp. 256-257.

10. U.S. Congress, Senate, *Hearings, Book 7,* (Exhibit 108), p. 3009. (Ken Clawson was the deputy director of communications.)

11. Ibid., p. 3010 (Exhibit 109).

12. U.S. Congress, Senate, *The Final Report of the Select Committee on Presidential Campaign Activities United States Senate,* pp. 34-35.

13. Ibid.

14. Ibid., p. 35. (The Haldeman was aide was Bruce Kehrli and the Dean aide was Fred Fielding.)

15. Ibid.

16. Ibid.

17. Ibid., p. 36.

18. Ibid.

19. Ibid.

20. Hunt, *Undercover,* p. 277.

21. U.S. Congress, Senate, *Hearings, Book 4,* p. 1622.

22. Rosen, *The Strong Man,* p. 308.

23. Ibid. (Frederick LaRue and Robert Mardian were the names of the Mitchell aides who attended the meeting.)

24. Ibid.

25. Colodny and Gettlin, *Silent Coup,* p. 189.

26. Ibid.

27. Bob Woodward and E.J. Bachinski, "White House Consultant Tied to Bugging Figure," *Washington Post,* June 20, 1972, p. A1.

28. Carl Bernstein and Bob Woodward, *All the President's Men,* (New York: Simon and Schuster, 1974), p. 72.

29. Nixon, *RN: The Memoirs of Richard Nixon,* p. 629.

30. H.R. Haldeman with Joseph DiMona, *The Ends of Power,* p. 14.

31. Colodny and Gettlin, *Silent Coup,* p. 191.

32. Haldeman with DiMona, *The Ends of Power,* p. 14.

33. Ibid.

34. Colodny and Gettlin, *Silent Coup,* p. 191.

35. Dean, *Blind Ambition,* p. 109.

36. U.S. Congress, Senate, *Hearings, Book 9,* pp. 3575-3576.

37. Ibid., 3576.

38. Dean, *Blind Ambition,* pp. 114-115.

39. Ibid., p. 115.

40. Ibid.

41. Liddy, *Will,* p. 263. (Fred LaRue was the Mitchell aide who contacted Liddy)

42. Ibid. (Robert Mardian was the name of the second Mitchell aide.)

43. U.S. Congress, Senate, *Hearings, Book 6,* p. 2358.

44. Ibid., pp. 2359-2360.

45. Ibid., p. 2358.

46. Ibid., p. 2360.

47. Ibid., p. 2363.

Chapter Seventeen

1. Nixon, *RN: The Memoirs of Richard Nixon,* p. 635.

2. Ibid., pp. 635-636.

3. Ibid., p. 636.

4. Lukas, *Nightmare,* p. 193.

5. U.S. Congress, Senate, *Hearings, Book 9,* p. 3450.

6. Ibid., pp. 3450-3451.

7. Ibid., p. 3451.

8. Ibid.

9. Ibid.

10. U.S. Congress, Senate, *The Final Report of the Select Committee on Presidential Campaign Activities United States Sen-*

ate, p. 37.

11. Ibid.

12. U.S. Congress, Senate, *Hearings, Book 9*, p. 3451

13. Nick Bryant, *The Franklin Scandal: A Story of Powerbrokers, Child Abuse, and Betrayal,* (Walterville: Trineday, 2012), p. 12.

14. Haldeman with DiMona, *The Ends of Power,* p. 29.

15. Ibid., pp. 29-30.

16. Ibid., p. 30.

17. Ibid.

18. Colodny and Gettlin, *Silent Coup,* p. 203

19. Conversation between President Nixon and H.R. Haldeman June 23, 1972, from 10:04 A.M. to 11:39 A.M., tape 741-002.

20. Rosen, *The Strong Man,* pp. 43-44.

21. Conversation between President Nixon and H.R. Haldeman June 23, 1972, from 10:04 A.M. to 11:39 A.M., tape 741-002.

22. Ibid.

23. Ibid.

24. Ibid.

25. Ibid.

26. Morely, *Scorpions' Dance,* pp. 153-155.

27. U.S. Congress, Senate, *Hearings, Book 8,* p. 3041.

28. Conversation between President Nixon and H.R. Haldeman June 23, 1972, from 1:04 P.M.-1:13 P.M., tape 741-010.

29. Haldeman with DiMona, *The Ends of Power,* p. 34.

30. Ibid.

31. Ibid., pp. 37-38.

32. Ibid., p. 38.

33. Ibid.

34. Ibid.

35. U.S. Congress, Senate, *Hearings, Book 7,* p. 2835.

36. Haldeman with DiMona, *The Ends of Power,* p. 38.

37. U.S. Congress, Senate, *Hearings, Book 4,* p. 1415.

38. U.S. Congress, Senate, Hearings, Book 9, p. 3452.

39. U.S. Congress, Senate, *Hearings, Book 5,* p. 3452.

40. Ibid.

41. Ibid.

42. Ibid.

43. Ibid.

44. Ibid.

Chapter Eighteen

1. U.S. Congress, Senate, *Hearings, Book 4,* p. 1646.

2. U.S. Congress, Senate, *Hearings, Book 6,* p. 2363. (Robert Mardian was the name of the Mitchell aide.)

3. Colodny and Gettlin, *Silent Coup,* p. 210.

4. U.S. Congress, Senate, *Hearings, Book 3,* p. 945-946.

5. U.S. Congress, Senate, *Hearings, Book 5,* p. 1900.

6. U.S. Congress, Senate, *Hearings, Book 6,* p. 2368. (Robert Mardian was the name of the Mitchell aide.)

7. U.S. Congress, Senate, *Hearings, Book 3,* p. 945-946.

8. U.S. Congress, Senate, *The Final Report of the Select Committee on Presidential Campaign Activities United States Senate,* p. 38-39.

9. Ibid., p. 38.

10. Ibid.

11. U.S. Congress, Senate, *Hearings, Book 3,* p. 947.

12. U.S. Congress, Senate, *The Final Report of the Select Committee on Presidential Campaign Activities United States Senate,* p. 38.

13. Ibid.

14. Ibid.

15. Ibid.

16. Ibid. p. 39.

17. U.S. Congress, Senate, *Hearings, Book 7,* p. 2835.

18. U.S. Congress, Senate, *Hearings, Book 3,* pp. 949-950.

19. Ibid., 950.

20. Ibid.

21. Ibid.

22. U.S. Congress, Senate, *Hearings, Book 4,* p. 1672.

23. Colodny and Gettlin, *Silent Coup,* p. 215.

24. George Lardner Jr., "Mitchell Resigns to Spend Time with His Family," *Washington Post,* July 2, 1972, p. A1.

25. U.S. Congress, Senate, *The Final Report of the Select Committee on Presidential Campaign Activities United States Senate,* p. 52. (Herbert Kalmbach was the

name of Nixon's personal attorney.)

26. Ibid.

27. U.S. Congress, Senate, *Hearings, Book 5*, p. 2097.

28. U.S. Congress, Senate, *The Final Report of the Select Committee on Presidential Campaign Activities United States Senate*, p. 52.

29. U.S. Congress, Senate, *Hearings, Book 5*, p. 2098.

30. U.S. Congress, Senate, *Hearings, Book 6*, p. 2220.

31. Ibid., p. 2221.

32. U.S. Congress, Senate, *The Final Report of the Select Committee on Presidential Campaign Activities United States Senate*, p. 55.

33. U.S., Congress, Senate. *Hearings, Book 6*, p. 2245.

34. Colodny and Gettlin, *Silent Coup*, p. 222.

35. Rosen, *The Strong Man*, p. 322.

36. Ibid., p. 323.

37. Ibid., pp. 322-323.

Chapter Nineteen

1. "Ex-F.B.I. Agent Named Bugging Case Witness," *New York Times*, September 17, 1972, p. 39.

2. Ibid.

3. Liddy, *Will*, p. 267.

4. Ibid., pp. 267-268.

5. U.S. Congress, Senate, *Hearings, Book 9*, p. 3481.

6. Colodny and Gettlin, *Silent Coup*, p. 224.

7. Ibid., p. 223.

8. Ibid. p. 226.

9. U.S. Congress, Senate, *Hearings, Book 2*, p. 803.

10. Ibid.

11. Magruder, *This American Life*, p. 250.

12. Ibid., pp. 247-248.

13. U.S. Congress, Senate, *Hearings, Book 2*, p. 803.

14. Magruder, *This American Life*, p. 250.

15. Rosen, *The Strong Man*, p. 331.

16. Magruder, *This American Life*, p. 251.

17 Rosen, *The Strong Man*, p. 331. (Henry Petersen was the assistant attorney general.)

18. U.S. Congress, Senate, *Hearings, Book 2*, p. 803.

19. U.S. Congress, Senate, *Hearings, Book 5*, p. 1859.

20. Rosen, *The Strong Man*, p. 330.

21. U.S. Congress, Senate, *The Final Report of the Select Committee on Presidential Campaign Activities United States Senate*, p. 46.

22. U.S. Congress, Senate, *Hearings, Book 2*, p. 804.

23. Ibid.

24. Ibid.

25. Agis Salpukas, "2 Nixon Ex-Aides Among 7 Indicted in Raid in Capital," *New York Times*, September 16, 1972, p. 1

26. Ibid.

27. Ibid.

28. Conversation among President Nixon, H.R. Haldeman, and John Dean September 15, 1972, from 5:27 P.M.-6:17 P.M., tape 779-002.

29. Ibid.

30. Ibid.

31. Ibid.

32. Nixon, *RN: The Memoirs of Richard Nixon*, p. 682.

33. Ibid.

34. Carl Bernstein and Bob Woodward, "F.B.I. Finds Nixon Aides Sabotaged Democrats: F.B.I. Finds Nixon Aides Sabotaged Democratic Candidates," *Washington Post*, October 10, 1973, p. A1.

35. Ibid.

36. Ibid.

37. Bernstein and Woodward, *All the President's Men*, pp. 130-135.

38. Rosen, *The Strong Man*, p. 335.

39. Lukas, *Nightmare*, p. 255.

40. Ibid.

41. Ibid.

42. Ibid., p. 256.

43. Ibid., p. 257.

44. Ibid.

45. U.S. Congress, Senate, *Hearings, Book 3*, p. 969.

46. Ibid.

47. U.S. Congress, Senate, *Hearings, Book 7*, p. 2852.

48. U.S. Congress, Senate, *Hearings, Book 3*, p. 970.

49. Rosen, *The Strong Man*, p. 337.

50. Ibid.

51. Ibid.

52. Ibid.

53. Ibid.

54. U.S. Congress, Senate, *Hearings, Book 3*, p. 970.

55. Ibid.

56. Ibid.

57. U.S. Congress House, Committee on the Judiciary. *A Resolution Authorizing and Directing the Committee on the Judiciary to Investigate Whether Sufficient Grounds Exist for the House of Representatives to Exercise its Constitutional Power to Impeach Richard M. Nixon, President of the United States of America, White House Surveillance Activities and Campaign Activities, Book III, Part 1 - Events Following the Watergate Break-In,* 93rd Congress., 2nd Session., (U.S. Government Printing Office: Washington, 1974), p. 36.

58. U.S. Congress, Senate, *Hearings, Book 3*, p. 970.

59. U.S., Congress, House, Committee on the Judiciary, *Book II: William O. Bittman, John N. Mitchell, and John W. Dean III*, p. 232.

60. Dean, *Blind Ambition*, p.163.

61. Ibid.

62. U.S., Congress, House, Committee on the Judiciary, *Book III, Part 1 - Events Following the Watergate Break-In*, p. 36. (William Bittman was the name of Hunt's attorney and Kenneth Parkinson was the C.R.P. counsel.)

63. Lukas, *Nightmare*, p. 265-266. (Gerald Alch was the name of McCord's lawyer.)

64. Ibid., p. 266.

65. Ibid.

66. Colodny and Gettlin, *Silent Coup*, p. 243.

67. Lukas, *Nightmare*, p. 267.

68. Carroll Kilpatrick, "Schlesinger to Get Helms' Post at C.I.A.," *Washington Post*, December 22, 1972, p. A1.

Chapter Twenty

1. Walter Rugaber, "Watergate Trial Opens; Jury Screening Begins," *New York Times*, January 9, 1973, Late City Edition, p. 26

2. Shepard, *The Real Watergate Scandal*, p. 13.

3. Bart Barnes, "John Sirica, Watergate Judge, Dies," *Washington Post*, August 15, 1992, p. A1.

4. John Sirica, "Growing Up Poor in the Nation's Capital," *Washington Post*, April 29, 1979, B1.

5. Ibid.

6. Ibid.

7. Ibid.

8. Ibid.

9. Ibid.

10. Ibid.

11. Ibid. (Jack Britton was the name of the former welterweight champion.)

12 Ibid.

13. Ibid.

14. Ibid.

15. Ibid.

16. Ibid.

17. Shepard, *The Real Watergate Scandal*, p. 13.

18. Sirica, "Growing Up Poor In the Nation's Capital."

19. Ibid.

20. Shepard, *The Real Watergate Scandal*, p. 13. (Edward Bennett Williams was the name of the prominent Democrat.)

21. Ibid.

22. Barnes, "John Sirica, Watergate Judge, Dies."

23. Howard Muson, "A Man for this Season: Sirica Likes his Country the Way Immigrants' Sons Do," *New York Times Magazine*, November 4, 1973, p. 34.

24. Shepard, *The Real Watergate Scandal*, p. 13.

25. Barnes, "John Sirica, Watergate Judge, Dies."

26. Shepard, *The Real Watergate Scandal*, pp. 13-14.

27. Lukas, *Nightmare*, p. 260.

28. Ibid., p. 261.

29. "News Summary and Index," *New York Times*, December 9, 1972, Late City Edition, p. 37.

30. Ibid.

31. Lukas, *Nightmare*, p. 260.

32. Hunt, *Undercover*, p. 283.

33. Lukas, *Nightmare*, p. 261.

34. Hunt, *Undercover*, p. 277.

35. Lukas, *Nightmare*, p. 260.

36. Hunt, *Undercover*, p. 277.

37. Dean, *Blind Ambition*, p. 182.

38. Walter Rugaber, "Hunt Admits all 6

Charges as Judge Bars Partial Plea," *New York Times,* January 12, 1973, Late City Edition, p.1.

39. Walter Rugaber, "4 More Admit Guilt as Spies in Watergate," *New York Times,* January 16, 1973, p. 1.

40. Barnes, "John Sirica, Watergate Judge, Dies."

41. Rugaber, "4 More Admit Guilt As Spies In Watergate."

42. Ibid.

43. Ibid.

44. Ibid.

45. Ibid.

46. Arthur Siddon, "4 Watergate Defendants Plead Guilty; 2 Still on Trial," *Chicago Tribune,* January 16, 1973, p. 3.

47. Liddy, *Will,* p. 279.

48. Colodny and Gettlin, *Silent Coup,* p. 243. (Jack Caufield was the name of the Dean underling.)

49. Ibid.

50. Shepard, *The Real Watergate Scandal,* p. 105.

51. Lawrence Meyer, "Ex-Aides of Nixon to Appeal: Jury Convicts Liddy, McCord In 90 Minutes," *Washington Post,* January 31, 1973, p. A1.

52. Liddy, *Will,* p. 275. (Peter Maroulis was the name of Liddy's lawyer.)

53. Colodny and Gettlin, *Silent Coup,* p. 143. (Earl J. Silbert was the assistant U.S. attorney who thought blackmail was integral to the Watergate caper.)

54. Ibid.

55. Lawrence Meyer, "Key U.S. Witness Tells of Bugging Democrats," *Washington Post,* January 18, 1973, p. A1. (Gerald Alch was the name of McCord's lawyer.)

56. Ibid.

57. Ibid. (Charles Morgan Jr., was the name of the attorney who made the objection.)

58. Colodny and Gettlin, *Silent Coup,* p. 143.

59. Ibid. (David Bazelon was the name of the appellate judge.)

60. Ibid.

61. Ibid.

62 Ibid., p. 144.

63. Ibid.

64. Meyer, "Ex-Aides of Nixon To Appeal: Jury Convicts Liddy, McCord in 90 Minutes."

65. Ibid.

66. Lukas, *Nightmare,* p. 269.

67. Ibid., p. 291.

68. Walter Rugaber, "Watergate Spy Says Defendants were Under 'Political Pressure' to Admit Guilt and Keep Silent," *New York Times,* March 24, 1973, p. 1.

69. Ibid.

70. Ibid.

71. Ibid.

72. Ibid.

73. Ibid.

74. Ibid. (Earl Silbert was the assistant U.S. attorney for D.C. who announced the reconvening of a grand jury to investigate McCord's allegations.)

Chapter Twenty-One

1. Conversation among President Nixon, H.R. Haldeman, and John Dean September 15, 1972, from 5:27 P.M.-6:17 P.M., tape 779-002.

2. Ibid.

3. Ibid.

4. Lukas, *Nightmare,* p. 277.

5. Ibid.

6. Ibid. (Sam Ervin, Daniel Inouye, Joseph Montoya, and Herman Talmadge were the Democratic senators on the Watergate Committee, and Howard Baker, Edward Gurney, and Lowell Weicker Jr., were the Republican senators on the Watergate Committee.

7. Stanford, *White House Call Girl,* p. 177.

8. Ibid.

9. Warren E. Leary, "Samuel Dash, 79, Counsel For Watergate Committee," *New York Times,* March 31, 2019, p. B7.

10. Elizabeth Mehren, "Taxing the Patience of Connecticut," *Los Angeles Times,* July 1, 1991, p. E1.

11. Ibid.

12. Dean, *Blind Ambition,* pp. 315-316.

13. Ibid., p. 316.

14. Stanford, *White House Call Girl,* p. 177.

15. Lukas, *Nightmare,* p. 280.

16. Conversation between President Nixon and John Dean March 17, 1973, from 1:25 P.M. to 2:10 P.M., tape 882-012.

17. Ibid.

18. Ibid.

19. Ibid.

20. Lukas, *Nightmare*, p. 291.
21. Ibid. (Paul O'Brien was the name of the C.R.P. counsel.)
22. U.S. Congress, Senate, *The Final Report of the Select Committee on Presidential Campaign Activities United States Senate*, p. 57.
23. Lukas, *Nightmare*, p. 291.
24. U.S. Congress, Senate, *The Final Report of the Select Committee on Presidential Campaign Activities United States Senate*, p. 57. (David Shapiro was the name of Colson's law partner.)
25. Ibid.
26. Ibid.
27. Conversation among President Nixon, H.R. Haldeman and John Dean March 21, 1973, from 10:12 A.M. -11:55 A.M., tape 886-008.
28. Ibid.
29. Ibid.
30. Ibid.
31. Ibid. (Larry Higby was the name of Haldeman's assistant.)
32. Ibid.
33. Ibid.
34. Ibid.
35. Ibid.
36. Ibid.
37. Ibid.
38. Ibid.
39. Ibid.
40. Ibid.
41. Ibid.
42. Ibid.
43. Ibid.
44. Ibid.
45. Conversation among President Nixon, H.R. Haldeman, John Ehrlichman and John Dean March 21, 1973, from 5:20 P.M.-6:01 P.M., tape 421-018.
46. Ibid.
47. Ibid.
48. Dean, *Blind Ambition*, pp. 166-167
49. Ibid., pp. 167-168.
50. Ibid., p. 168.
51. Conversation among President Nixon, John Mitchell, H.R. Haldeman, John Ehrlichman, and John Dean March 22, 1973, 1:57 P.M. to 3:43 P.M., tape 442-033.
52. Ibid.
53. John M. Crewdson, "Gray Testifies that Dean 'Probably' Lied to F.B.I.," *New York Times*, March 23, 1973, p. 1.
54. Ibid.
55. Dean, *Blind Ambition*, p. 212.
56. Ibid., p. 213.
57. Ibid., p. 214.
58 Ibid.

Chapter Twenty-Two

1. Dean, *Blind Ambition*, p. 218.
2. Ibid.
3. Ibid., p. 216.
4. Ibid.
5. Ibid., p. 221.
6. U.S. Congress, Senate, *Hearings, Book 3*, (Exhibit 34-40), pp. 1258-1259.
7. Colodny and Gettlin, *Silent Coup*, p. 277.
8. U.S. Congress, Senate, *Hearings, Book 3*, (Exhibit 34-42), p. 1262. (The name of Liddy's attorney was Peter Maroulis.)
9. Dean, *Blind Ambition*, p. 222. (Tommy Hogan was the friend Dean phoned.)
10. Ibid.
11. Rosen, *The Strong Man*, p. 294.
12. Dean, *Blind Ambition*, p. 222.
13. U.S. Congress, Senate, *Hearings, Book 3*, p. 1006.
14. Ibid.
15. U.S. Congress, Senate, *Hearings, Book 2*, p. 804.
16. Ibid. p, 807.
17. U.S. Congress, Senate, *Hearings, Book 3*, p. 1007.
18. Rosen, *The Strong Man*, p. 363.
19. Ibid.
20. Ibid.
21. U.S. Congress, Senate, *Hearings, Book 3*, p. 1009.
22. Sam Roberts, "Charles N. Shaffer Jr., 82, Whose Client Helped Make Case Against Nixon, Dies," *New York Times*, March 24, 2015. P. B15. (Charles Shaffer was the name of Dean's attorney.)
23. Ibid.
24. Hougan, *Secret Agenda*, p. 240. (Robert McCandless was the name of Dean's co-counsel.)
25. Ibid.

26. Dean, *Blind Ambition,* p. 290.

27. U.S. Congress, Senate, *Hearings, Book 3,* p. 1009.

28. Ibid.

29. Ibid.

30. Ibid.

31. Ibid., pp. 1010-1011.

32. Ibid., p. 1011.

33. Ibid.

34. U.S. Congress, Senate, *The Final Report of the Select Committee on Presidential Campaign Activities United States Senate,* p. 91.

35. Dean, *Blind Ambition,* p. 256.

36. Colodny and Gettlin, *Silent Coup,* p. 241.

37. U.S., Congress, House, Committee on the Judiciary, *Book IV, Part 2 - Events Following the Watergate Break-In,* p. 1016.

38. Dean, *Blind Ambition,* pp. 256-257.

39. U.S., Congress, House, Committee on the Judiciary, *Book IV, Part 2 - Events Following the Watergate Break-In,* (Exhibit 27), p. 1016. (Earl Silbert was the name of the assistant U.S. attorney prosecuting Watergate and Henry Petersen was the assistant attorney general.)

40. U.S. Congress, Senate, *Hearings, Book 6,* (Exhibit 93), pp. 2652-2653.

41. U.S. Congress, Senate, *Hearings, Book 9,* p. 3631

42. Ibid.

43. Martin Arnold, "Evidence Snarls Ellsberg Trial," *New York Times,* April 27, 1973, p. 1.

44. Fred P. Graham, "Ellsberg Offers 2 Views on Delay," *New York Times,* August 2, 1972, p. 6.

45. U.S. Congress, Senate, *Hearings, Book 6,* p. 2618. (William Byrne Jr., was the name of Ellsberg's trial judge.)

46. John M. Crewdson, "Nixon Withdraws Gray Nomination as F.B.I. Director," *New York Times,* April 6, 1973, Late City Edition, p. 1.

47. U.S. Congress, Senate, *Hearings, Book 6,* p. 2618.

48. Associated Press, "William Byrne Jr., 75, Judge in Ellsberg Case," *New York Times,* January 15, 2006, p. 31.

49. U.S. Congress, Senate, *Hearings, Book 9,* p. 3631.

50. Ibid.

51. Colodny and Shachtman, *The Forty Years War,* p. 171.

52. Martin Arnold, "Trial Will Go On," *New York Times,"* April 28, 1973, Late City Edition, p. 1.

53. Ibid.

54. "Text of Ruling by Judge in Ellsberg Case," *New York Times,* May 12, 1973, p. 14

55. Ibid.

56. R. W. Apple Jr., "2 Aides Praised: Counsel Forced Out – Leonard Garment Takes Over Job," *New York Times,* May 1, 1973, Late City Edition, p. 1.

57. Ehrlichman, *Witness to Power,* p. 390.

58. Ibid.

59. Ibid.

60. Ibid.

61. Apple Jr., "2 Aides Praised: Counsel Forced Out – Leonard Garment Takes Over Job."

62. Ibid.

63. Ibid. (Leonard Garment was the new counsel to the president)

Chapter Twenty-Three

1. Bob Woodward and Carl Bernstein, "Wiretaps Put on Phones of 2 Reporters," *Washington Post,* May 3, 1973, p. A1.

2. James Hohmann, "Soldier-Statesman was High-Profile Aide to Presidents," *Washington Post,* February 21, 2010, p. A1.

3. Ibid.

4. Ibid.

5. Dick Polman, "Al Haig, the Long Goodbye," *Philadelphia Inquirer,* February 22, 2010, https://www.philly.com/philly/blogs/americandebate/Al_Haig_the_long_goodbye.html. Accessed September 14, 2019.

6. Ibid.

7. Ibid.

8. Ibid.

9. Hohmann, "Soldier-Statesman was High-Profile Aide to Presidents."

10. Ibid.

11. Ibid.

12. Ibid.

13. Polman, "Al Haig, the Long Goodbye."

14. Hohmann, "Soldier-Statesman was High-Profile Aide to Presidents."

15. Colodny and Gettlin, *Silent Coup*, p. 88.
16. Polman, "Al Haig, the Long Goodbye."
17. Ibid.
18. Ibid.
19. Ibid.
20. Ibid.
21. Ibid.
22. Ibid.
23. Ibid.
24. Ibid.
25. Ibid.
26. Ibid.
27. Hohmann, "Soldier-Statesman was High-Profile Aide to Presidents."
28. Polman, "Al Haig, the Long Goodbye," *Philadelphia Inquirer."*
29. Colodny and Gettlin, *Silent Coup*, p. 54.
30. Ibid.
31. Ibid.
32. Ibid.
33. Ehrlichman, *Witness to Power,* p. 308.
34. Colodny and Gettlin, *Silent Coup*, p. 301.
35. Hougan, *Secret Agenda*, p. 286.
36. Polman, "Al Haig, the Long Goodbye."
37. Colodny and Shachtman, *The Forty Years War*, p. 134.
38. Bob Woodward and Carl Bernstein, *The Final Days,* (New York: Simon and Schuster, 1976), p. 197.
39. Ibid.
40. Colodny and Shachtman, *The Forty Years War*, pp. 175-176.
41. Ibid., p. 176.
42. Colodny and Gettlin, *Silent Coup,* pp. 299-300.
43. Colodny and Shachtman, *The Forty Years War*, p. 176.
44. Peter Kihss, "Fred Buzhardt Jr., Nixon's Counsel in Watergate, Dies," *New York Times*, December 17, 1978, p. 44.
45. Ibid.
46. Ibid.
47. Colodny and Shachtman, *The Forty Years War*, pp. 50-51.
48. Ibid.
49. Ibid., p. 51.
50. Kihss, "Fred Buzhardt Jr., Nixon's Counsel in Watergate, Dies."
51. Colodny and Shachtman, *The Forty Years War*, p. 56.
52. Colodny and Gettlin, *Silent Coup*, p. 63.
53. Colodny and Shachtman, *The Forty Years War*, p. 129-130. (Don Stewart was the name of the Pentagon investigator.)
54. Ibid., p. 129.
55. Ibid., p. 179.
56. Ibid.
57. Ibid.
58. Ibid.
59. Ibid.
60. Ibid., p. 180.
61. Ibid.
62. Ibid.
63. Ibid.
64. Ibid., pp. 180-181.
65. Ibid.
66. Ibid., p. 181.
67. Ibid.
68. Ibid.
69. Ibid.
70. Ibid.
71. Ibid., pp. 181-182.
72. Ibid., p. 182.
73. Ibid.
74. Ibid. (Stuart Symington was the name of the Democratic senator.)
75. Morely, *Scorpions' Dance*, p. 210. (The name of Helm's secretary was Elizabeth C. Dunlevy.)

Chapter Twenty-Four

1. Adrian Havill, *Deep Truth: The Lives of Bob Woodward and Carl Bernstein,* (New York: Birch Lane Press, 1993), p. 6.
2. Ibid.
3. Ibid.
4. Colodny and Gettlin, *Silent Coup*, p. 72.
5. Havill, *Deep Truth,* p. 7.
6. Ibid.
7. Ibid., p. 10.
8. Colodny and Gettlin, *Silent Coup*, p. 73.
9. Havill, *Deep Truth,* p. 9.
10. Ibid.
11. Colodny and Gettlin, *Silent Coup,* p. 73.
12. Ibid., p. 76.
13. Havill, *Deep Truth,* p. 63.
14. Colodny and Gettlin, *Silent Coup,* p. 74.
15. Ibid., p. 75.

16. Ibid. (Kathleen Woodward is the name of Woodward's first wife.)

17. Ibid., p. 81.

18. Ibid., p. 85.

19. Ibid., pp. 76-79.

20. Ibid., pp. 80-81.

21. Ibid., p. 71.

22. Ibid., p. 90.

23. Ibid., p. 71.

24. Ibid., p. 84. (Melvin Laird was the secretary of defense, and Jerry Friedheim was the name of his aide.)

25. Ibid., p. 85.

26. Ibid.

27. Havill, *Deep Truth,* p. 63.

28. Colodny and Gettlin, *Silent Coup,* p. 85.

29. Havill, *Deep Truth,* p. 64.

30. Colodny and Gettlin, *Silent Coup,* pp. 85-86. (Harry Rosenfeld was the name of the *Washington Post* editor, and Roger B. Farquhar was the name of *The Montgomery Sentinel* editor.)

31. Ibid., p. 86.

32. Havill, *Deep Truth,* p. 64.

33. Ibid., p. 65.

34. Ibid.

35. Ibid., p. 64.

36. Ibid., p. 65.

37. Ibid.

38. Ibid., p. 66.

39. Ibid., p. 69.

40. Carl Bernstein and Bob Woodward, *All the President's Men*, p. 13.

41. Ibid., p.16.

42. Ibid., p. 17. (Joseph Rafferty Jr., was the name of the burglars' "attorney of record.")

43. Alfred E. Lewis, "5 Held in Plot to Bug Democrats' Office Here, *Washington Post,* June 18, 1972, p. A1.

44. Ibid.

45. Bernstein and Woodward, *All the President's Men,* p. 20.

46. Ibid.

47. Ibid., pp. 21-22.

48. Ibid., p. 15.

49. Ibid., p. 21.

50. Ibid., p. 22.

51. Ibid.

52. Bob Woodward and Carl Bernstein, "GOP Security Aide Among 5 Arrested in Bugging Affair," *Washington Post,* June 19, 1972, p. A1.

53. Bernstein and Woodward, *All the President's Men,* p. 22.

54. Ibid.

55. Ibid., pp. 22-25.

56. Ibid., p. 24.

57. Ibid., pp. 24-25. (Ken Clawson was the deputy director of White House communications.)

58. Ibid., p. 25. (Robert F. Bennett was the president of the Mullen Company.)

59. Ibid., p. 23.

60. Ibid., p. 25.

61. Bob Woodward and E.J. Bachinski, "White House Consultant Tied to Bugging Figure," *Washington Post,* June 20, 1972, p. A1.

62. John D. O'Connor, "I'm the Guy They Called Deep Throat," *Vanity Fair,* July 2005, https://archive.vanityfair.com/article/2005/7/im-the-guy-they-called-deep-throat. Accessed on September 14, 2019.

63. Christopher Hitchens, "The Insider," *New York Times,* July 24, 2005, p. F8.

64. Bernstein and Woodward, *All the President's Men,* p. 72.

65. Tim Weiner, "W. Mark Felt, F.B.I. Official Who Became 'Deep Throat' is Dead at 95," *New York Times,* December 19, 2008, Late Edition, p. B 11.

66. Bernstein and Woodward, *All the President's Men,* p. 73.

67. Weiner, "W. Mark Felt, F.B.I. Official Who Became 'Deep Throat' is Dead at 95."

68. Mark Washburn, "Watergate History For Sale at Webster House in Dupont Circle," D.C. Condo Boutique," April 27, 2011, https://www.dccondoboutique.com/blog/watergate-history-for-sale-at-webster-house-in-dupont-circle.html. Accessed September 14, 2019.

69. Hougan, *Secret Agenda,* p. 292.

70. Ibid.

71. Weiner, "W. Mark Felt, F.B.I. Official Who Became 'Deep Throat' is Dead at 95."

72. Bernstein and Woodward, *All the President's Men,* p. 333.

73. Stephen C. Fehr, "In this House Lived Deep Throat," *Washington Post,* June 9, 2005, Final Edition, Fairfax Extra, p. T03.

74. Havill, *Deep Truth,* pp. 78-79.

75. Ibid., p. 79.

76. Ibid., pp. 78-79.

77. Ibid, p. 79.

78. Bernstein and Woodward, *All the President's Men*, p. 72.

79. Havill, *Deep Truth,* p. 79.

80. Ibid.

81. Bernstein and Woodward, *All the President's Men,* p. 72.

82. Ibid., p. 132.

83. U.S. Congress, Senate, *Hearings, Book 4,* p. 1613.

84. Bernstein and Woodward, *All the President's Men,* p. 244.

85. Ibid., p. 270.

86. Hougan, *Secret Agenda*, p. 241.

87. John D. O'Connor, "I'm the Guy They Called Deep Throat."

88. Ronald Ostrow, "Ex-F.B.I. Agent Said to be Data Source in Watergate Case," *Los Angeles Times,* September 17, 1972, p. 1.

89. Hougan, *Secret Agenda*, p. 264.

90. Bernstein and Woodward, *All the President's Men,* pp.108-110. (C.I.A. agent or asset Robert Foster Bennett was the C.E.O. of the Robert Mullin Company, and he would become a U.S. senator from Utah.)

91. Hougan, *Secret Agenda*, p. 6.

92. Ibid., p. 264. (Robert Bennett was the C.E.O. of the Robert Mullin Company and also a U.S. senator.)

93. Ibid. (Robert Bennett's case officer was Martin Lukoskie, and the C.I.A. director was Richard Helms.)

94. Ibid.

95. Ibid.

96. Russ Baker, *Family of Secrets: The Bush Dynasty, the Powerful Forces That Put It in the White House, and What Their Influence Means for America,* (New York: Bloomsbury Press, 2009), p. 207. (Senator Howard Baker was the Watergate Committee's ranking Republican, and Fred Thompson was the name of the Watergate Committee's counsel.)

97. Ibid.

98. Ibid. (William Colby was the C.I.A. director.)

99. Ibid.

Chapter Twenty-Five

1. Havill, *Deep Truth,* pp. 14-15.

2. Ibid., p. 17.

3. Ibid.

4. Ibid.

5. Ibid.

6. Ibid., p. 16.

7. Ibid.

8. Ibid., p. 15.

9. Ibid., p. 22.

10. Ibid., p. 23.

11. Ibid., p. 34.

12. Ibid.

13. Ibid., p. 36

14. Ibid.

15. Ibid.

16. Ibid.

17. Ibid.

18. Ibid.

19. Ibid., p. 37.

20. Ibid., p. 39.

21. Ibid., p. 38

22. Ibid., p. 39.

23. Ibid.

24. Ibid.

25. Ibid.

26. Ibid.

27. Ibid., p. 40.

28. Ibid.

29. Hougan, *Secret Agenda,* p. 322.

30. Ibid.

31. Ibid.

32. Ibid. (John Paisley was the name of the C.I.A.'s liaison to the Plumbers.)

33. Havill, *Deep Truth,* p. 120.

34. Ibid.

35. Ibid., p. 108. (Nora Ephron was the name of the woman Bernstein married in 1976.)

36. Ibid., p. 125.

37. Stuart Schoffman, "Marriage and Ephrontery: A New Woman Strikes Back," Los *Angeles Times, The Book Review,* April 17, 1983, p. 52.

38. Nora Ephron, *Heartburn,* (New York: Vintage Books, 1983/1996), p. 13.

39. Bernstein and Woodward, *All the President's Men*, p. 79 (The treasurer of the C.R.P. was Hugh Sloan.).

40. Ibid.

41. Ibid.

42. Havill, *Deep Truth*, p. 86.

43. Bernstein and Woodward, *All the President's Men*, p. 81.

44. Havill, *Deep Truth*, p. 86.

45. Bernstein and Woodward, *All the President's Men,* p. 260.

46. Ibid.

47. Ibid.

48. Ibid.

49. Havill, *Deep Truth*, pp. 86-87.

50. Ibid., p. 87.

51. Ibid.

52. Bernstein and Woodward, *All the President's Men,* p. 212.

53. Jeff Himmelman, "The Red Flag in the Flowerpot; Four Decades after Watergate, There's Something that Still Nags at Ben Bradlee about Deep Throat," *New York,* May 7, 2012.

54. Bernstein and Woodward, *All the President's Men*, p. 212.

55. Himmelman, "The Red Flag in the Flowerpot; Four Decades after Watergate, There's Something that Still Nags at Ben Bradlee about Deep Throat."

56. Bernstein and Woodward, *All the President's Men,* p. 210-211.

57. Himmelman, "The Red Flag in the Flowerpot; Four Decades after Watergate, There's Something that Still Nags at Ben Bradlee about Deep Throat."

Chapter Twenty-Six

1. John J. O'Connor, "TV Radio: Watergate: N.B.C. Says Over 9 Million Viewed Opening of Hearings on 3 Channels," *New York Times,* May 18, 1973, Late City Edition, p. 75.

2. Dean, *Blind Ambition,* p. 312.

3. Lukas, *Nightmare,* p. 377.

4. Ibid.

5. Nixon, *RN: The Memoirs of Richard Nixon*, p. 501.

6. Ray Locker, *Haig's Coup: How Richard Nixon's Closest Aide Forced Him from Office,* (Lincoln: Potomac Books, 2019) pp. 33-34.

7. Colodny and Shachtman, *The Forty Years War,* p. 189. (Larry Higby was the name of the Haldeman-Haig apparatchik.)

8. Ibid.

9. Ibid.

10. U.S., Congress, House, Committee on the Judiciary, *Book I: Alexander Butterfield, Paul O'Brien, and Fred C. LaRue,* p. 8.

11. Ibid.

12. Colodny and Gettlin, *Silent Coup*, p. 330.

13. Ibid.

14. Haldeman with DiMona, *The Ends of Power,* pp. 203-204.

15. Bernstein and Woodward, *All the President's Men,* pp. 195-196.

16. Ibid., p. 214. (Hugh Sloan was the name of the C.R.P.'s treasurer.)

17. Ibid., p. 330.

18. Ibid.

19. Ibid.

20. Ibid.

21. Ibid.

22. Colodny and Gettlin, *Silent Coup*, p. 333.

23. Colodny and Shachtman, *The Forty Years War,* pp. 189-190. (One of the Watergate staffers who questioned Butterfield was Scott Armstrong: He was a boyhood friend of Woodward, and Woodward had recommended him to the Watergate Committee.)

24. Bernstein and Woodward, *All the President's Men,* p. 331.

25. Colodny and Shachtman, *The Forty Years War,* p. 190.

26. Bernstein and Woodward, *All the President's Men,* pp. 330-331.

27. Ibid., p. 331.

28. Ibid.

29. Ibid., p. 332.

30. Ibid.

31. Colodny and Shachtman, *The Forty Years War,* p. 190.

32. Ibid., p. 190. (Fred Thompson was the name of the Watergate Committee counsel.)

33. Colodny and Gettlin, *Silent Coup*, p. 341.

34. Colodny and Shachtman, *The Forty Years War,* p. 190.

35. Nixon, *RN: The Memoirs of Richard Nixon*, p. 899.

36. Ibid.

37. Ibid., pp. 899-900.

38. Ibid., p. 900.

39. Ibid., p. 901.

40. Ibid.

41. Ibid.

42. Ibid., 902.

43. Deborah Davis, *Katharine the Great: Katherine Graham and The Washington Post,* (Bethesda: National Press, 1987), p. VII.

44. Michael Moore, "Stopping the Presses: The Anatomy of the Book Burning Business," *Multinational Monitor,* September 1987, https://www.multinationalmonitor. org/hyper/issues/1987/09/moore.html. Accessed September 15, 2019.

45. Davis, *Katharine the Great,* pp. 142-143.

46. Ibid., p. XI.

47. Ibid.

48. Ibid., p. VII.

49. Ibid., p. XI.

50. Ibid.

51. Ibid., pp. 142-43.

52. Ibid.

53. Ibid.

Chapter Twenty-Seven

1. Neil Lewis, "Elliot Richardson Dies at 79; Stood Up to Nixon and Resigned In 'Saturday Night Massacre," *New York Times,* January 1, 2000, Late Edition, p. B7

2. "Archibald Cox, Special Watergate Prosecutor, Dies at 92," *New York Times,* May 31, 2004, Late Edition, p. B7.

3. Anthony Ripley, "Senate Speedily Confirms Richardson by 82-3 Vote," *New York Times,* May 24, 1973, Late City Edition, p. 1.

4. Lewis, "Elliot Richardson Dies at 79; Stood Up to Nixon and Resigned In 'Saturday Night Massacre."

5. Ibid.

6. Ibid.

7. Ibid.

8. Ibid.

9. Ibid.

10. Ibid.

11. Ibid. (Felix Frankfurter was the name of the supreme court justice.)

12. Ibid.

13. Ibid.

14. Ibid.

15. Anthony Ripley, "Cox and Richardson Given Oaths in Contrasting Rites," *New York Times,* May 26, 1973, Late City Edition, p. 11.

16. John M. Crewdson, "Near the End of a Career, a Job to be Done: Archibald Cox," *New York Times,* August 26, 1973, Section 4, Late City Edition, p. E2.

17. "Archibald Cox, Special Watergate Prosecutor, Dies at 92."

18. Ibid.

19. Ibid.

20. Ibid.

21. Crewdson, "Near the End of A Career, a Job To be Done: Archibald Cox."

22. Anthony Ripley "Special Prosecutor Decides to Seek Legal Action Rather Than Resign Over Move to Block His Inquiry," July 24, 1973, *New York Times,* Late City Edition, p. 17.

23. Ibid.

24. Susanna McBee, "Cox's Tapes Stand Rests on 4 Issues," *Washington Post,* August 6, 1973, p. A1.

25. Ripley, "Special Prosecutor Decides to Seek Legal Action Rather than Resign Over Move to Block His Inquiry."

26. Locker, *Nixon's Gamble,* p. 250.

27. Warren Weaver, "Tape Case Argued in Federal Court," *New York Times,* August 23, 1973, Late City Edition, p. 1.

28. Ibid. (Charles Wright was the name of the attorney representing Nixon.)

29. Ibid.

30. Ibid.

31. "Text of Judge Sirica's Opinion in Ordering the President to Submit Tapes," *New York Times,* August 30, 1973, Late City Edition, p. 20.

32. Ibid.

33. Lesley Oelsner, "Judges Rule 5-2: Historic Decision Finds President Not Above Law's Commands," *New York Times,* October 13, 1973, Late City Edition, p. 1.

34. Locker, *Nixon's Gamble,* p. 251.

35. United Press International, "Cox Appoints 4 Lawyers to Investigatory Team," *New York Times,* September 4, 1973, Late City Edition, p. 25.

36. Lukas, *Nightmare,* p. 421.

37. Ibid.

38. Ibid.

39. Ibid., p. 422.

40. Ibid.

41. Ibid. p. 424.
42. Ibid.
43. Ibid., pp. 424-425.
44. Ibid., p. 425.
45. Ibid.
46. Ibid.
47. Ibid.
48. Locker, *Nixon's Gamble*, p. 251. (Senator John Stenis was the name of the "Undertaker.")
49. Lukas, *Nightmare,* p. 425.
50. Ibid.
51. Ibid., pp. 425-426.
52. Ibid., p. 426.
53. Colodny and Gettlin, *Silent Coup,* p. 354.
54. Nixon, *RN: The Memoirs of Richard Nixon*, p. 930.
55. Lukas, *Nightmare,* p. 426.
56. Ibid.
57. Ibid., p. 427.
58. Ibid.
59. Ibid., p. 428.
60. Ibid.
61. Ibid.,
62. Ibid. (Charles Wright was the name of the attorney aiding Nixon.)
63. Ibid., pp. 428-429.
64. Ibid., 429.
65. Ibid.
66. Colodny and Gettlin, *Silent Coup,* p. 357.
67. Lukas, *Nightmare,* p. 432.
68. Nixon, *RN: The Memoirs of Richard Nixon,* p. 931.
69. Lukas, *Nightmare,* pp. 431-432.
70. Ibid., p. 432.
71. Ibid.
72. Ibid.
73. Ibid., p. 431.
74. Ibid., p. 432.
75. Ibid.
76. Ibid.
77. Ibid.
78. Ibid.
79. Nixon, *RN: The Memoirs of Richard Nixon,* p. 932.
80. Lukas, *Nightmare*, p. 434.
81. Ibid.
82. Ibid.
83. Ibid.
84. Ibid., p. 435.
85. Warren Weaver, "Cox News Conference," *New York Times,* October 21, 1973, Late City Edition, p. 60.
86. Ibid.
87. Lukas, *Nightmare,* p. 437.
88. Ibid.
89. Ibid.
90. Ibid., p. 439. (William Ruckelshaus was the deputy attorney general.)
91. Ibid., pp. 439-440. (Robert Bork was the solicitor general.)
92. Ibid., p. 440. (Ron Ziegler was the name of Nixon's press secretary.)
93. Ibid., p. 441.
94. Ibid.
95. Ibid., p. 445.
96. Nixon, *RN: The Memoirs of Richard Nixon*, p. 937.
97. Ibid.
98. United Press International, "Agnew Said to Hold Long Discussions About Resigning," *New York Times,* September 18, 1973, Late City Edition, p. 32.
99. Christopher Lydon, "Agnew Says 'Damned Lies' to Report of Kickbacks; Doubts He'll be Indicted," *New York Times,* August 9, 1973, Late City Edition, p.1.
100. James M. Naughton, "Judge Orders Fine, 3 Years' Probation," *New York Times,* October 11, 1973, Late City Edition, p.1.
101. Ibid.
102. Ibid.
103. Helen Dudar, "Agnew: I Quit Because I Feared for My Life," *Washington Post,* April 20, 1980, https://www.washingtonpost.com/archive/opinions/1980/04/20/agnew-i-quit-because-i-feared-for-my-life/b3ebc16c-a0ab-4a41-ae4d-db76aa-136ba9. Accessed September 4, 2019.
104. David E. Rosenbaum, "Panel Hears I.R.S. Weighed Fraud Charge for Nixon," *New York Times,* June 21, 1974, Late City Edition, p. 17.
105. Ibid.
106. Ibid.

Chapter Twenty-Eight

1. Lukas, *Nightmare,* p. 562.

2. Ibid.

3. Ibid.

4. Ibid.

5. John Herbers, "Nixon Names Saxbe Attorney General; Jaworski Appointed Special Prosecutor," *New York Times,* November 2, 1973, Late City Edition, p. 1. (William Saxbe was the new acting attorney general.)

6. Anthony Ripley, "Jaworski Assumes Office; Bork Praises Prosecutor," *New York Times,* November 6, 1973, Late City Edition, p. 23.

7. Linda Charlton, "Key Role in Nixon Case: Leon Jaworski, Watergate Lawyer, Dies," *New York Times,* December 10, 1982, Late Edition, p. A1.

8. Ibid.

9. Ibid.

10. Ibid.

11. Ibid.

12. Lukas, *Nightmare,* p. 446.

13. New York Times, "Jaworski Reportedly Had Role in Setting Up C.I.A. Aid Conduit," *New York Times,* November 6, 1973, p. 25.

14. Ibid.

15. Ibid.

16. Ibid.

17. Lukas, *Nightmare,* p. 446.

18. Ibid., p. 447.

19. Ibid., p. 445.

20. Locker, *Haig's Coup,* p. 198.

21. Nixon v. Sirica, 1973 U.S. Appeals D.C. LEXIS (1973)

22. Lukas, *Nightmare,* p. 458. (Rose Mary Woods was the name of Nixon's personal secretary.)

23. Colodny and Gettlin, *Silent Coup,* p. 373.

24. Ibid.

25. Ibid.

26. Ibid.

27. Lukas, *Nightmare,* p. 458.

28. Ibid.

29. Ibid.

30. Warren Weaver Jr., "Court Informed: The Talks were Those President had with Mitchell and Dean," *New York Times,* November 1, 1973, Late City Edition, p. 1.

31. Ibid.

32. Ibid.

33. Colodny and Shachtman, *The Forty Years War,* p. 208.

34. Warren Weaver Jr., "A 'Gap' in Tapes Reported by Aide," *New York Times,* November 8, 1973, Late City Edition, p. 1. (John C. Bennet was the name of the presidential aide.)

35. Colodny and Gettlin, *Silent Coup,* p. 372.

36. United Press International, "Rose Mary Calls Some Tapes Poor, Impossible to Copy: She-Disputes in Court that She Discovered 'Gap,'" *Los Angeles Times,* November 8, 1973, p. 2.

37. Carl Bernstein and Bob Woodward, "Parts 'Inaudible': Nixon Tape Portions 'Inaudible and Uneven,'" *Washington Post,* November 8, 1973, p. A1.

38. Ibid.

39. Ibid.

40. Bernstein and Woodward, *All the President's Men,* p. 333.

41. Ibid.

42. Ibid.

43. Locker, *Nixon's Gamble,* p. 250.

44. Stephen C. Fehr, "In This House Lived Deep Throat," *Washington Post,* June 9, 2005, Fairfax Extra, p. T3.

45. "Deep Throat: Narrowing the Field," *Time,* May 3, 1976, p. 19.

46. Colodny and Gettlin, *Silent Coup,* p. 379. (Samuel Powers was the name of the attorney.)

47. Ibid., pp. 373-374.

48. Ibid., p. 379.

49. Ibid.

50. Ibid.

51. Nixon, *RN: The Memoirs of Richard Nixon,* p. 949.

52. David E. Rosenbaum, "Another Section of Tapes is Blank, A Nixon Aide Says," *New York Times,* November 22, 1973, Late City Edition, p. 1.

53. George Lardner Jr., "Haig Tells of Theories on Erasure," *Washington Post,* December 7, 1973, p. A1.

54. Linda Mathews, "White House Discloses Lapse in Key Watergate Recording," *Los Angeles Times,* November 22, 1973, p. 1.

55. Lukas, *Nightmare,* p. 463.

56. Ibid.

57. Ibid.

58. Ibid.

59. Ibid., p. 462.

60. Ibid.

61. Colodny and Gettlin, *Silent Coup,* p. 381.

62. Nixon, *RN: The Memoirs of Richard Nixon,* pp. 631-632.

63. Ibid., p. 632.

64. Ibid.

65. "White House Finds Jaworski No Easier Than Cox," *New York Times,* December 1, 1973, Late City Edition, p. 16.

66. Leon Jaworski, *The Right and the Power: The Prosecution of Watergate,* (New York: Reader's Digest Press, 1976), p. 81.

67. Colodny and Gettlin, *Silent Coup,* pp. 386-387.

68. Ibid., p. 387.

69. Nixon, *RN: The Memoirs of Richard Nixon,* p. 991.

70. Jaworski, *The Right and the Power: The Prosecution of Watergate,* pp. 55.

71. Ibid.

72. Colodny and Gettlin, *Silent Coup,* p. 395.

73. Ibid.

74. Ibid.

75. Woodward and Bernstein, *The Final Days,* p. 114.

76. Ibid., p. 115.

77. Ibid.

78. Ibid.

79. Ibid.

80. Ibid.

81. Nixon, *RN: The Memoirs of Richard Nixon,* p. 991.

82. Ibid.

83. Anthony Ripley, "Jaworski Asserts Nixon Withholds Requested Tapes," *New York Times,* February 15, 1974, Late City Edition, p. 1.

84. Ibid.

85. Lesley Oelsner, "New Subpoena for Tapes Delivered to White House," *New York Times,* April 19, 1974, Late Jersey Edition, p. 1.

86. Ibid.

87. Nixon, *RN: The Memoirs of Richard Nixon,* p. 999.

88. Ibid., pp. 999-1000.

89. Ibid., p. 1000.

90. Ibid., p. 1001.

91. Warren Weaver Jr., "Supreme Court Agrees to Decide Now if Nixon can Withhold Evidence," *New York Times,* June 1, 1974, Late City Edition, p.1.

92. Warren Weaver Jr., "Opinion by Burger: Name of President is Left in Indictment as a Co-Conspirator," *New York Times,* July 25, 1974, Late City Edition, p. 1.

93. Colodny and Shachtman, *The Forty Years War,* p. 223.

94. Ibid. (John Rhodes was the House Minority Leader.)

95. Ibid.

96. "Transcript of President Nixon's Address to the Nation Announcing His Resignation," *New York Times,* August 9, 1974, Late City Edition, p. 2.

Chapter Twenty-Nine

1. Jim Squires, "Probers Charge Pentagon Spied on Kissinger in 1971: Report Chiefs got Secrets," *Chicago Tribune,* January 11, 1974, p. 1.

2. Bob Woodward and Carl Bernstein, "Pentagon Got Secret Data Of Kissinger's: Secret Kissinger Data Passed to Pentagon," *Washington Post,* January 12, 1974, p. A1.

3. Ibid.

4. Ibid.

5. Seymour M. Hersh, "Report on Data Leak Said to Have Named Moorer," *New York Times,* January 14, 1974, Late City Edition, p. 1.

6. Colodny and Gettlin, *Silent Coup,* pp. 400-401.

7. Ibid.

8. Ibid., p. 400.

9. Ibid., p. 401.

10. Ibid., p. 402

11. Ibid.

12. Ibid.

13. Ibid., pp. 406-407.

14. Ibid. p. 407.

15. Ibid., p. 402.

16. Ibid., p. 410.

17. Ibid.

18. Ibid., p. 411.

19. Ibid., p. 412.

20. Ibid. (Harold Hughes was the name of the senator.)

21. Ibid.

22. Ibid.

23. Anthony Ripley, "Federal Grand Jury Indicts 7 Nixon Aides on Charges of Conspiracy on Watergate; Haldeman, Ehrlichman, Mitchell on List," *New York Times,* March 2, 1974, Late City Edition, p. 1.

24. Ibid.

25. Ibid.

26. Ibid.

27. Ibid.

28. Ibid.

29. Ibid.

30. Ibid.

31. Shepard, *The Real Watergate Scandal,* p. 57.

32. Ibid., p. 54.

33. Ibid.

34. Ibid., p. 175.

35. Ibid., p. 176.

36. Ibid., p. 175.

37. Ibid., pp. 168-169.

38. Ibid., p. 149.

39. "Text of Indictment Handed Up to Judge Sirica by Watergate Grand Jury," *New York Times,* Mar 2, 1974, Late City Edition, p. 14.

40. Ibid.

41. Ibid.

42. Ibid.

43. Ibid.

44. Colodny and Gettlin, *Silent Coup,* p. 170.

45. Ibid., p. 168.

46. "Text of Indictment Handed Up to Judge Sirica by Watergate Grand Jury."

47. U.S. Congress, Senate, *Hearings, Book 3,* p. 950.

48. U.S. Congress, Senate, *Hearings, Book 4,* p. 1672.

49. "Text of Indictment Handed Up to Judge Sirica by Watergate Grand Jury."

50. Rosen, *The Strong Man,* p. 318. (George Frampton was the W.S.P.F. lawyer who wrote the memo.)

51. Ibid.

52. Ibid., p. 319.

53. Ibid., pp. 430-431.

54. Lesley Oelsner, "Proceeding Grim: Panel Deliberated for 15 Hours on 3 days – Appeals Planned," *New York Times,* January 2, 1975, Late City Edition, p. 1.

55. Lesley Oelsner, "Dean Sentenced to 1 to 4 Years in Cover-Up Case," *New York Times,* August 3, 1974, Late City Edition, p. 1.

56. Ibid.

57. Shepard, *The Real Watergate Scandal,* p. 128.

58. "Judge Sirica's Mercy," *New York Times,* January 10, 1975, Late City Edition, p. 36

59. Associated Press, "Dean and Magruder Say Telling the Truth has 'Cleansed' Them," *New York Times,* January 13, 1975, Late City Edition, p. 20.

Epilogue

1. Hougan, *Secret Agenda,* pp. 11-12.

2. Doug Stanglin, "C.I.A. Formerly Admits Role in 1953 Iranian Coup," *USA Today,* August 20, 2013, https://www.usatoday.com/story/news/nation/2013/08/20/cia-iran-coup-documents-acknowledges-classified/2675911. Accessed September 21, 2019.

3. Douglas Martin, "Emilio Colombo, 93, Dies; Former Italian Premier," *New York Times,* July 2, 2013, Late Edition, p. A 21.

4. Tim Weiner, "C.I.A. Opening Files on Cold War Role," *New York Times,* August 29, 1993, Late Edition, p. 7.

5. Philip Agee, *Inside the Company: C.I.A. Diary* (Middlesex: Penguin Books, 1975), pp. 103-316.

6. Gaylord Shaw, "Where is the Truth?: The C.I.A.'s 29 Years Successes, Failures," *Los Angeles Times,* February 22, 1976, p. 1.

7. Ibid.

8. Jeff Gerth, "C.I.A. has Long Sought to Sway Foreign Voters," *New York Times,* May 13, 1984, Late Edition, p. 12.

9. David Aronson, "Kabilla or Chaos," *Washington Post,* November 12, 1997, p. A23. (Mobuto Sese Seko was the Congo's C.I.A.-installed dictator.)

10. Andre Mwamba Kapanga, "The Congo Held Hostage: Taking Exception," *Washington Post,* October 15, 1997, p. A21.

11. Kerry Luft, "Military Maintains its Grip on Chile: Former Dictator Still Influential," *Chicago Tribune,* November 13, 1995; Section 1, p. 12. (Augusto Pinochet was the Chilean dictator.)

12. Jonathan Kandell, "Augusto Pinochet, 91, Dictator Who Ruled by Terror in Chile,

Dies," *New York Times,* December 11, 2006, Late Edition, p. A1. (Augusto Pinochet was the Chilean dictator.)

13. Anthony Faiola, "U.S. Allies in Drug War in Disgrace," *Washington Post,* May 9, 2001, p. A1. (Alberto K. Fujimori was the Peruvian dictator.)

14. Simon Romero, "Chileans Order Peru's Ex-Chief Home For Trial,"*New York Times,* September 22, 2007, Late Edition, p. A1.

15. Serge F. Kovaleski, "Panamanians Split on Legacy of U.S. Stay," *Washington Post,* January 16, 2000, p. A29. (Manual Noriega was the Panamanian dictator.)

16. "The Bodies in Panama," *New York Times,* February 20, 2001, Late Edition, p. A20.

17. Tim Weiner, "C.I.A. Formed Haitian Unit Later Tied to Narcotics Trade," *New York Times,* November 14, 1993, Late Edition, p. 2. (François "Papa Doc" Duvalier and his son Jean-Claude Duvalier nicknamed "Baby Doc" were the Haitian dictators.)

18. Randal C. Archibold, "The Brutal Baby Doc of Haiti, A Second-Generation Dictator," *New York Times,* October 5, 2014, Late Edition, p. 1.

19. "Arms Deal Put U.S. on Both Sides of War," *Chicago Tribune,* December 16, 1986, p. 4. (Saddam Hussein was the Iraqi dictator.)

20. Kathy Kadane, "U.S. Officials' Lists Aided Indonesian Bloodbath in '60s," *Washington Post,* May 21, 1990, p. A5. (General Suharto was the Indonesian dictator.)

21. Joshua Oppenheimer, "Suharto's Purge, Indonesia's Silence," *New York Times,* September 30, 2015, Late Edition, p. A25.

22. Kadane, "U.S. Officials' Lists Aided Indonesian Bloodbath in '60s."

23. Colodny and Gettlin, *Silent Coup,* pp. 90-91.

24. Ibid., p. 91.

25. Locker, *Haig's Coup,* p. 347.

26. Ibid.

27. Ibid., p. 350.

28. Ibid., p. 349.

29. Ibid., p. 352.

30. Ibid., p. 349.

31. Ibid., p. 352.

32. Ibid., p. 348.

33. Deirdre Carmody, "Book on Nixon's Last Months in Office Challenged on Methods and Accuracy," *New York Times,* April 3, 1976, Late City Edition, p. 14.

34. Robert G. Kaiser, "Carl Bernstein Will Resign from Post to Write Books," *Washington Post,* December 9, 1976, p. A3.

35. Carl Bernstein, "The C.I.A. and the Media," *Rolling Stone,* September 20, 1977.

36. Walt Harrington, "Still Carl After All These Years," *Washington Post Magazine,* March 19, 1989.

37. Havill, *Deep Truth,* p. 155.

38. Ibid., p. 128.

39. Harrington, "Still Carl After All These Years."

40. Ibid.

41. Ibid.

42. Havill, *Deep Truth,* p. 151. (Roone Arledge was the president of ABC news.)

43. Ibid., p. 166.

44. Ibid., p. 136.

45. Ibid., p. 137.

46. Janet Cooke, "Jimmy's World: 8-Year-Old Heroin Addict Lives for a Fix," *Washington Post,* September 28, 1980, p. A1.

47. Havill, *Deep Truth,* pp. 139-140. (Janet Cooke was the name of the reporter who wrote "Jimmy's World.")

48. Ibid., p. 144.

49. Ibid.

50. Ibid.

51. Cass Peterson, "Post Writer Wins Pulitzer for Story on Child Addict," *Washington Post,* April 14, 1981, p. A1.

52. Havill, *Deep Truth,* p. 147.

53. Ibid.

54. Cheryl Lavin, "Falling Star," *Chicago Tribune Magazine,* May 23, 1982, p. 16.

55. Havill, *Deep Truth,* pp. 176-177.

56. Ibid, p. 176.

57. Ibid., p. 177.

58. Ibid.

59. Ibid.

60. Ibid.

61. Ibid.

62. Ibid., p. 178.

63. Ibid.

64. Ibid.

65. Ibid.

66. Ibid.

67. Ibid.

68. Ibid., pp. 178-179.

69. Ibid., p. 150. (Donald Graham was *The Washington Post's* publisher.)

70. Ibid.

71. Lou Cannon, "Reshaping the White House," *Washington Post,* May 19, 1975, p. A1.

72. Ibid.

73. Philip Shabecoff, "Ford's Primary Losses Divide White House Staff as Factions Trade Charges of Laxity," *New York Times,* May 24, 1976, Late City Edition, p. 18.

74. Michael Getler, "Percy Subpoenas Indexes, Logs for Haig-Nixon Tapes," *Washington Post,* January 12, 1981, p. A1.

75. Bob Woodward, "Don't Subpoena the Tapes," *Washington Post,* January 15, 1981, p. A19.

76. Ibid.

77. Associated Press, "Nixon Moves to Bar Senate Access to Tapes," *Washington Post,* January 17, 1981, p. A4.

78. Helen Dewar, "Senate Confirms Haig to be Secretary of State, 93 to 6," *Washington Post,* January 22, 1981, p. A12.

79. "George Tenet Resigns," *New York Times,* June 4, 2004, Late Edition, p. A26.

80. "Lawsuit Over a Watergate Book Could Put Scandal Back in Court." *New York Times,* June 15, 1992, Late Edition, p. A14.

81. Associated Press, "Watergate Figure John Dean Sues Liddy, Others," January 30, 1992.

82. Phil Willon and Michael Fechter, "Watergate; The Untold Story," *Tampa Tribune,* Metro Edition, January 19, 1997, p 1.

83. Ibid.

84. Ibid.

85. Ibid.

86. Ibid.

87. George Lardner Jr., "Watergate Libel Suit Settled; John Dean and St. Martin's Press Come to Terms Over 'Silent Coup,'" *Washington Post,* July 23, 1997, p. C1.

88. Ibid.

89. Ibid.

90. Ibid.

91. James Rosen, "Under Watergate," *Washington City Paper,* May 25, 2001, https://

www.washingtoncitypaper.com/arts/books/article/13022221/under-watergate. Accessed on September 23, 2019.

92. Lardner Jr., "Watergate Libel Suit Settled; John Dean and St. Martin's Press Come to Terms Over 'Silent Coup,"

93. Ibid.

94. Michael Fechter, "Watergate; Although 25 Years have Passed Since the Watergate Break-in that Toppled President Nixon, Questions Remain about the Culpability of John Dean," *Tampa Tribune,* June 15, 1997, p. 4.

95. Ibid.

96. Russ Baker, "Watergate Revelations: The Coup Against Nixon, Part 3 of 3," *WhoWhatWhy,* May 10, 2012, https://whowhatwhy.org/2012/05/10/watergate-revelations-the-coup-against-nixon-part-3-of-3. Accessed September 23, 2019.

97. Jacqueline Soteropoulos, "Watergate Book Lawsuit Settled," *Tampa Tribune,* September 28, 1999, Final Edition, p. 1.

98. Ibid. (Emmet G. Sullivan was the name of the U.S. district court judge.)

99. Rosen, "Under Watergate."

100. Soteropoulos, "Watergate Book Lawsuit Settled." (John M. Garrick was the name of the Deans' attorney.)

101. Len Colodny and Robert Gettlin, *Silent Coup: The Removal of a President,* (Walterville: Trineday, 2015)

102. Rosen, "Under Watergate."

103. Fechter, "Watergate; Although 25 Years have Passed Since the Watergate Break-in that Toppled President Nixon, Questions Remain about the Culpability of John Dean."

104. Manuel Roig-Franzia, "Arguments in Liddy Trial Focus on Dean: Jury Begins Deliberations in Defamation Suit," *Washington Post,* February 1, 2001, p. A6.

105. Seth Hettena, "Liddy Blasts Former Nixon Counsel," Associated Press Online, January 31, 2001.

106. "The Courts and History," *Washington Post,* Editorial, February 4, 2001, p. B6.

107. Hettena, "Liddy Blasts Former Nixon Counsel."

108 Manuel Roig-Franzia, "Mistrial Declared in Case Against Liddy," *Washington Post,* February 2, 2001, p B1.

109. Seth Hettena, "Attorney: Dean is Pulling the Strings in Liddy Lawsuit," Associated

Press, January 31, 2001.

110. Manuel Roig-Franzia, "Liddy Concludes Testimony in Md. Lawsuit," *Washington Post,* January 31, 2001, p. B3.

111. Hettena, "Liddy Blasts Former Nixon Counsel."

112. Hettena, "Attorney: Dean is Pulling the Strings in Liddy Lawsuit."

113. Ibid. (John B. Williams was the name of Liddy's attorney.)

114. Roig-Franzia, "Mistrial Declared in Case Against Liddy."

115. Ibid.

116. Ibid.

117. "The Courts and History," *Washington Post,* February 4, 2001, p. B6.

118. Ibid.

119. Ibid.

120. Darragh Johnson, "Second Trial Opens in Watergate Case: Ex-D.N.C. Worker Suing Gordon Liddy," *Washington Post,* June 25, 2002, p. B5.

121. Canadian Press, "Judge Dismisses Defamation Suit Against Watergate Plumber G. Gordon Liddy," *Press News Limited,* July 3, 2002.

122. Rosen, *The Strong Man,* 2008.

123. Stanford, *White House Call Girl,* 2013.

124. Stone with Colapietro, *Nixon's Secrets,* 2014.

125. Locker, *Nixon's Gamble,* 2016

126 Joseph Abrams, "Watergate Figure John Dean Threatens to Sue Historian Over Damaging Tape Recordings," FOX News, July 10, 2009, https://www.foxnews.com/story/watergate-figure-john-dean-threatens-to-sue-historian-over-damaging-tape-recordings. Accessed September 23, 2019.

127. Dean with Gorey, *Mo: A Woman's View of Watergate,* 1977, p. 48.

128. Ibid., pp. 49-50.

129. Stephanie Mansfield, "Sex! Power! Mo Dean! And Sex!: The Stockbroker Turns Novelist with Her Racy 'Washington Wives.'"

130. Mark Shields, "Our Last Liberal President," *Washington Post,* August 4, 1996, p. C7.

131. Ibid.

132. Ibid.

133 Ibid.

134. Ibid.

135. Ibid.

136. Ibid.

137. Ibid.

138. Ibid.

139. Ibid.

140. Ibid.

141. Bob Herbert, "After the War was Over," *New York Times,* July 7, 2009, Late Edition, p. A23.

142. Colman McCarthy, "Nixon and His Mythmakers," *Washington Post,* April 26, 1001, p. O14.

143. Thomas Lippman, "After the Eulogies: Nixon Critics Recall Vietnam," *Washington Post,* May 1, 1994, p. A11.

144. Peter S. Goodman," Repressed Memories: The Hypocrisy of U.S. Policy in War Torn Cambodia," *Washington Post,* January 10, 1999, p. C2.

145. United Press International, "Suharto Put U.S. Aid on 'Shopping List,'" *Los Angeles Times,* December 2, 1970, p. A7.

146. Vernon Loeb, "C.I.A. had Covert Tie to Letelier Plotter," *Washington Post,* September 20, 2000, p. A3.

147. United States Office of Management and Budget, *Historical Tables,* (Washington, D.C.: U.S. Government Printing Office, 1997), pp. 45-46.

148. Nan Tian, Diego Lopes Da Silva, Xiao Liang, Lorenzo Scarazzato, Lucie Béraud-Sudreau, Ana Carolina De Oliveira Assis. Trends in World Military Expenditures, 2022. (Solna: Stockholm International Peace Research Institute, 2023), p. 2.

149. Ibid.

150. Ibid.

151. Pieter D. Wezeman, Justine Gadon, Siemon T. Wezeman. *Trends in International Arms Transfers,* 2022.(Solna: Stockholm International Peace Research Institute, 2023), p. 2.

BIBLIOGRAPHY

Abrams, Joseph. "Watergate Figure John Dean Threatens to Sue Historian Over Damaging Tape Recordings." FOX News, July 10, 2009. https://www.foxnews.com/story/watergate-figure-john-dean-threatens-to-sue-historian-over-damaging-tape-recordings.

Abramson, Rudy. "From Beginning to End, Nixon Was a Fighter." Los Angeles Times, April 24, 1994.

Agee, Philip. Inside the Company: CIA Diary. Middlesex. Penguin Books, 1975

Alcindor, Yamiche. "John Conyers to Leave Congress Amid Harassment Claims." New York Times, December 5, 2017. https://www.nytimes.com/2017/12/05/us/politics/john-conyers-election.html.

Anderson, Patrick. "Rushing Toward a Footnote in History." New York Times Magazine, July 8, 1973.

Apple, R. W., Jr. "2 Aides Praised: Counsel Forced Out—Leonard Garment Takes Over Job." New York Times, May 1, 1973.

"Archibald Cox, Special Watergate Prosecutor, Dies at 92." New York Times, May 31, 2004.

Archibold, Randal C. "The Brutal Baby Doc of Haiti, A Second-Generation Dictator." New York Times, October 5, 2014.

"Arms Deal Put U.S. on Both Sides of War." Chicago Tribune, December 16, 1986.

"Arnie Ally Ducks Film Awards," New York Post, October 1, 2004.

Arnold, Martin. "Evidence Snarls Ellsberg Trial." New York Times, April 27, 1973.

Arnold, Martin. "Trial Will Go On," New York Times, April 28, 1973.

Aronson, David. "Kabila or Chaos." Washington Post, November 12, 1997.

Associated Press. "Dean and Magruder Say Telling the Truth has 'Cleansed' Them." New York Times, January 13, 1975.

Associated Press. "Nixon Moves to Bar Senate Access to Tapes." Washington Post, January 17, 1981.

Associated Press. "Watergate Figure John Dean Sues Liddy, Others." January 30, 1992.

Associated Press. "William Byrne Jr., 75, Judge in Ellsberg Case." New York Times, January 15, 2006.

Baker, Russ. Family of Secrets: The Bush Dynasty, America's Invisible Government, and the Hidden History of the Last Fifty Years. New York: Bloomsbury Press, 2009.

Baker, Russ. "Watergate Revelations: The Coup Against Nixon, Part 3 of 3." WhoWhatWhy, May 10, 2012. https://whowhatwhy.org/2012/05/10/watergate-revelations-the-coup-against-nixon-part-3-of-3.

Bamford, James. Body of Secrets: Anatomy of the Ultra-Secret National Security Agency. New York: Doubleday, 2001.

Barnes, Andrew. "GOP's Birely Named to County Council; Power Shift Seen." Washington Post, December 29, 1965.

Barnes, Bart. "Carmine Bellino Dies at 84; was Congressional Investigator." Washington Post, February 28, 1990.

Barnes, Bart. "John Sirica, Watergate Judge, Dies." Washington Post, August 15, 1992.

Beecher, William. "Raids in Cambodia By U.S. Unprotested." New York Times, May 9, 1969.

"Bennett, John C. "56; Nixon Aide Testified on Watergate Tapes." New York Times, May 6, 1980.

Bernstein, Carl. "The CIA and the Media." Rolling Stone, September 20, 1977.

Bernstein, Carl and Bob Woodward. All the President's Men. New York: Simon and Schuster, 1974.

Bernstein, Carl and Bob Woodward. "FBI Finds Nixon Aides Sabotaged Democrats." Washington Post, October 10, 1973.

Bernstein, Carl and Bob Woodward. "Parts 'Inaudible': Nixon Tape Portions 'Inaudible and Uneven.'" Washington Post, November 8, 1973.

Bosman, Julie Phillips. "Woman Says Her Brother was Victim of Hastert: Sex Abuse Hidden For Years, She Adds." New York Times, June 6, 2015.

Bruskin, Robert. "New Congress Members Hit Housing Lack." Washington Post. December 29, 1946.

Bryant, Nick. The Franklin Scandal: A Story of Powerbrokers, Child Abuse, and Betrayal. Walterville: Trineday, 2012.

Campbell Robertson. "In Louisiana, Tainted Senator Rides Anti-Obama Sentiment." New York Times, September 11, 2009.

Canadian Press. "Judge Dismisses Defamation Suit Against Watergate Plumber G. Gordon Liddy." Press News Limited, July 3, 2002.

Cannon, Lou. "Reshaping the White House." *Washington Post,* May 19, 1975.

Carmody, Deirdre. "Book on Nixon's Last Months in Office Challenged on Methods and Accuracy." *New York Times,* April 3, 1976.

Charlton, Linda. "Key Role in Nixon Case: Leon Jaworski, Watergate Lawyer, Dies." *New York Times,* December 10, 1982.

Cochrane, Emily. "G.O.P. Congressman to Retire After Reports He Asked Woman to have Abortion." *New York Times,* October 4, 2017. https://www.nytimes.com/2017/10/04/us/politics/representative-tim-murphy-retire-abortion.html.

Cochrane, Emily. "Texas Congressman Who Settled Harassment Case with Taxpayer Funds Resigns." *The New York Times,* April 6, 2018. https://www.nytimes.com/2018/04/06/us/politics/farenthold-harassment-case-resigns.html.

Cohen, Adam. "Editorial Observer: Larry Craig's Great Adventure: Suddenly, He's a Civil Libertarian." *New York Times,* September 24, 2007.

Collins, Gail. "Sex Scandals to Learn By." *New York Times,* March 18, 2010.

Colodny, Len and Robert Gettlin. *Silent Coup: The Removal of a President.* New York: St. Martin's Paperbacks, 1992.

Colodny, Len and Tom Shachtman. *The Forty Years War: The Rise and Fall of the Neocons, from Nixon to Obama.* New York: HarperCollins, 2009.

Condon, Tom. "From Hartford 25 Years Later, A Watergate Player Reflects." *Hartford Courant,* June 15, 1997.

Conklin, William R. "Hiss Is Sentenced to Five-Year Term; Acheson Backs Him." *New York Times,* January 26, 1950.

Cooke, Janet. "Jimmy's World: 8-Year-Old Heroin Addict Lives for a Fix." *Washington Post,* September 28, 1980.

Cornwell, Rupert. "Obituary: John Ehrlichman." *Independent.* February 17, 1999. https://www.independent.co.uk/arts-entertainment/obituary-john-ehrlichman-1071331.html.

Crewdson, John M. "Gray Testifies that Dean 'Probably' Lied to FBI." *New York Times,* March 23, 1973.

Crewdson, John M. "Near the End of a Career, a Job To Be Done: Archibald Cox." *New York Times,* August 26, 1973.

Crewdson, John M. "Nixon Withdraws Gray Nomination as F.B.I. Director." *New York Times,* April 6, 1973.

Davis, Deborah. *Katharine the Great: Katharine Graham and Her Washington Post Empire.* Bethesda: National Press, 1987.

Dean, John, III. *Blind Ambition: The White House Years.* New York: Simon and Schuster, 1976.

Dean, John. *Worse than Watergate: The Secret Presidency of George W. Bush.* New York: Little, Brown & Company, 2004.

Dean, Maureen with Hays Gorey. *Mo: A Woman's View of Watergate.* New York: Simon and Schuster, 1977.

"Deep Throat: Narrowing the Field." *Time,* May 3, 1976.

Dewar, Helen. "Senate Confirms Haig to be Secretary of State, 93 to 6." *Washington Post,* January 22, 1981.

Dowd, Maureen. "Pharisees on the Potomac." *New York Times,* July 19, 2009.

Ehrlichman, John. *Witness to Power: The Nixon Years.* New York: Simon and Schuster, 1982.

"Ex-F.B.I. Agent Named Bugging Case Witness." *New York Times,* September 17, 1972.

Faiola, Anthony. "U.S. Allies in Drug War in Disgrace." *Washington Post,* May 9, 2001.

Fandos, Nicholas and Jonathan Martin. "Congressman Caught in Storm Over Explicit Photo." *New York Times,* November 23, 2017.

Fandos, Nicholas. "House Republican Trent Franks Resigns Amid Harassment Investigation." *New York Times,* December 7, 2017. https://www.nytimes.com/2017/12/07/us/politics/trent-franks-house-member-resigns.html.

Fechter, Michael. "Watergate; Although 25 Years have Passed Since the Watergate Break-in that Toppled President Nixon, Questions Remain about the Culpability of John Dean." *Tampa Tribune,* June 15, 1997.

Fehr, Stephen C. "In this House Lived Deep Throat." *Washington Post,* June 9, 2005.

Feron, James. "Poughkeepsie Recalls Liddy: Gung-Ho Deputy Prosecutor." *New York Times,* July 13, 1973.

Feuer, Alan. "From a Bright Past to a Cloudy Future: D.W.I. Arrest, a Secret Child. So What's Next for Fossella?" *New York Times,* May 10, 2008.

Finney, John W. "Defense Recalls 'Checkers' Speech

By Nixon." *New York Times,* July 31, 1972.

Fitzgibbon, William. "The Hiss-Chambers Case: A Chronology Since 1934." *New York Times,* June 12, 1949.

Frankel, Max. "It All Adds Up for Richard Nixon." *New York Times,"* August 11, 1968.

"George Tenet Resigns." *New York Times,* June 4, 2004.

Gerth, Jeff. "C.I.A. Has Long Sought to Sway Foreign Voters." *New York Times,* May 13, 1984.

Getler, Michael. "Percy Subpoenas Indexes, Logs for Haig-Nixon Tapes." *Washington Post,* January 12, 1981.

Gibson, Gail. "Dean won't Take Stand in Liddy Defamation Lawsuit." *Baltimore Sun,* January 29, 2001.

Gibson, Gail. "Jury Rejects Claim that Liddy Hurt Reputation; Repeating Watergate Call-Girl Ring Theory didn't Defame ex-DNC Secretary." *Baltimore Sun,* July 4, 2002.

Giraldi, Phillip. "Did Foreign Governments Blackmail Denny Hastert?" *The American Conservative,* October 20, 2015.

Goodman, Peter S. "Repressed Memories: The Hypocrisy of U.S. Policy in War Torn Cambodia." *Washington Post,* January 10, 1999.

Goodman, Walter. "Revelations about J. Edgar Hoover." *New York Times,* February 9, 1993.

Goodnough, Abby and Kate Zernike. "A Complex and Hidden Life Behind Ex-Representative's Public Persona." *New York Times,* October 5, 2006.

Graham, Fred P. "Ellsberg Offers 2 Views on Delay." *New York Times,* August 2, 1972.

Haldeman, H.R. with Joseph DiMona. *The Ends of Power.* New York: Times Books, 1978.

Harrington, Walt. "Still Carl After All These Years." *Washington Post Magazine,* March 19, 1989.

Harwood, Richard. "Business Leaders are Tied to CIA's Covert Operations." *Washington Post,* February 18, 1967.

Havill, Adrian. *Deep Truth: The Lives of Bob Woodward and Carl Bernstein.* New York: Birch Lane Press, 1993.

Hefling, Kimberly. "Congressman Sherwood Settles Suit Filed by Mistress, Lawyer Says." Associated Press State and Local Wire, BC Cycle, November 8, 2005.

Herbers, John. "Nixon Names Saxbe Attorney General; Jaworski Appointed Special Prose-cutor." *New York Times,* November 2, 1973.

Herbert, Bob. "After the War was Over." *New York Times,* July 7, 2009.

Hersh, Seymour M. "Report on Data Leak Said to Have Named Moorer." *New York Times,* January 14, 1974.

Hettena, Seth. "Liddy Blasts Former Nixon Counsel." Associated Press Online, January 31, 2001.

Hettena, Seth. "Attorney: Dean is Pulling the Strings in Liddy Lawsuit." Associated Press, January 31, 2001.

Hill, Gladwin. "Nixon Denounces Press as Biased." *New York Times,* November 8, 1962.

Himmelman, Jeff. "The Red Flag in the Flowerpot; Four Decades after Watergate, There's Something that Still Nags at Ben Bradlee about Deep Throat." *New York,* May 7, 2012.

Hitchens, Christopher. "The Insider." *New York Times,* July 24, 2005.

Hohmann, James. "Soldier-Statesman was High-Profile Aide to Presidents." *Washington Post,* February 21, 2010.

Hougan, Jim. *Secret Agenda: Watergate, Deep Throat, and the CIA.* New York: Random House, 1984.

Huebner, Lee. "The Checkers Speech After 60 Years." *The Atlantic,* September 22, 2012.

Hulse, Carl. "Citing Affair, Republican Gives Up House Seat." *New York Times,* May 19, 2010.

Hulse, Carl. "Once-Calming Leader and a Stunning Turn." *New York Times,* May 30, 2015.

Hunt, E. Howard. *Undercover: Memoirs of an American Secret Agent.* New York: Putnam, 1974.

Jackson, David. "Most Still Believe in JFK Assassination Conspiracy." *USA Today,* November 17, 2013.

Janson, Donald. "The Violence that Hurt the Ticket." *New York Times,* September 1, 1968.

Jaworski, Leon, *The Right and the Power: The Prosecution of Watergate.* New York: Reader's Digest Press, 1976.

"John N. Mitchell Dies at 75; Major Figure in Watergate." *New York Times,* November 10, 1988.

Johnson, Darragh. "Second Trial Opens in Watergate Case: Ex-DNC Worker Suing Gordon Liddy." *Washington Post,* June 25, 2002.

"Judge Sirica's Mercy." *New York Times,* January 10, 1975.

Kadane, Kathy. "U.S. Officials' Lists Aided Indonesian Bloodbath in '60s." *Washington Post,* May 21, 1990.

Kahn, Chris. "Appeals Court Orders New Trial in Defamation Suit Against Watergate Burglar G. Gordon Liddy." Associated Press, March 1, 2002.

Kaiser, Robert G. "Carl Bernstein will Resign from Post to Write Books." *Washington Post,* December 9, 1976.

Kandell, Jonathan. "Augusto Pinochet, 91, Dictator Who Ruled by Terror in Chile, Dies." *New York Times,* December 11, 2006.

Kapanga, Andre Mwamba. "The Congo Held Hostage: Taking Exception." *Washington Post,* October 15, 1997.

Kaplan, Thomas. "Pennsylvania Congressman Who Settled Harassment Case Resigns Amid Ethics Inquiry." *New York Times,* April 27, 2018.

Kihss, Peter. "Fred Buzhardt Jr., Nixon's Counsel in Watergate, Dies." *New York Times,* December 17, 1978.

Kilpatrick, Carroll. "Schlesinger to Get Helms' Post at CIA." *Washington Post,* December 22, 1972.

Kovaleski, Serge F. "Panamanians Split on Legacy of U.S. Stay." *Washington Post,* January 16, 2000.

Langer, Emily. "Steven LaTourette, Ohio Republican with an Independent Streak, Dies; He Served Nine Terms in Congress Before Stepping Down in 2012, Citing Rancorous Partisanship." *Washington Post,* August 4, 2016.

Lardner, George Jr. "Haig Tells of Theories on Erasure: Erasure Theories Described by Haig." *Washington Post,* December 7, 1973.

Lardner, George Jr. "Watergate Libel Suit Settled; John Dean and St. Martin's Press Come to Terms Over 'Silent Coup.'" *Washington Post,* July 23, 1997.

Lavin, Cheryl. "Falling Star." *Chicago Tribune Magazine,* May 23, 1982.

"Lawsuit Over a Watergate Book Could Put Scandal Back in Court." *New York Times,* June 15, 1992.

Leary, Warren E. "Samuel Dash, 79, Counsel For Watergate Committee." *New York Times,* March 31, 2019.

Lewis, Neil. "Elliot Richardson Dies at 79; Stood Up to Nixon and Resigned in 'Saturday Night Massacre.'" *New York Times,* January 1, 2000.

Liddy, G. Gordon. *Will: The Autobiography of G. Gordon Liddy.* New York: St. Martin's Press, 1980.

Lippman, Thomas. "After the Eulogies: Nixon Critics Recall Vietnam." *Washington Post,* May 1, 1994.

Locker, Ray. *Haig's Coup: How Richard Nixon's Closest Aide Forced Him from Office.* Lincoln: Potomac Books, 2019.

Locker, Ray. *Nixon's Gamble: How a President's Own Secret Government Destroyed His Administration.* Guilford: Lyons Press, 2016.

Locker, Ray. "Watergate Figure Jeb Magruder Dies at 79." *USA Today,* May 16, 2014. https://www.usatoday.com/story/news/nation/2014/05/16/jeb-magruder-watergate-figure-dies-at-79/9174989.

Loeb, Vernon. "CIA had Covert Tie to Letelier Plotter." *Washington Post,* September 20, 2000.

Luft, Kerry. "Military Maintains its Grip on Chile: Former Dictator Still Influential." *Chicago Tribune,* November 13, 1995.

Lukas, Anthony J. *Nightmare: The Underside of the Nixon Years.* Athens: Ohio University Press, 1999.

Lydon, Christopher. "Agnew Says 'Damned Lies' to Report of Kickbacks; Doubts He'll be Indicted." *New York Times,* August 9, 1973.

MacDonald, Elizabeth. "The Kennedys and the IRS," *Wall Street Journal.* January 28, 1997.

Magruder, Jeb Stuart. *This American Life: One Man's Road to Watergate.* New York: Atheneum, 1974.

Mansfield, Stephanie. "Sex! Power! Mo Dean! And Sex!: The Stockbroker Turns Novelist with Her Racy 'Washington Wives.'" *Washington Post,* October 24, 1977.

Mansnerus, Laura. "Timothy Leary, Pied Piper of Psychedelic 60's, Dies at 75." *New York Times,* June 1, 1996.

Martin, Douglas. "Emilio Colombo, 93, Dies; Former Italian Premier." *New York Times,* July 2, 2013.

Martin, Douglas. "Jack Caulfield, 83, Bearer of a Watergate Message." *New York Times,* June 22, 2012.

Martin, Douglas. "Jeb Magruder, 79, Nixon Aide Jailed for Watergate, Dies." *New York Times,* May 17, 2014.

Mathews, Linda. "White House Discloses Lapse in Key Watergate Recording." *Los Angeles Times,* November 22, 1973.

McBee, Susanna. "Cox's Tapes Stand Rests on 4 Issues." *Washington Post,* August 6, 1973.

McCarthy, Colman. "Nixon and His Mythmakers." *Washington Post,* April 26, 1994.

Mehren, Elizabeth. "Taxing the Patience of Connecticut." *Los Angeles Times,* July 1, 1991.

Meyer, Lawrence. "Ex-Aides of Nixon to Appeal: Jury Convicts Liddy, McCord In 90 Minutes." *Washington Post,* January 31, 1973.

Meyer, Lawrence. "Key U.S. Witness Tells of Bugging Democrats." *Washington Post,* January 18, 1973.

Miller, John. "Idaho Senator Quits Amid Sex Scandal." *Sunday Gazette-Mail,* September 2, 2007.

Milligan, Susan. "Shirtless Christopher Lee Shows More Class than Other Scandal Pols." *US News and World Report,* February 10, 2011.

Morely, Jefferson. *Scorpions' Dance: The President, the Spymaster, and the CIA.* New York: St. Martin's Press, 2022.

Moore, Michael. "Stopping the Presses: The Anatomy of the Book Burning Business." *Multinational Monitor,* September 1987.

Morris, Roger. *Richard Milhous Nixon: The Rise of an American Politician.* New York: Henry Holt and Company, 1990.

Muson, Howard. "A Man for this Season: Sirica Likes his Country the Way Immigrants' Sons Do." *New York Times Magazine,* November 4, 1973.

Naughton, James M. "Arguments to be Heard Today Federal Warrant is Issued for the Arrest Ellsberg." *New York Times,* June 26, 1971.

Naughton, James M. "Judge Orders Fine, 3 Years' Probation." *New York Times,* October 11, 1973.

Naughton, James M. "Poll Finds Nixon Rating Lowest After Saigon's Invasion of Laos." *New York Times,* Mar 4, 1971.

"News Summary and Index." *New York Times,* December 9, 1972.

New York Times Staff. *The Watergate Hearings: Break-in and Cover-up.* New York: Bantam Books, 1973.

Nixon, Richard. *RN: The Memoirs of Richard Nixon.* New York: Grosset & Dunlap, 1978.

"Nixon motto: 'The worst thing a politician can be is dull.'" *Chicago Tribune,* April, 24, 1994.

O'Connor, John D. "I'm the Guy They Called Deep Throat." *Vanity Fair,* July 2005.

O'Connor, John J. "TV Radio: Watergate: N.B.C. Says Over 9 Million Viewed Opening of Hearings on 3 Channels," *New York Times,* May 18, 1973.

Oelsner, Lesley. "Dean Sentenced to 1 to 4 Years in Cover-Up Case." *New York Times,* August 3, 1974.

Oelsner, Lesley. "Judges Rule 5-2: Historic Decision Finds President not Above Law's Commands." *New York Times,* October 13, 1973.

Oelsner, Lesley. "New Subpoena for Tapes Delivered to White House." *New York Times,* April 19, 1974.

Oelsner, Lesley. "Proceeding Grim: Panel Deliberated for 15 Hours on 3 days—Appeals Planned." *New York Times,* January 2, 1975.

Oppenheimer, Joshua. "Suharto's Purge, Indonesia's Silence." *New York Times,* September 30, 2015.

Pace, Eric. "Carl M. Shoffler 51, Officer Who Arrested Burglars at Watergate." *New York Times,* July 16, 1996.

Peterson, Cass. "Post Writer Wins Pulitzer for Story on Child Addict." *Washington Post,* April 14, 1981.

Polman, Dick. "Al Haig, the Long Goodbye." *Philadelphia Inquirer,* February 22, 2010.

Reston, James. "Nominee Asks Unity at Home and Just, Sure Peace Abroad." *New York Times,* July 12, 1952.

Ripley, Anthony. "Cox and Richardson Given Oaths in Contrasting Rites." *New York Times,* May 26, 1973.

Ripley, Anthony. "Federal Grand Jury Indicts 7 Nixon Aides on Charges of Conspiracy on Watergate; Haldeman, Ehrlichman, Mitchell on List." *New York Times,* March 2, 1974.

Ripley, Anthony. "Jaworski Assumes Office; Bork Praises Prosecutor." *New York Times,* November 6, 1973.

Ripley, Anthony. "Senate Speedily Confirms Richardson by 82-3 Vote." *New York Times,* May 24, 1973.

Ripley, Anthony. "Special Prosecutor Decides to Seek Legal Action Rather than Resign Over Move to Block His Inquiry." *New York Times,* July 24, 1973.

Roberts, Sam. "Charles N. Shaffer Jr., 82, Whose Client Helped Make Case Against Nixon, Dies." *New York Times,* March 24, 2015.

Robertson, Campbell. "In Louisiana, Tainted Senator Rides Anti-Obama Sentiment." *New York Times,* September 11, 2009.

Robertson, Campbell. "Politicians are Slowed by Scandal, but Many Still Win the Race." *New York Times,* July 18, 2013.

Rockefeller Commission. *Report to the President by the Commission on CIA Activities Within the United States.* Washington: Government Printing Office, 1975.

Roig-Franzia, Manuel. "Arguments in Liddy Trial Focus on Dean: Jury Begins Deliberations in Defamation Suit." *Washington Post,* February 1, 2001.

Roig-Franzia, Manuel, "Liddy Concludes Testimony in Md. Lawsuit," *Washington Post,* January 31, 2001.

Roig-Franzia, Manuel. "Mistrial Declared in Case Against Liddy." *Washington Post,* February 2, 2001.

Roig-Franzia, Manuel. "Plaintiff Testifies of Harm by Liddy." *Washington Post,* January 19, 2001.

Romero, Simon. "Chileans Order Peru's Ex-Chief Home For Trial." *New York Times,* September 22, 2007.

Rosen, James. "Under Watergate." *Washington City Paper,* May 25, 2001.

Rosen, James. *The Strong Man: John Mitchell and the Secrets of Watergate.* New York: Doubleday, 2008.

Rosenbaum, David E. "Another Section of Tapes is Blank, A Nixon Aide Says." *New York Times,* November 22, 1973.

Rosenbaum, David E. "Panel Hears I.R.S. Weighed Fraud Charge for Nixon." *New York Times,* June 21, 1974.

Rugaber, Walter. "4 More Admit Guilt as Spies In Watergate." *New York Times,* January 16, 1973.

Rugaber, Walter. "Hunt Admits all 6 Charges as Judge Bars Partial Plea." *New York Times,* January 12, 1973.

Rugaber, Walter. "Watergate Spy Says Defendants were Under 'Political Pressure' to Admit Guilt and Keep Silent." *New York Times,* March 24, 1973.

Rugaber, Walter. "Watergate Trial Opens; Jury Screening Begins." *New York Times,* January 9, 1973.

Salisbury, Harrison E. "Nixon: Then and Now." *New York Times,* September 16, 1968.

Salpukas, Agis. "2 Nixon Ex-Aides Among 7 Indicted in Raid in Capital." *New York Times,* September 16, 1972.

Schlesinger, Arthur, Jr. "A Skeptical Democrat Looks at President Nixon." *New York Times, Sunday Magazine,* November 17, 1968.

Schmidt, Michael S., et al. "Gaetz Said to Face U.S. Inquiry Over Sex With an Underage Girl." *New York Times,* March 31, 2021.

Schoffman, Stuart. "Marriage and Ephrontery: A New Woman Strikes Back." *Los Angeles Times, The Book Review,* April 17, 1983.

Schudel, Matt. "Nixon Operative Devised Some 'Dirty Tricks.'" *Washington Post,* June 24, 2012.

Scott, Austin. "Haig Picked as Head of Nixon Staff." *Washington Post,* May 5, 1973.

Seelye, Katherine. "Oregon Congressman Named in Sex Case, Says He'll Resign." *New York Times,* July 27, 2011.

Semple, Robert B., Jr. "Presidential Race: Nixon's View: It's Not in the Bag—Not Yet." *New York Times,* September 22, 1968.

"Senator, Arrested in an Airport Bathroom, Pleads Guilty." *New York Times,* August 28, 2007.

Severo, Richard, "H.R. Haldeman, Nixon Aide Who had Central Role in Watergate, is Dead." *New York Times,* November 13, 1993.

Severson, Kim. "Candidate, Philanderer and Juggler, Too: Edwards Trial Shows Deception's Strains." *New York Times,* May 21, 2012.

Shabecoff, Philip. "Ford's Primary Losses Divide White House Staff as Factions Trade Charges of Laxity." *New York Times,* May 24, 1976.

Shanker, Thom. "U.S. Leads Arms Market with Sales of $40 Billion." *New York Times,* December 27, 2016.

Shaw, Gaylord. "Where is the Truth?: The CIA's 29 Years Successes, Failures." *Los Angeles Times,* February 22, 1976.

Shear, Michael D. "Race in Va.'s 2nd District Turns Fierce." *Washington Post,* October 29, 2004.

Shear, Michael D. and Michael S. Schmidt. "Hastert Payouts Said to be Linked to Sexual Abuse." *New York Times,* May 30, 2015.

Sheehan, Neil. "Vietnam Archive: Pentagon Study Traces 3 Decades of Growing U. S. Involvement." *New York Times,* June 13, 1971.

Shepard, Geoff. *The Real Watergate Scandal: Collusion, Conspiracy, and the Plot that Brought Nixon Down.* Washington, D.C.: Regency History, 2015.

Shields, Mark. "Our Last Liberal President." *Washington Post,* August 4, 1996.

Siddon, Arthur. "4 Watergate Defendants Plead Guilty; 2 Still on Trial." *Chicago Tribune,* January 16, 1973.

Silk, Mark. "Before the Scandal Broke," *Smithsonian,* November 2016.

Sirica, John. "Growing Up Poor in the Nation's Capital." *Washington Post,* April 29, 1979.

Soteropoulos, Jacqueline. "Watergate Book Lawsuit Settled." *Tampa Tribune,* September 28, 1999.

Squires, Jim. "Probers Charge Pentagon Spied on Kissinger in 1971: Report Chiefs got Secrets." *Chicago Tribune,* January 11, 1974.

Stanford, Phil. *White House Call Girl: The Real Watergate Story.* Port Townsend: Feral House, 2013.

Stanglin, Doug. "CIA Formerly Admits Role in 1953 Iranian Coup." *USA Today,* August 20, 2013.

Stolberg, Sheryl Gay, "First-Term Democrat, Rising Star in House, Denies Relationship With an Aide." *New York Times,* October 23, 2019, p. A19.

Stolberg, Sheryl Gay, Yamiche Alcindor, and Nicholas Fandos. "Al Franken to Resign From Senate Amid Harassment Allegations." *New York Times,* December 7, 2017,

Stone, Roger with Mike Colapietro. *Nixon's Secrets: The Rise, Fall, and Untold Truth about the President, Watergate, and the Pardon.* New York: Skyhorse, 2014.

Stout, David. "John D. Ehrlichman, Nixon Aide Jailed for Watergate, Dies at 73." *New York Times,* February 16, 1999.

Summers, Anthony. *Official and Confidential: The Secret Life of J. Edgar Hoover.* New York: G. P. Putnam's Sons, 1993.

Tavernse, Sabrina. "Thomas H. Moorer, 91, Dies; Head of Joint Chiefs in 70's." *New York Times,* February 7, 2004.

"Text of Indictment Handed Up to Judge Sirica by Watergate Grand Jury." *New York Times,* Mar 2, 1974.

"Text of Judge Sirica's Opinion in Ordering the President to Submit Tapes." *New York Times,* August 30, 1973.

"Text of Ruling by Judge in Ellsberg Case." *New York Times,* May 12, 1973.

"Text of Senator Nixon's Broadcast Explaining Supplementary Expense Fund." *New York Times,* September 24, 1952.

"The Bodies in Panama." *New York Times,* February 20, 2001.

"The Courts and History." *Washington Post,* Editorial, February 4, 2001.

"The Ensign Investigation, to be Continued." *New York Times,* May 14, 2011.

Thomas, Evan, *Being Nixon: A Man Divided.* New York: Random House, 2015.

Tian, Nan and Aude Fleurant, Alexandra Kuimova, Pieter D. Wezeman, and Siemon T. Wezeman. *Trends in World Military Expenditures. 2018.* Solna: Stockholm International Peace Research Institute, 2019.

"Transcript of President Nixon's Address to the Nation Announcing His Resignation," *New York Times,* August 9, 1974.

Trip, Gabriel and Isabella Grullon Paz, "North Carolina Survey Gives Democrats Edge." *New York Times,* October 30, 2020.

Trussell, C. P. "Alger Hiss Admits Knowing Chambers; Meet Face to Face." *New York Times,* August 18, 1948.

Turner, Wallace. "California Curbs Mental State as Trial Defense: Odd Twist to Defense." *New York Times,* September 13, 1981.

U.S., Congress, House, Committee on the Judiciary. *A Resolution Authorizing and Directing the Committee on the Judiciary to Investigate Whether Sufficient Grounds Exist for the House of Representatives to Exercise its Constitutional Power to Impeach Richard M. Nixon, President of the United States of America, White House Surveillance Activities and Campaign Activities, Book I: Alexander Butterfield, Paul O'Brien, and Fred C. LaRue.* 93rd Congress, 2nd Session. Washington: U.S. Government Printing Office, 1974.

U.S., Congress, House, Committee on the Judiciary. *A Resolution Authorizing and Directing the Committee on the Judiciary to Investigate Whether Sufficient Grounds Exist for the House of Representatives to Exercise its Constitutional Power to Impeach Richard M. Nixon, President of the United States of America, White House Surveillance Activities and Campaign Activities, Book II: William O. Bittman, John N. Mitchell, and John W. Dean III.* 93rd Congress, 2nd Session. Washington: U.S. Government Printing Office, 1974.

U.S. Congress, House, Committee on the Judiciary. *A Resolution Authorizing and Directing the Committee on the Judiciary to Investigate Whether Sufficient Grounds Exist for the House of Representatives to Exercise its Constitutional Power to Impeach Richard M. Nixon, President of the United States of America, White House Surveillance Activities and Campaign Activities, Book III, Part 1 - Events Following the Watergate*

Break-In, 93rd Congress, 2nd Session. Washington: U.S. Government Printing Office, 1974.

U.S., Congress, House, Committee on the Judiciary. *A Resolution Authorizing and Directing the Committee on the Judiciary to Investigate Whether Sufficient Grounds Exist for the House of Representatives to Exercise its Constitutional Power to Impeach Richard M. Nixon, President of the United States of America, White House Surveillance Activities and Campaign Activities, Book IV, Part 2 - Events Following the Watergate Break-In*. 93rd Congress, 2nd Session. Washington: U.S. Government Printing Office, 1974.

U.S., Congress, Senate. *Hearings before the Select Committee on Presidential Campaign Activities: Watergate and Related Activities, Book 1*, 93rd Congress, 1st Session. Washington: U.S. Government Printing Office, 1973.

U.S., Congress, Senate. *Hearings before the Select Committee on Presidential Campaign Activities: Watergate and Related Activities, Book 2*, 93rd Congress, 1st Session. Washington: U.S. Government Printing Office, 1973.

U.S., Congress, Senate. *Hearings before the Select Committee on Presidential Campaign Activities: Watergate and Related Activities, Book 3*, 93rd Congress, 1st Session. Washington: U.S. Government Printing Office, 1973.

U.S., Congress, Senate. *Hearings before the Select Committee on Presidential Campaign Activities: Watergate and Related Activities, Book 4*, 93rd Congress, 1st Session. Washington: U.S. Government Printing Office, 1973.

U.S., Congress, Senate. *Hearings before the Select Committee on Presidential Campaign Activities: Watergate and Related Activities, Book 5*, 93rd Congress, 1st Session. Washington: U.S. Government Printing Office, 1973.

U.S., Congress, Senate. *Hearings before the Select Committee on Presidential Campaign Activities: Watergate and Related Activities, Book 6*, 93rd Congress, 1st Session. Washington: U.S. Government Printing Office, 1973.

U.S., Congress, Senate. *Hearings before the Select Committee on Presidential Campaign Activities: Watergate and Related Activities, Book 7*, 93rd Congress, 1st Session. Washington: U.S. Government Printing Office, 1973.

U.S., Congress, Senate. *Hearings before the Select Committee on Presidential Campaign Activities: Watergate and Related Activities, Book 8*, 93rd Congress, 1st Session. Washington: U.S. Government Printing Office, 1973.

U.S., Congress, Senate. *Hearings before the Select Committee on Presidential Campaign Activities: Watergate and Related Activities, Book 9*, 93rd Congress, 1st Session. Washington: U.S. Government Printing Office, 1973.

U.S., Congress, Senate. *The Final Report of the Select Committee on Presidential Campaign Activities United States Senate*, 93d Congress, 2nd Session. Report No. 93-981. Washington: U.S. Government Printing Office, 1974.

United Press International. "Agnew Said to Hold Long Discussions about Resigning." *New York Times*, September 18, 1973.

United Press International. "Cox Appoints 4 Lawyers to Investigatory Team." *New York Times*, September 4, 1973.

United Press International. "Paper Says Girl was Sent to Kill Castro." *Los Angeles Times*, June 13, 1976.

United Press International. "Rose Mary Calls Some Tapes Poor, Impossible to Copy: She-Disputes in Court that She Discovered 'Gap.'" *Los Angeles Times*, November 8, 1973.

United Press International. "Suharto Put U.S. Aid on 'Shopping List.'" *Los Angeles Times*, December 2, 1970.

United States. Office of Management and Budget, *Historical Tables*.

Urbina, Ian. "Arrest Near in 2001 Killing of Intern, Authorities Say." *New York Times*, February 22, 2009.

Urbina, Ian, "Sex Scandal Shakes Race for Congress in Florida." *New York Times*, October 14, 2008.

Vinson, Henry with Nick Bryant. *Confessions of a DC Madam: The Politics of Sex, Lies, and Blackmail*. Walterville: Trineday, 2014.

Washburn, Mark. "Watergate History For Sale at Webster House in Dupont Circle." DC Condo Boutique," April 27, 2011.

Weaver, Warren, Jr. "A 'Gap' in Tapes Reported by Aide." *New York Times*, November 8, 1973.

Weaver, Warren, Jr. "Court Informed: The Talks were Those President had with Mitchell and Dean." *New York Times*, November 1, 1973.

Weaver, Warren, Jr., "Opinion by Burger: Name of President is Left in Indictment as a Co-Conspirator. *New York Times*, July 25, 1974.

Weaver, Warren, Jr. "Supreme Court Agrees to Decide Now if Nixon can Withhold Evidence." *New York Times*, June 1, 1974.

Weaver, Warren. "Tape Case Argued in Federal

Court." *New York Times,* August 23, 1973.

Weiner, Tim. "C.I.A. Formed Haitian Unit Later Tied to Narcotics Trade." *New York Times,* November 14, 1993.

Weiner, Tim. "C.I.A. Opening Files on Cold War Role." *New York Times,* August 29, 1993.

Weiner, Tim. "E. Howard Hunt, Agent Who Organized Botched Watergate Break-in, Dies at 88." *New York Times* January 24, 2007.

Weiner, Tim. "W. Mark Felt, F.B.I. Official Who Became 'Deep Throat' is Dead at 95." *New York Times,* December 19, 2008.

Weiser, Benjamin. "Anthony Weiner Gets 21 Months in Prison for Sexting with Teenager." *New York Times,* September 25, 2017. https://www.nytimes.com/2017/09/25/nyregion/anthony-weiner-sentencing-prison-sexting-teenager.html.

Weisman, Jonathan. "Despite Ethics Pledge, Response by G.O.P. Varies." *New York Times,* April 29, 2014.

Chris Whipple. *The Spymasters: How the CIA Directors Shape History and the Future.* New York: Scribner, 2020.

"White House Finds Jaworski No Easier than Cox." *New York Times,* December 1, 1973.

Willon, Phil and Michael Fechter. "Watergate; The Untold Story." *Tampa Tribune,* January 19, 1997.

Witte, Brian. "Jury Rejects Defamation Lawsuit Against Watergate Conspirator G. Gordon Liddy." Associated Press, BC Cycle, July 3, 2002.

Woodward, Bob. "Don't Subpoena the Tapes." *Washington Post,* January 15, 1981.

Woodward, Bob and Carl Bernstein. "GOP Security Aide Among 5 Arrested in Bugging Affair." *Washington Post,* June 19, 1972.

Woodward, Bob and Carl Bernstein. "Pentagon Got Secret Data of Kissinger's: Secret Kissinger Data Passed to Pentagon." *Washington Post,* January 12, 1974.

Woodward, Bob and Carl Bernstein. *The Final Days.* New York: Simon and Schuster, 1976.

Woodward, Bob and Carl Bernstein. "Wiretaps Put on Phones of 2 Reporters." *Washington Post,* May 3, 1973.

Woodward, Bob and E.J. Bachinski. "White House Consultant Tied to Bugging Figure." *Washington Post,* June 20, 1972.

Zeleny, Jeff. "Report Finds Negligence in Foley Case: Ethics Inquiry Faults Republicans, but Cites No Rule Violations." *New York Times,* December 9, 2006.

Index